birth

birth

Caterine Milinaire

with Barbara Aria

Reviewed for Medical Accuracy
by Joseph Berger, M.D.

revised and updated

Harmony Books / New York

Publisher's Note: This book contains case histories of several pregnancies and general suggestions relating to questions that may arise during pregnancy. The instructions in this work are not intended as a substitute for professional medical advice.

Copyright ©1987, 1974 by Caterine Milinaire
All rights reserved. No part of this book may be reproduced or transmitted in any form or by any means, electronic or mechanical, including photocopying, recording, or by any information storage and retrieval system, without permission in writing from the publisher.

Published by Harmony Books, a division of Crown Publishers, Inc., 225 Park Avenue South, New York, New York 10003, and represented in Canada by the Canadian MANDA Group.
HARMONY and colophon are trademarks of Crown Publishers, Inc.
Manufactured in the United States of America

Library of Congress Cataloging-in-Publication Data
Milinaire, Caterine.
  Birth: facts and legends.
  Bibliography: p.
  Includes index.
  1. Prenatal care. 2. Childbirth. 3. Infants—Care and hygiene. I. Aria, Barbara. II. Title.
RG525.M457   1987   612.2′ 4   86–22802
ISBN 0-517-54347-8

10 9 8 7 6 5 4 3 2 1
First Revised Edition

Dedicated to all those who become another through birth

©Barbara Nessim '11-85

Acknowledgments

I wish to express my gratitude to all the mothers and fathers who contributed their experiences to *Birth*. With the help and enthusiasm of midwives, doctors, nutritionists and exercise teachers this new edition has become an even more fascinating and resourceful companion for future parents than the previous one.

As I have conceived it, *Birth* is addressed to anyone interested in the subject of childbirth, including some childless artists who have contributed generously of their photographs and drawings.

To the Harmony team and all my supportive friends along the decades, thank you.

In addition to all of the people mentioned in this book, especially in the "Birth Experiences" chapter, I would particularly like to thank Moun and Ian • Henri • Mati • Gilles • Manuella • Freddy • David Rosensweet, M.D. and Ricky • Colette and Peter • B & M Margetts • Vicky McLaughlin • David Padwa • Bruce and Susan Harris • Deni Bank • Candice Bolbech • Alison Ozer • Ulla Kristiina Laasko • Jaclyn Israel • Barbara Mortimer • Jamie Jackson • Fred Cushing. And thank you again to Dr. Joseph Berger for giving me a better understanding of the medical aspects of maternity.

Contents

©K. Haring

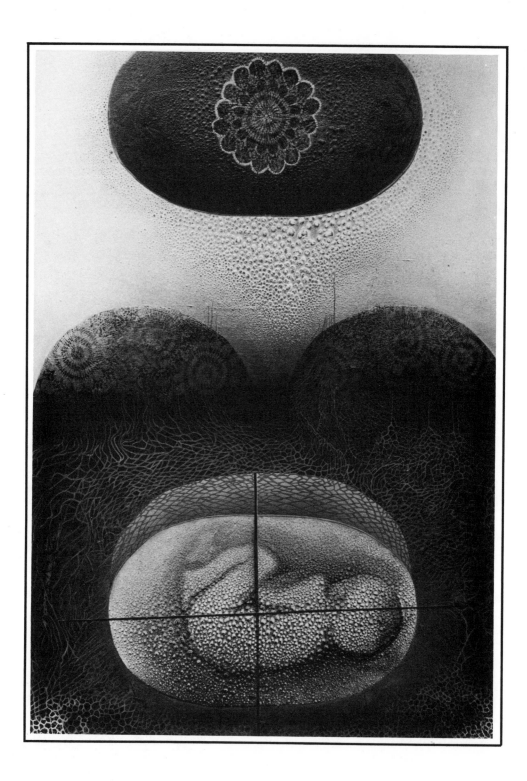

Forethoughts

PREFACE TO THE ORIGINAL EDITION

Think deeply—a baby—think about it.... What a joy, but what a commitment!

Every woman (and man) in this world thinks about having a baby at one time or another. Some think about it more often, even to the point of obsession. It does not mean that all women wish to become pregnant. Changing life-styles have made it hard for many women to bear and raise a child. It is a long-term commitment that involves devotion, patience and strength (mental and physical), among other qualities. Childbearing in a world of exploding population is becoming a smaller part in women's lives. This is especially true in countries where contraception and abortion are readily available (which in turn help focus attention on the quality of prenatal care, birth and childcare). There is no more rushing into having children; there is plenty of time to prepare for this special experience.

Giving birth is life's most powerful realization of a miracle. It is so fantastic an event that it is always surrounded with the greatest expectation. Yet men and women never feel quite well informed enough to let go—to give fully—to be carried away by the exploding forces of new life, to relax and let nature take its course at birthtime.

Birth is still the taboo event of human life. Only recently have women and men begun to probe, expose and seek alternatives to the birth-consciousness that has been imposed upon them for centuries. Today it seems as though men and women are seeking knowledge about every phase of childbearing from friends, doctors and parents. It is only through expanding their knowledge of childbearing that people can fully understand and celebrate the miracle of birth.

A great deal of material can be found on the subject of physical development during pregnancy and the different phases of giving birth, all written by professional people and experts in the field. But little has been recorded, in written or visual form, about people's personal experiences and about the spiritual preparation essential for a high state of mind during pregnancy and actual delivery. This is the fundamental focus of *Birth*: parents' stories in which they relate their personal experiences with pregnancy, birth and childbearing. We learn best how to cope with birth from listening to our bodies, our friends, our doctors, mostly from men and women who have gone through the birth experience. From their stories we shape our expectations. There are many different ways to choose from, and we want to know as much as possible; the good, the bad, spoken in everyday language. The subject of birth is exciting and, in many respects, vastly unexplored. To anyone with a little curiosity it becomes a fascinating probe. After all, this is where we all started, and to give someone else a good start in life is the least we can do.

This book does not advocate that the best way to give birth is at home, in the hospital, with or without drugs. It merely says that you have a choice; each has its advantages and drawbacks. Birth does not belong exclusively to the medical domain, which for all its knowledge still does not know how to transform the impersonal, depressing, blank environment of hospitals. There is much to be thankful for in the progress of modern obstetrics and great empathy for a person who has studied long years to achieve such skills. However, this is no excuse for the almost mechanized treatment received in the large medical establishments. On the other hand, birth at home with all its personal care, relaxed atmosphere and lack of hospital germs can quickly turn into a drama if a serious complication arises endangering both the life of the mother and the child for lack of equipment that is on hand in a medical delivery room. A pleasant environment and the freedom to follow one's own birth rhythm is important, but so is the assurance that all possible safety measures are readily available.

More than ever babies of the future will be conceived in joy, rather than out of a sense of duty, as a burst of emotion transforming the meeting of two spirits into a new life. Pregnancy becomes a transition, a passage so special it requires a great deal of patience, humor, self-love, good nutrition and physical care. Finally, childbirth can be a pleasure, a time of sensual fulfillment, a gathering of unknown forces and pure creation.

Birth, however eventful, is always an act of love. Whether we choose home or hospital as a location, the idea is to be well prepared and to have a totally positive experience.

C. M., 1974

PREFACE TO THIS REVISED AND UPDATED EDITION

Upon rereading my motherly impressions, I realize a great deal has happened concerning attitudes toward childbirth since I wrote *Birth* some fifteen years ago.

Today women know and want to know more about pregnancy and birthing. Mothers-to-be have a better comprehension of how preventive nutrition, prenatal exercise and potential health hazards can affect the fetus. From giving birth in water, to a hospital with technology's most sophisticated equipment, the wide choices of birthing possibilities are today a reality. Birthing rooms in many hospitals are now an accepted alternative to the traditional surgical delivery room. More community childbearing centers have opened across the nation. A growing number of working women decide to have their children in their thirties and forties. Responsible adult women may choose to have and raise children without permanent partners—sometimes through artificial insemination—increasing the already huge number of single mothers across the nation who do not always plan their pregnancies. Certified nurse-midwives, who have gained wide acceptance, face a three-steps-forward–two-steps-backward syndrome as their liability coverage is either not renewed or increased to sums they cannot afford. There has been widespread awakening to the physiological importance of parental-infant bonding—the intense attachment that develops between the newborn and its parents during the first hours and days after birth.

Dedicated fathers share in the daily physical tasks of infant care. Concerned people are demanding legislative reforms to meet the real needs of working mothers and improve the state of day care in this country. Parents now realize that pregnancy and birth are emotional times, which open up the creative realm and the understanding of a greater and different sensuality.

Because of these issues, an updated edition of *Birth* is essential. The encouraging letters I received from readers through the years, the many parents who expressed joy with the help they derived from the book and the fact that *Birth* is still selling in bookstores, over a decade after its publication, have convinced me that it is time to bring this book into a closer focus with the kind of life we lead at the end of this century.

C. M., 1987

AUTHOR'S NOTE

In describing the baby's development within the mother's womb we will use the word "it" to identify the fetus, the embryo, the growing individual. The English language has beautifully provided neutral ground for description with the pronoun "it," which encompasses both the masculine and feminine gender.

A warm, human "it" defined from the start as a person will elude misinterpretations.

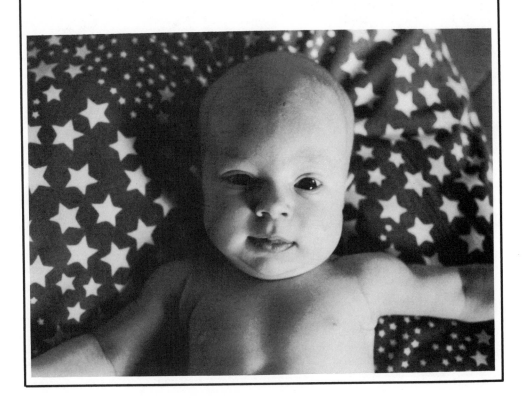

Inside Stories

The beginning of a new person starts at conception with the meeting of the egg and the sperm in fertilization which is the union of the female & male cell into one, the beginning of a new person

DETAILS OF THE PARTICIPATING CELLS AT CONCEPTION

Female Germ Cell or the egg, also called ovum. One egg is ripe every month in the egg storage: the ovaries. The pituitary, a small gland situated at the base of the brain, secretes stimulating hormones into the blood. This causes the follicle, a protective bubble for the maturing egg, to burst. The ripe egg falls away from the 250,000 immature eggs stored in the ovaries since birth and is pulled toward the abdominal cavity by the seaweedlike ends of the fallopian tube. The egg floats through one of the tubes, alternating between one and the other each month. It is moved slowly by little hairs called cilia toward the mother's womb: the uterus, the nest.

The egg can be fertilized in the fallopian tube six to twenty-four hours after ovulation.

Male Germ Cell. The sperm (short for spermatozoon) is much smaller than the egg and is effective for approximately forty-eight hours. The male cells are produced in the testicles; twenty to five hundred million are released with each ejaculation. Only a small number reach the environment of the egg. A few will manage to peel off the protective membrane of the egg; but only the first one that reaches the center, the nucleus, can fertilize the egg.

Fertilization takes place in a little more than an hour.

The Two Germ Cells. Magnetically drawn together, the two germ cells fuse. The twenty-three chromosomes of the female cell blend with the twenty-three chromosomes of the male cell to shape a new cell. In the following brief half-hour a great deal of the new person's physical and mental attributes are established. They are drawn from the inherited characteristics of each parent and their ancestors.

THE NEW CELL

Made up of forty-six chromosomes, the new cell begins to move wildly, as if agitated by a great force. It becomes so violent a rumble that an explosion follows and the fertilized egg divides into two cells of the same type. This is the start of embryo growth.

The Division of Cells.   The cells continue to divide; they become smaller within the original envelope. Slowly, they are moved down through the narrow fallopian tube by liquid secretions and little hairlike projections. Three to five days later the tiny cluster has reached its nest, the uterus, where it will wander in the salty fluid for a few days. By approximately the sixth day, the cluster of 150 cells resembles in formation the mulberry fruit (or *morula* from Latin) and is the size and color of a tiny freckle.

The Embryonic Vesicle.   A liquid secreted from the center of the cluster pushes the cells away, leaving a hollow space and a multilayered envelope called the embryonic vesicle. The vesicle is composed of two different layers of cells. The external layers eventually become the food vehicle for the embryo in the form of placenta and bag of waters. The inner layers will shape the body of the child.

Lining of the Uterus.   Meanwhile, the uterus has been preparing itself, as it does every cycle, to receive and feed the fertilized egg by building up a thick spongy lining of nourishing tissues. When fertilization does not occur, the cycle ends with menstruation, the shedding of the uterine lining.

Nesting.   By the seventh day after ovulation the fertilized egg is ready to nest in the prepared wall of the uterus.

The aggressive external layer of cells eats away and absorbs a section of the fresh lining, breaking tiny bloody vessels and preparing a space for the entire embryonic vesicle. Fingerlike projections (villi roots) grow from

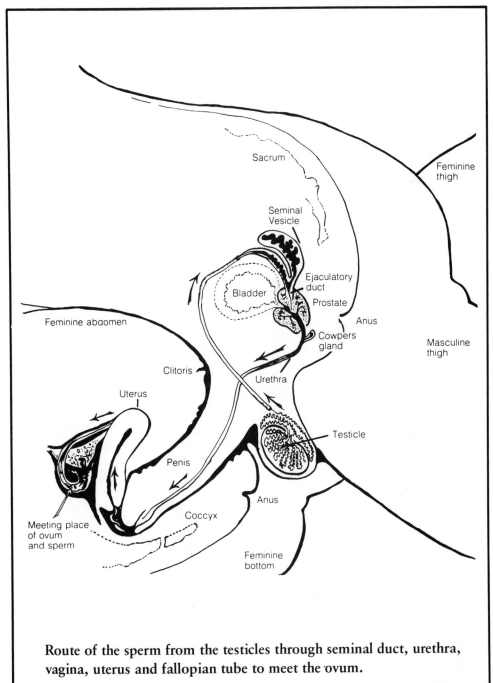

Route of the sperm from the testicles through seminal duct, urethra, vagina, uterus and fallopian tube to meet the ovum.

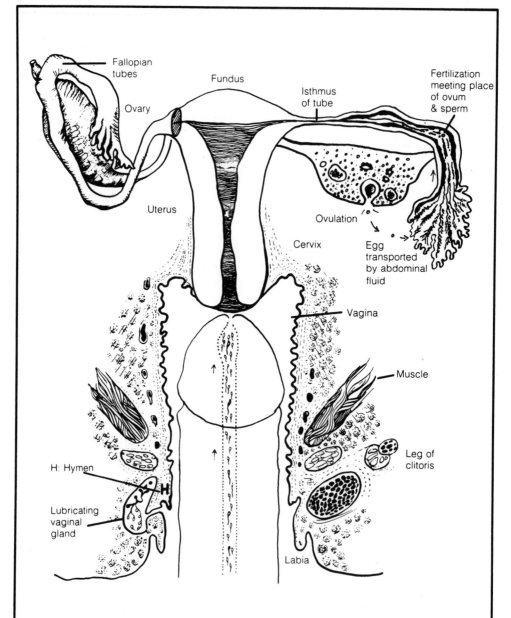

The path followed by the egg from ovary through fallopian tube to uterus (the right part and the uterus are laid open), and the sperm on the way to fallopian tube.

the tiny vesicle-embryo in order to anchor the cluster securely as it sinks deeper into the uterus.

The Feeding Circuit is established between mother and child through the villi roots. They will also function as lungs and digestive organs until the embryo grows further and the cord and placenta are formed. All forms of the child's nourishment received from the mother's blood filter through the walls of this structure, as does the sterile waste matter which moves in the opposite direction.

Growing from Cell to Embryo. The nesting cluster of cells multiplies and transforms rapidly within the vesicle envelope. It is now buried deep under the surface of the uterine lining. By the second week after fertilization, groups of cells begin to look very different from each other. Large and small cells take up their position in shaping the human being. Brain cells, bone cells, blood and skin cells start to form. The large cells are shaping the embryo which resembles, at this stage, a small disk of tissues. A transparent sheath starts to grow around the embryo. This is the amniotic sac, or bag of waters, which will contain the fluid to cushion, warm, supply drink and provide a wading pool for the fetus.

The Embryo Elongates. By the third week, the embryo is tubular-shaped; it is growing a spinal column of sorts and then bending over upon itself. The large rounded head-end almost touches the tail. The brain and nervous system are developing. The head shows traces of eyes and sprouting ears. The cheeks and jaws often look like gills at this stage. Shortly, by the fourth week, a basic structure pulsates and pumps blood through an independent microscopic circulatory system. The digestive tract is a little tube that begins at the mouth and goes into the developing stomach and intestines. On the embryo's side, tiny buds of finlike shapes appear, soon to be arms and legs.

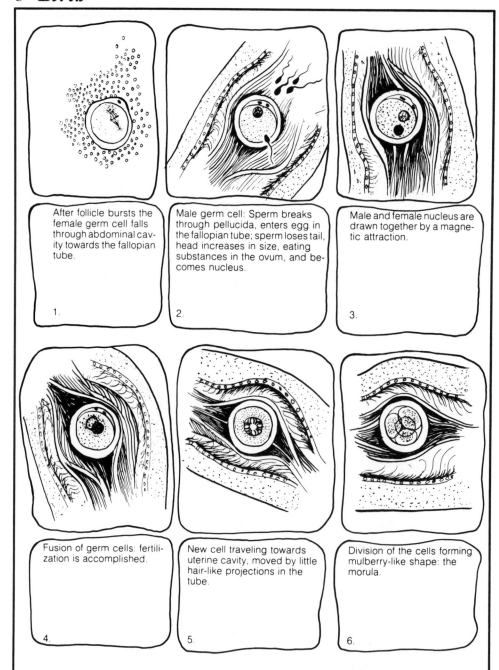

1. After follicle bursts the female germ cell falls through abdominal cavity towards the fallopian tube.

2. Male germ cell: Sperm breaks through pellucida, enters egg in the fallopian tube; sperm loses tail, head increases in size, eating substances in the ovum, and becomes nucleus.

3. Male and female nucleus are drawn together by a magnetic attraction.

4. Fusion of germ cells: fertilization is accomplished.

5. New cell traveling towards uterine cavity, moved by little hair-like projections in the tube.

6. Division of the cells forming mulberry-like shape: the morula.

Fertilization and travels of the fertilized cell through the fallopian tube.

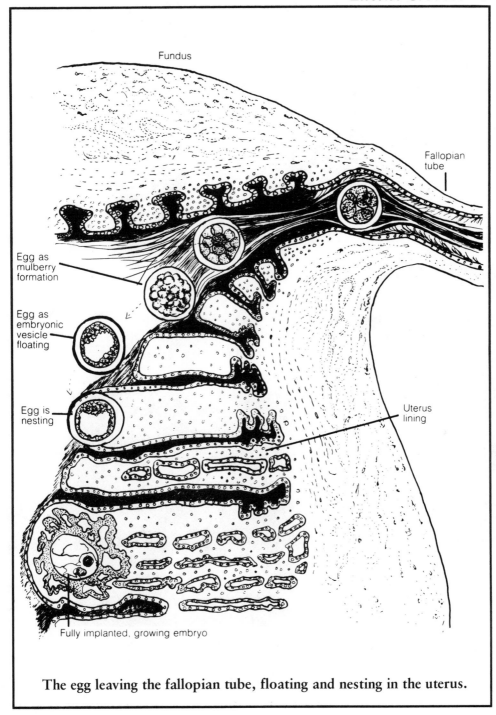

Fundus

Fallopian tube

Egg as mulberry formation

Egg as embryonic vesicle floating

Egg is nesting

Uterus lining

Fully implanted, growing embryo

The egg leaving the fallopian tube, floating and nesting in the uterus.

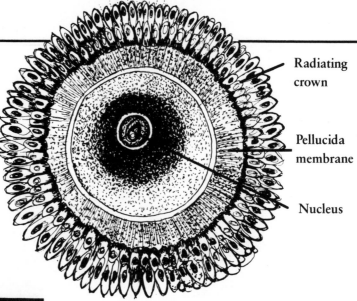

Fully developed
unfertilized
female egg

Radiating
crown

Pellucida
membrane

Nucleus

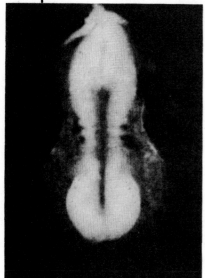

Embryo (dorsal aspect) at approximately 21 days: size, 2.1mm.

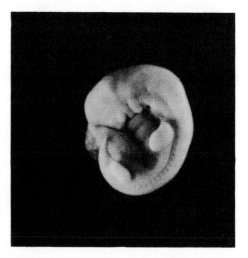

Embryo at 34 days: size, 8mm or 5/16
inch.

As the First Lunar Month Ends the finely structured creature is a quarter of an inch (5mm) long; it is growing into a recognizable human being at an incredibly fast pace.

By this time the first period is approximately two weeks late. The embryo is one month old fourteen days after the first missed period, since conception usually only takes place ten to fourteen days after menstruation. This is based on a regular twenty-eight-day lunar cycle. However, the physician will start counting the pregnancy from the last day of the previous period.

Since the memory of each evolving cell—and we all started as one cell—is the story of all that has transpired universally, it is interesting to think about the possibilities of having first evolved through the various species before modifications and specialization formed us into the genetically coded human body.

Recommendation. Almost needless to say is that it's important to be super healthy at this stage. The embryo, growing at a speed it will never again repeat, is drawing from the mother the basic elements for its structure and is very susceptible to communicable diseases.

In addition, X rays during this (or any other) stage of pregnancy are strictly taboo. Even if you only suspect that you are pregnant, be sure to let your doctor know. This includes dental X rays as well. In absolute emergencies, a dental X ray may be performed if the abdomen is shielded, but even this should be avoided if possible.

SECOND LUNAR MONTH

The embryo's nest is now well covered with tissues and roots. The embryo feeds through a primitive umbilical cord and the little body floats in the amniotic sac. Currents of gelatinous cells modify and specialize into the nose and ears, the arms, elbows, fingers, and, a while later, the legs, knees, feet and toes. The sex organs are apparent (sixth week) but not distinct enough to differentiate as either male or female. The eyes are

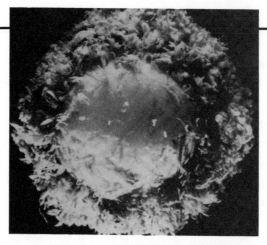

Embryo at 5 weeks within its embryonic vesicle.

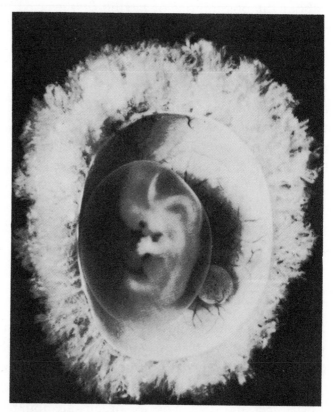

42-day-old fetus, ½ inch long.

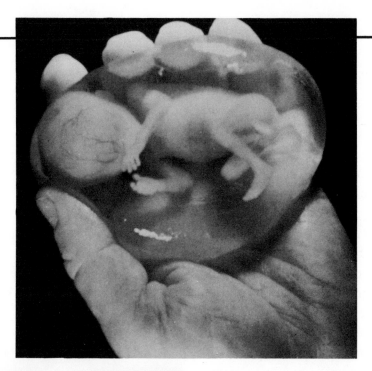

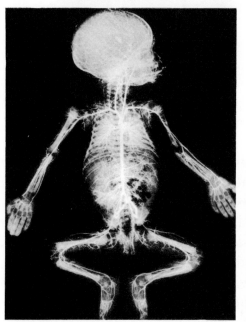

(Above) 12-week-old fetus in amniotic sac, showing size relative to adult hand.

(Left) Circulatory system of 30-week-old fetus.

(Below) 7-month-old fetus, umbilical cord and placenta.

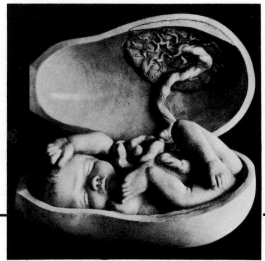

getting their pigmentation; a dark circle is forming and above that is the vague indication of an eyelid. The tail is still quite prominent but will soon disappear. The internal organs, the stomach, liver and kidneys are getting ready to function. By the eighth week the embryo is covered with a thin layer of tissue and a transparent layer of skin. The little body is 1 inch long (2.54cm) and weighs about $1/30$ of an ounce (1g). The heart has started to beat.

Abortion. Even though you may have planned this baby, there may be some strong emotional or financial reasons that have recently occurred to make you doubtful about continuing with the pregnancy. If you feel you want to have an abortion, it is best to have it now, via suction curettage. It is a simple, fast method that can be performed up until the twelfth week of pregnancy. After this period of time the methods become more emotionally taxing, tedious, painful, expensive and hazardous.

THIRD LUNAR MONTH

The offspring (translation of fetus from Latin) is now refining; cells are transforming the cartilage of the skeleton into bones. Finishing touches such as nails appear as a fine membrane on the fingertips; teeth sockets are laid down in the jawbone. Externally, the sexual organs are strikingly alike. Both have the same glands and similar skinfolds—a slit and tissue folds on either side with a small round bud in the middle. It remains almost the same for the female sex. The clitoris bud stays small and the folds surrounding it become the labia. Development continues for the male sex; the bud grows into a penis, the tissue folds join and swell into the scrotum. The internal reproductive organs already contain a few primitive eggs or sperm cells. By the twelfth week the eyelids close over the eyes only to open again around the seventh month. The mother does not yet feel anything as the fetus only weighs an ounce (28g) and its muscles are not big enough for strong movements.

FOURTH LUNAR MONTH

The major systems are now developed even though there will be many little changes before birth. The main process from now on is for the baby to grow strong enough to be able to live on its own. The fetus is now about 6 inches long (15cm) and neatly secured in the amniotic membrane. Surrounded with beneficial fluid that keeps renewing itself, the fetus is cuddling up to the growing placenta. The baby is growing so fast now that when it stretches the mother may feel the movement faintly. It spends its time drinking, floating about and sleeping. The little oxygen needed by the baby is carried in the red blood corpuscles from the placenta through the umbilical cord to the little heart which pumps it through the entire body. The placenta, rooted in the lining of the uterus, is now the same size as the fetus. A dark red mass of tissues and arteries, the placenta performs the important task of digesting the necessary materials for the child (proteins, vitamins, minerals, fats) and releasing the amount needed in a simpler form. The placenta also produces the progesterone hormone in sufficient quantity to maintain pregnancy and prepare for the milk. A fine downy growth of hair (called lanugo) develops as a covering over most of the fetus, almost all of which will be shed before birth.

FIFTH LUNAR MONTH

The baby's heartbeat is now loud enough to be heard through a stethoscope. The baby is very sensitive to noise and may respond by vigorous kicking if very loud music or other noises disturb it. The scalp and eyebrows are more marked. Eyelashes appear and nails harden. Breasts shape out with pale pink nipples.

By the twentieth week the average fetus weighs one pound (500g) and is 12 inches long (30cm). It is making the mother's abdomen protrude externally because the uterus needs more room to expand.

Some spotting or bleeding may occur even at this advanced stage in pregnancy.

SIXTH LUNAR MONTH

The miniature baby can grip firmly with its hands and suck its thumb. It is small enough to turn around completely in the womb. The skin is wrinkled and red; there is not quite enough of that tissue underneath the skin which gives babies that plump look. To protect itself against abrasion, through long submersion, the skin secretes a greasy protective varnish, similar to cream cheese, called vernix.

SEVENTH LUNAR MONTH

The baby is now two-thirds grown in the uterus. Born prematurely, one in four can survive if there is enough stored fat, if the liver, kidneys and lungs have matured enough to function independently and if it is kept in an incubator. The amniotic fluid that has been increasing steadily will now start decreasing in order to make room for the growing baby who will weigh two and a half pounds (1kg) by the end of this month. Enclosing the baby in the amniotic fluid is the amnion, a thick shimmering membrane. It is water-tight and hermetically sealed around the umbilical cord. The cord starts at the baby's navel, travels through the waters and the amniotic membrane to the placenta which functions outside the sac. The amniotic fluid is renewed completely every two hours. The cells of the amnion continue to divide from the original layer and grow along with the baby.

The baby exercises, stretching arms and legs in all directions. The mother feels these movements as slippery slides and little kicks.

EIGHTH LUNAR MONTH

Most of the body hair has been shed by now, but the hairs on the head and eyebrows are lengthening. A little fat has accumulated and the skin has a smoother appearance. The eyelids have reopened. All the organs are sufficiently formed to function independently. Contrary to certain old superstitions, if born prematurely now, it has an even better chance of survival than it did the month before; but it definitely needs all the growing it can get inside of the uterus for health and strength. Towards the end of the month, it is a big 16 inches (38cm). On rare occasions, it can still do somersaults but usually it only moves from side to side. At this point, it might settle in a head-down position, crowned by the pelvic bones.

NINTH LUNAR MONTH

Still perfecting and growing, the mature infant sleeps and eats quietly. When it changes position, the mother may see bulges moving around her abdomen which may be an elbow or a knee. The neatly folded legs are shorter than the arms; the hands now have distinctive little nails. The breasts of both baby boy or baby girl may be protruding as it receives the same substance (estrogen) that makes the mother's breasts enlarge in preparation for the milk. In the last month, the baby has also been receiving special combatting proteins: the antibodies. They will keep it immune to most diseases during the early part of babyhood. Born now, the chances of survival are almost equal to full-term birth.

TENTH LUNAR MONTH

(Forty weeks). The meeting of the two cells blended into one has produced some hundred million cells in the short time span of ten lunar months. Full term is reached approximately in the middle of this month. The child has gathered all it needs to live outside the mother's womb. It cannot grow or move much anymore. Growth stops about a week before birth as the cramped placenta's feeding efficiency lessens. This brings about a change in the hormonal balance which sets in motion the actual

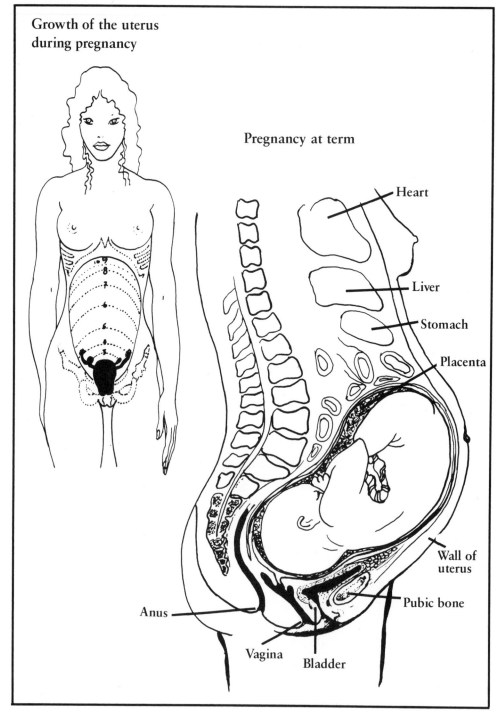

Growth of the uterus
during pregnancy

Pregnancy at term

Heart

Liver

Stomach

Placenta

Wall of
uterus

Pubic bone

Anus

Vagina

Bladder

birth process. Soon the uterine muscles will start contracting. The uterus, expanded to maximum size, drops down a few inches from last month's position. The child at term usually weighs seven to seven and a half pounds (3½kg) and measures an average of nineteen inches (45cm). The head, or bottom, becomes further engaged in the tight pelvic bone passage. It moves through the slowly dilating cervix and the expanding vagina. It is ready for the big journey out . . .

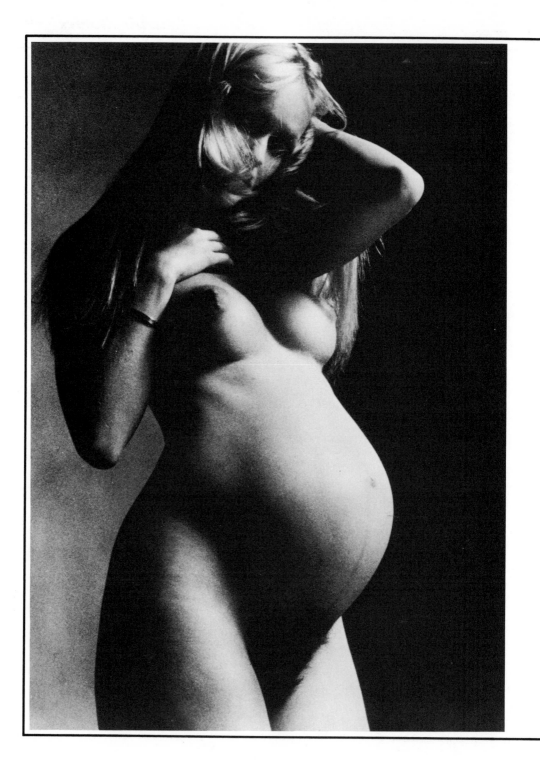

Body Care

Pregnancy . . . preparation

**so long as one feels
that one is the doer
one cannot escape
from the wheels of birth
—Buddha**

Since you are going to have this child with a positive attitude and in a relaxed manner, it makes sense—during this unique period—to give a lot of attention to the body that is producing a new person.

Harmony is the state to achieve and maintain

HARMONY INSIDE By knowing the details of the baby's development, by eating healthy foods, by understanding the process of reproduction with clarity.

HARMONY OUTSIDE By keeping the body supple, strong, alert, clean, by wearing easy and pleasant clothes, by getting involved in activities outside of your emotions.

Limbering Exercises

Total Relaxation. Before doing any exercises, it's best to give the body a layback period to relax: unwinding and breathing.

When to Start. Most childbirth exercise classes begin toward the middle of the seventh month. But it takes time to become aware of the body, to learn to control muscles and respiration, to know how to distribute energies and relieve pressures. Ideally, exercises are already part of every woman's routine. It is really a good idea to start exercising as soon as possible if you do not already have a regular fitness routine. Muscles are not strengthened in a few days. Fifteen minutes a day (before breakfast or dinner) are preferable to one hour a week in a rush. If you find it boring to do the same exercises daily, add variations, stretching movements of your own invention that feel good. For giving birth a woman needs flexibility, strength and endurance, and this is where gymnastic training can be helpful. Daily physical activities can be performed consciously to reinforce the strengthening of muscles (i.e., picking up things from the floor, reaching for high shelves, climbing stairs).

Purpose
- To tone muscles and keep them supple.
- To lessen the strains of pregnancy and birth.
- To help control relaxation consciously and decrease awareness of labor discomfort.

Clothing for Exercises. Minimal or none, in a warm environment. In cooler places, wear leotards or body suits that will stretch to accommodate your growth. A tee shirt and bikini pants, cotton longjohns or even sweatpants are also comfortable.

Begin by Lying Flat on Your Back.

(Or lie on your side in the late stages of pregnancy.) If you do not have a carpeted area and the floor feels too hard, fold a blanket in two, lengthwise. A cushion can support your head if that makes you more comfortable. Some people feel even more relaxed with a pillow placed under the thighs near the knees. Exercise mats can be purchased in many places.

1. Lie at ease . . . Breathe slowly . . . In . . . Out . . . Let the whole body go loose from head to toe . . . Let the hands open up and find an easy position . . . Roll the legs a little from side to side . . . The feet will probably point outward when settling . . . Stay loose a few minutes . . . Take a deep cleansing breath through your nostrils and sigh it out through your lips . . .

2. Once the body is at rest, the mind quieted, and a few deep breaths inhaled and released, you are ready to start the limbering exercises.
From the lying flat position bring both legs up as in the above photograph.

Bend your knees and bring the right leg up to the side of your abdomen, hold for thirty seconds and put the leg down. This helps to stretch the pelvic floor muscles.

Repeat five to ten times. End this set of exercises by bringing up both knees at the same time.

Return to total relaxation position. . . . Breathe slowly and deeply.

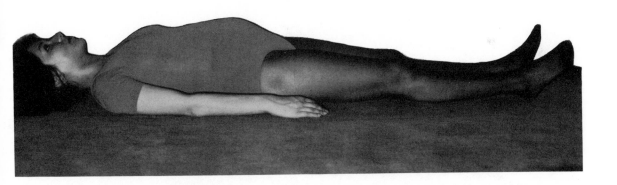

3. Let your head roll from side to side, untangle the neck.

Then, stop moving your head.

Close your eyes.

Erase the lines on the forehead.

Unclench your teeth.

Breathe regularly.

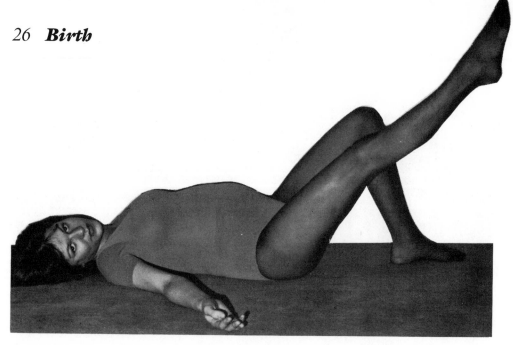

4. Bend left leg. (Note the position of the arm and open hand.)
Lift the right leg, keeping it straight and pointed in an outward right position, hold for a few seconds.
Repeat the movement with the left leg, keeping the right leg bent.
Repeat five to ten times.

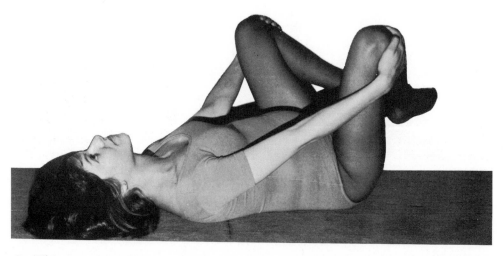

5. This exercise will be useful during the expulsion phase—the second stage of labor—when you push the baby out.
(For more comfort, place a pillow or two at shoulder level.)
Starting from the total relaxation position, draw your legs up against your abdomen, grab the knees or thighs,
take a deep breath...

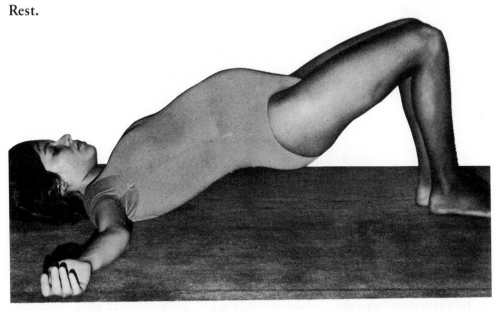

...Raise your head, blow out.

Take another deep breath and hold (or pant).

This will be the stage during which you push at birth. DON'T PUSH NOW!

Exhale and let your head go back.

Take another deep breath, hold it, head forward. (Ready for another push as if a contraction had come.)

Rest.

6. This exercise will help to strengthen the back muscles. Lie on your back, and bend your legs. Gently pressing down on the feet and stretched-out arms, raise up your bottom and arch your back in the shape of a bridge. Inhale as you go up, exhale slowly on the way down...Repeat...Relax.

7. DISASSOCIATION EXERCISES Usually, we use our muscles in a co-ordinated way, one muscle reacting in direct response to the other. Although this works fine for everyday activities, this coordinated response wastes energy during labor. For example, if your body can remain relaxed while the uterus is contracting, you can channel the saved energy into a form of deep breathing which will relieve the strain.

Check yourself on disassociation at exercise time or while lying on your bed before or after sleep. Concentrate on special areas of your body. For instance, make a tight fist with your right hand and then tighten the muscles in your left leg. Now, check the rest of your body. Is the back of your neck loose? Is the left arm at rest? Check it, or better still, have someone else see if it is really relaxed. . . . Let go. . . Repeat, this time tightening other parts of your body.

A moderation of exercises that involve prolonged periods on the back is recommended, as the womb in this position may compress major blood vessels and impede circulation.

8. RELIEVING ABDOMINAL PRESSURE Stand on hands and knees, breathe in, pull the abdomen inward, round the back, tighten up the bottom, lower the head slightly.

Breathe out, let the belly go slowly, decontract the abdominal muscles, let the back curve in gently, relax the bottom.

9. TONING THE MUSCLES OF THE BACK AND ABDOMEN Starting from the hand and knee position, straighten out the right leg, hold a few seconds and kneel again. Do the same with the left leg. Repeat both exercises five to ten times, taking great care not to strain yourself.

10. TOTAL RELAXATION Concentrate on decontracting every muscle in your body: starting with the scalp, then the forehead, the brows, the eyelids, the cheeks, the nostrils, the jawbone, the neck, the nape of the neck, the spine, the shoulders, the right arm and hand, the left arm and hand (all the way down to the fingers), the solar plexus, the torso, the stomach, the abdomen, the hips, the buttocks, the thighs, the calves and the feet.

11. KEGEL EXERCISE The muscles surrounding the vaginal opening and the perineal area used to be strong when we squatted to relieve ourselves instead of sitting on toilets. These muscles need to be—and can be—strengthened with a simple exercise that can be done anytime and anywhere, waiting for a bus, brushing your teeth, standing on line at the post office. . . .

Contract the muscles around the vagina as if you were trying to stop or hold from urinating. (These are the muscles to work on!) Hold them tight for a few seconds and release slowly.

This is an excellent exercise to do before, during and after birth. During labor, the pressure is on the pelvic floor and the opening needs to be relaxed in order to let the baby through. You can help if you learn to control these muscles. This same little exercise can be useful in toning up and firming the whole area starting a week or two after the baby is born.

LEG STRETCH   1. Roll onto your side, fold one leg and tuck foot in back. Keeping the other leg straight, lift ten times without resting it on the floor in between. To maintain balance, put palm of hand flat on floor at chest level.

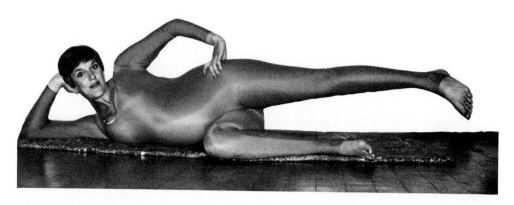

2. To stretch a different set of muscles, shift weight of body and fold leg at floor level. Keeping other leg straight and raised above the floor, point toe toward floor, give eight little lifts—rest, breathe and go for two more sets of eight. Breathe and roll to the other side to repeat both sets of exercises.

UPPER SPINE ROLL   Fold legs a little and with both arms straight out, lift head off floor, exhaling all the while. Hold a moment, feel abdominal muscles gently pull, and roll back. Repeat four times.

LOWER SPINE STRETCH   Lift both legs and fold one to the side of belly. Hold this position to the count of eight, release and repeat with other leg. Breathe out and lower legs slowly.

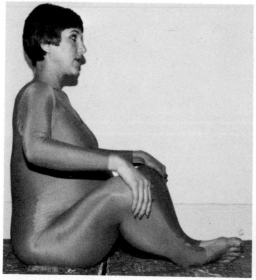
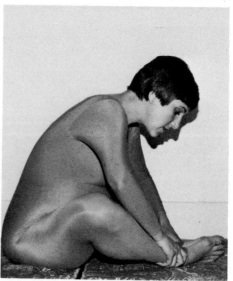

SPINE STRETCH   Sitting in tailor position, shift hands from knees to ankles and press with elbows on knees. Slowly bend forward feeling the inner leg muscles stretching. Stay in this position to the count of ten. Straighten slowly and breathe.

Shift weight to the back. With hands on top of knees hold yourself from rolling back. Feel the shoulder area stretching. Hold to the count of ten. Straighten slowly and breathe.

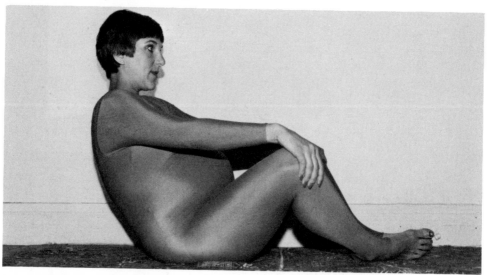

SIDE STRETCH 1. Sitting in tailor position, feet joined flat in middle, extend arms overhead. Stretch from waist. Swaying gently from left to right alleviates pressure on rib cage and aches in higher back. Repeat ten to twenty times.

2. With palms of hands on knees, press knees down using upper torso strength. Push knees back up using lower torso strength. These movements will help stretch leg ligaments and relieve back pressure. Try eight to ten times with each leg.

BACK AND LEG STRETCH   Still sitting on floor, spread both legs as far apart as possible. After straightening them, point one toe and lean upper body sideways to touch toe. Or grasp ankle and pull forward slowly. Repeat on the other side. Raise and lower torso, ten times on each side. Breathe in between.

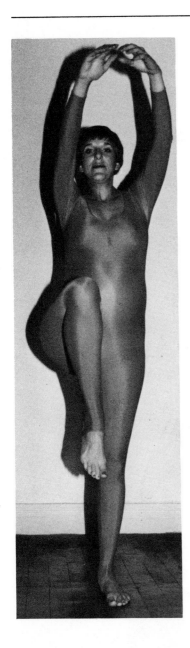 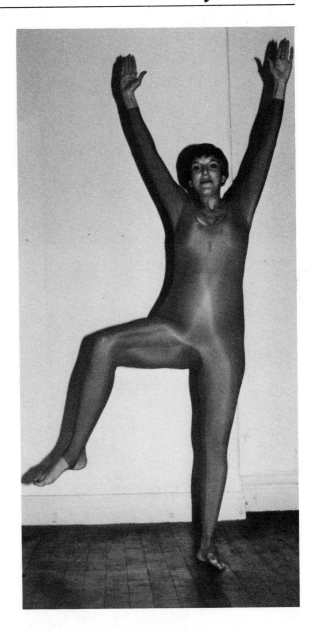

STRETCH STAND   With arms above head, stretch high and wiggle finger tips. Lift up folded leg and shift leg to the side and let the arms come down slowly. Bring down leg slowly, bring feet back together. Repeat ten times, back and forth—from right to left and left to right.

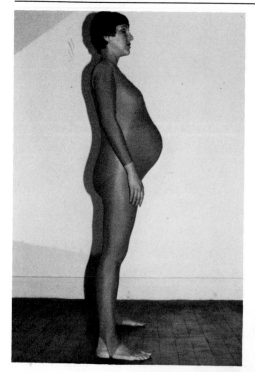
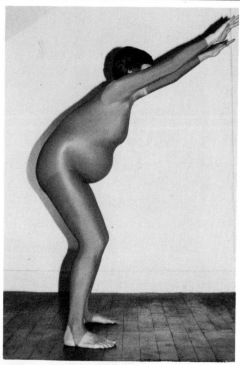
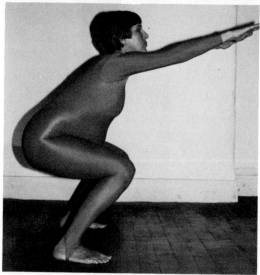

STRENGTHEN AND TONE   Stand with legs apart, raise arms and arch
back. Bend legs and hold to the count of ten. Rise slowly, breathe. Repeat three
times. This movement works tummy muscles, back, and strengthens legs.

If you have been practicing yoga, many of the exercises will be familiar to you. But remember, whether you are doing yoga or any of the limbering exercises already mentioned, always exercise slowly without forcing or straining your body.

HELPFUL HINTS

- Do not exercise on a mattress or soft ground. This will disturb your equilibrium.
- Do not wear anything stiff or hard while exercising. Glasses, tight clothing, jewelry, etc., would be constricting.
- Jumpy and jerky movements should be avoided.
- Empty your bladder before exercising.
- Do not exercise for at least two hours after eating.
- Do not force yourself to exercise if you are in a hurry, feverish, nauseous or have breathing problems. If you have any pain, take it as a warning to stop.
- You may find it easier to relax and exercise after a warm bath.
- Swimming is one of the best workouts.
- Try to allow for a rest period at the end of the session, wrapping yourself in a blanket to keep warm.
- Think about joining a postdelivery fitness program. It can help you keep your body in shape, and it is a good way to meet and talk with other mothers.

Breathing: The Rhythm of Life

Notice the way you are breathing now as you read this. In a quiet regular rhythm? Is there a tense muscle in your body? Shoulder muscles perhaps? Concentrate on relaxing them by breathing slowly. Breathe in through the nose. . . . Exhale through the mouth. Again. The tension will soon be gone, replaced by a warm mellow feeling.

Conscious breathing can be the magic key to an easier childbirth. It will help you through times of stress without wasting precious energy. Also, conscious breathing will make it easier for you to handle tension and excitement without the use of drugs. It is a good idea to learn how to relax through breathing as early as possible in pregnancy so that you will be well prepared when labor begins; and you will be able to participate full time in the birth of your baby. Deep breathing may also prove useful at other times when dealing with pain or tension.

There are many organized classes given to teach breathing and preparation for childbirth. Six lessons usually cost between $25 and $80 and will prove to be very useful to you. (Find the location of a class near you by looking in the telephone book or check the Resources section in this book.) Some hospitals and many birth centers offer classes as part of their programs. Hospital classes are generally Lamaze-oriented, while classes at birth centers may combine a variety of approaches. But you don't have to wait for the classes to begin. Start practicing now. The three basic kinds of breathing are deep, shallow and pant breathing.

It is a good idea to practice your breathing regularly at home, but in between scheduled practice sessions do your breathing exercises whenever you remember. Practice while you're sitting in traffic, while you're waiting for your prenatal exam or for the bus.

To begin, sit in a tailor position. Focus your attention on one specific point or object. At birthtime, place your chosen object or image in your room at home or in the hospital. It will remind you to open up.

DEEP BREATHING

Close your eyes. Free your mind of all thoughts.

Breathe in deeply through the nose. The air will go down the back of your throat, swell the lungs, and expand the abdomen (see it rise).

Release the breath very slowly.

A good cleansing of the respiratory tract takes place.

When the first abdominal contractions occur (which may be at labor time or just as a warning, tuning-up days before D-Day), you can override them smoothly with deep breathing. Each breathing exercise can be conveniently timed to last one minute, assuming it is a contraction. However, contractions do not necessarily last exactly one minute. Sometimes they are longer, sometimes shorter.

When real labor contractions begin, try to breathe normally for as long as possible, until you feel the need to use your deep breathing. If you start too soon, you may unnecessarily exhaust yourself.

SHALLOW BREATHING

As labor advances and the contractions get stronger, you need to relieve the pressure on the abdominal walls. Deep breathing will only be used at the beginning and end of the stronger contractions. To alleviate the more intense contractions, you can practice shallow breathing.

Start with deep breathing.

Relax the whole body. Breathe shallow, from the chest only. Put your hands on the rib cage. See and feel it rise.

Breathe not too fast, lightly, effortlessly, in through the nose, out through the mouth, letting out a faint sigh.

Gradually breathe slower. End with deep breathing.

You will notice that if you do this exercise too fast it will make you high. Don't let yourself get dizzy or you will lose the beneficial rhythm and you may even faint. If you get dizzy, take a short deep breath and hold it for ten seconds. Vertigo should disappear. Start shallow breathing again at a slower pace.

During the first week of practicing shallow breathing ask someone to time you. When your friend gives you the signal to start, go through the motions described above until the minute is over. Take a deep breath. You are in total relaxation, as you will be between every contraction during this phase of labor.

PANT BREATHING

When delivery is near, you may have to hold your urge to push until the time is really right. To prevent the diaphragm from pressing on the abdomen you will breathe in small puffs. Pant breathing can also be used to prevent yourself from pushing as the baby's head crowns. This will help you to avoid perineal tearing and episiotomy.

Breathe in and out through your mouth.
Breathe-pant in a regular rhythm, quite quickly to make it effective, but not too fast or you may become dry-mouthed and dizzy.
Rest when the contraction is over.

It takes a while to find out the correct way of panting. In the course of practicing you will find your own comfortable rhythm.

A variation to this panting exercise, which you may find easier, is to pant and then blow out the air (as if blowing out a candle).

Breathe quickly with mouth opened.

A few fast pants (1, 2, 3, 4, 5) and blow out.

Repeat, like the refrain to a tune, not too fast.

Stop a minute later (or when the desire to push is gone).

Deep sigh, Ahhhhh . . . relax.

Activities

Unless you have a special condition and your doctor has advised against certain activities, anything that you used to do before you were pregnant is fine now too.

If dancing feels all right then do it. The same goes for sports. But, there is no need for competitions which accelerate the heart and circulation unnecessarily. Obviously, riding a motorcycle is uncomfortable and not recommended. Snow or water skiing is dangerous because of the alteration in the balance of your weight and the possibility of falling.

Swimming feels the best during pregnancy and walking at least an hour a day is good exercise. Many women take jet airplanes up to the last weeks of pregnancy without any problems, but others say that the pressure and lack of oxygen interferes with their breathing. Airlines will not, knowingly, board women in their ninth month. Also, the restricted amount of space on long flights can be most uncomfortable and claustrophobic. Even though stewardesses have training in emergency childbirth, it's better to delay a trip if a few contractions have already occurred or if it's really close to due date. Moving by car is the unavoidable way of everyday life for many women. Remember that going at an easy speed may reduce sudden stopping, which is a real danger for women prone to miscarriages. Safety belts are now mandatory in many states.

PHYSICAL LOVING

It begins with loving your own body. As your body grows into this extraordinary shape, you get flashes of established attitudes from past and present fashion-conscious people who believe that a pregnant woman is unattractive! But these are only superficial fashion statements that cramp your style. What could be more fantastic than to see and feel this miraculous transformation which will happen perhaps just once or only a very few times in your life. Examine your preconceived prejudices, open your mind and then take a long look at the full, rounded shape of a pregnant woman. There are many women who feel more sensual when they become pregnant. Some women find that there are periods during their pregnancy, particularly in the first three months, when they don't want to make love. You may feel tired and tense, unaccustomed to your changing body. Your hormonal balance may be in a state of change. But there are many ways to express love and tenderness, if you recognize this as a small phase, not a change in your lives as lovers. Humor can be an erotic ingredient.

Some women are frightened that sex will hurt the baby, which it cannot if love is a harmonious exchange. Try different positions so the man's weight does not make you uncomfortable. Use extra pillows to

support your head, buttocks, back, wherever it helps you to relax and move your body. Experiment, use your imagination, and communicate openly with each other. You may find by the end of these few months that you have learned more than ever before about each other's bodies and desires. If you feel timid, just touch each other. Show him how to caress your belly with the round soft strokes (called effleurage) that you will do while in labor to relax your abdominal muscles. Feel free to love and to be loved.

Gentle lovemaking is the best and most natural preparation for birthing. If you can feel your whole body opening up and experience the complete release of orgasm, you will know what it is to open up and relax in labor. The sensation of giving birth, when the process is not impeded by anxiety or complications, is not far from the feeling of orgasmic burst. Your breasts, extra-sensitive in the last few months, are probably tingling with the need to be touched. By touching, squeezing, sucking them, he will be preparing your nipples for breast-feeding, in the most pleasurable way. When your body is ripe and ready for labor, stimulation of your nipples, and intercourse, will often help labor to start. And if you can add flexibility to the patterns of your love life, so that you make love at times when you are most relaxed instead of in those tired and tense nights, you will be well prepared for the days when you become lovers again between feedings, at nap time, whenever the calm of a sleeping baby allows it.

However, if there is any bleeding, if the waters have already broken or if you have an irritation, any penetration could be dangerous. In these instances, call your physician or midwife. Also if you have had a previous miscarriage it is best to abstain in the early months, especially during the weeks when your period would be due.

MASSAGE

A good way to relieve the fatigue that will sometimes come from carrying a baby inside of you is with a gentle, sensual massage. Also, your companion, in helping you, may feel closer to and more familiar with the unborn child. If he does not feel like doing it, try asking a good friend.

After a warm bath or shower (in the same manner as for the exercises) lie on a surface that is not too soft. Place a towel or a washable cloth under you. Put on some music. Make sure you are in a warm place and that you won't be disturbed. The person massaging you must have clean hands. She/he could start with the head; running her/his fingers through the hair, softly pulling on it by the handful. Then, with the thumbs pressing lightly on the forehead and temple, massage in a rotating motion. . . . With flat hands move down the neck and chin. . . . With both hands massage the back of the neck and head. . . . Up in the hair, down to the shoulders, where all the tension gathers. All the tight muscles of that area should be worked over until your facial expression is truly relaxed. Then massage the shoulders and arms all the way to the tips of each finger. Smooth the flesh with warm oil or a good cream. Slide along the muscles of the upper arm, press the palms around the shoulders. Brush–caress toward the chest. The looser you are when being massaged, the better it feels. With flat hands press down to the breasts and around. Come back with both hands between the breasts to the base

of the neck and reverse the movement, pressing with the tip of the fingers.

Go easy on the abdomen. Spread on some warm oil. Use soft circular strokes round and round with cupped hands from the base of the belly to the top, and down again with a brushing of the fingertips. Next come the legs. Knead the thighs and calves strongly to stimulate the circulation. They have been supporting the weight of the whole body and need to feel relieved. Press down on the thighs with both hands from the hip to the knee and in a downsweep to the foot, up and down making a halt at the knee. Work on the kneecap with the thumbs. Give special attention to the calf as it can get quite tense from walking. Massage the feet with both hands all the way to each individual toe.

Turn to the side for a back massage. The lower back may need extra care because of the abdominal pull. Repeat firm strokes from the spine to the hips with the flat of the hands, and press with the palms. Vibrate the buttocks with a shivery hand, then rotate each well-oiled buttock with separate hands, fast or slow, in the same or different direction, as desired. Finger press the base of the spine, then work up the spine over all the dorsal muscles. Use long strokes for long muscles, running each index finger along the sides of the spine. Knead the short muscles running from shoulder to neck. Turn over to the other side for a repeat performance. At the end, use the fingertips to play piano all over the back—this will feel great. Terminate with a soft brushing before wrapping her up in a blanket to keep her warm.

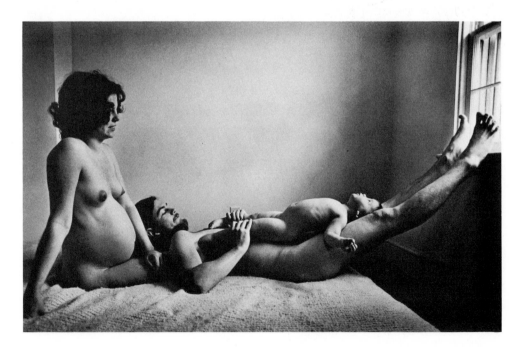

Ointments. The most ancient skin-care secret is refined olive oil. It has been treasured by people around the Mediterranean for thousands of years as a complete body massage ointment. If you live in a cold place, warm the oil to body temperature. One of the ways to keep it warm during a massage is in a container surrounded with very hot water. Midwives in many parts of the world anoint the perineum with warm olive oil to ease the stretching just before the baby's head is about to pop out. Coconut and almond oil smell delicious if they have been refined the natural way. Apricot kernel is also very good for the skin. A health-food store will usually stock any of these oils or can order one for you. If you do not have such a store near you, check the local pharmacy. Vegetable oils can also be used for massaging. Sesame and safflower are excellent, but corn, peanut and walnut are too thick and sticky. You could use lanolin oil, scentless or with a few drops of your favorite perfume or essence extract. Spread the oil first on your hands in small quantity and then spread it on your body. You can also break up a pearl of vitamin E and lubricate your skin with the contents. However, this will be more expensive and quite messy.

Remember to care regularly for your breasts, hips, buttocks and abdomen. Massage once a day with oil or a fluid cream to help the elasticity, as the skin will stretch during the progression of the pregnancy.

This is a good time to learn some songs or practice an instrument: recorder, guitar. Tunes to cool you, your companion or the baby when the going gets rough.

PALPATION

Palpation is the external method used to feel the position of the baby inside the uterus. Your doctor or midwife may do it during your regular prenatal visits, but in between visits it is simple for you to try it at home, perhaps at the end of a massage. As you discover what may feel like a hand, a head, an elbow, you may find that this is your first form of communication with your baby.

To feel the shape of the baby inside your uterus, apply firm but gentle pressure with your fingertips or your palms, starting at the top of the uterus and working down both sides of the abdomen. Press alternately with your right, and then your left hand, feeling first for the buttocks which will feel soft and unevenly rounded. Next you may feel the back, a gentle C-curve which resists the side-to-side pressure of your hands. You should feel the head above your pelvic bone—a firm, flexible, round shape that can be bobbed from side to side with alternate pressure. Of course, your baby may be in any position and may change position frequently, particularly before the last month of pregnancy when most babies decide to get into a head down position ready for birth. As you explore the form of your baby, you may feel arms and legs, knees and elbows moving in response to your touch. You needn't worry that you are hurting your baby—he or she is simply enjoying this intrauterine massage.

SHIATSU

Shiatsu is an ancient Japanese form of therapeutic massage in which pressure is applied with the fingers or thumbs to specific points over the surface of the body. These pressure points, and the meridians along which they lie, are the same as those used in acupuncture.

In the Orient, where shiatsu has been practiced for centuries, it is commonly believed that one-third of a person's adult functioning is determined by his or her life in the womb. Based on this belief, shiatsu has traditionally been practiced in pregnancy as a form of embryo education (*tai kyo*). Pressure applied to points over the abdomen is used to gently stimulate the fetus. When a man performs shiatsu on his partner in pregnancy, he is not only helping the pregnant woman, he is also nurturing his unborn child.

Besides *tai kyo,* shiatsu has many advantages in pregnancy. It can be used in place of medications, to treat common aches and pains— headache, backache, leg cramps, morning sickness, etc. It can be used to relieve pain in labor by applying specific pressure to the sacrum, to the neck and ankles, and to the neck and toes. And it can be useful as a preparation for childbirth by helping a woman develop control over parts of her body that she previously felt were uncontrollable, and by making her aware of muscular connections within her body—for instance, between the pelvis and the ribcage.

Shiatsu is quickly emerging as a recognized form of therapeutic massage in this country. Shiatsu therapists in the United States are generally trained, but there are also books available which can teach the lay person how to perform basic shiatsu for particular ailments on others or on him/herself.

PERINEAL MASSAGE

Very often, the tissue of the vaginal opening is not capable of stretching to allow the birth of the baby's head, and a small cut, or episiotomy, has to be made in the perineum. In cultures where women haul water and squat rather than sit to cook, weave or perform natural functions, tears and episiotomies are rare. But in our culture, with its comforts and conveniences, women who want to avoid tearing or being cut must exercise and condition the perineum in preparation for birth.

Make sure you have plenty of vitamin E in your diet and get plenty of exercise. Swim, dance, ride a bike, walk, and squat rather than kneel when wiping the floor or picking up an object. Practice your Kegel and pelvic relaxation exercises whenever you remember during the day, so that you will be able to control a slow and gentle birthing of your baby's head. Between four and six weeks before your due date, you should begin a daily massage of your vagina and perineal area. Ask your partner to help. It may become one of the intimate pleasures you can share at a time when making love is difficult. He should start by inserting one or two fingers into your vagina, moving them back and forth in a semicircular shape along the floor of the vaginal passage. Tell him when you feel tension or a burning sensation. He should apply pressure gently, so that the tissues can slowly stretch. As he feels them stretch, day by day, he can add more fingers. At the same time he will be able to check the

effectiveness of your Kegel and pelvic relaxation exercises by feeling your increasing ability to relax the muscles during massage. At the beginning or end of your massage, ask your partner to rub the whole of your perineal area with a natural (olive, coconut, almond) oil, massaging until all the lubricant has been absorbed.

You should tell your birth attendant if you are hoping to avoid an episiotomy, so that he/she can help during labor.

Preparation for Breast-Feeding

For some women, breast-feeding is inconvenient, unpleasant and, considering the available commercial substitutes, may even seem "backward." However, there are a great number of women who feel it is part of the continuous process of growing and nurturing the seed: feeding and watering the growing baby from their own well. It doesn't take a special kind of woman to breast-feed. Anyone who feels like it can do it. However, it is true that living in a city and working at a job are not conducive to nursing. This doesn't mean that all city mothers wanting to breast-feed their babies should move to the country, but they should allow themselves time after the birth to enjoy it in an unhurried manner. You will need time to discover what works best between mother and baby concerning supply and demand, and time for the breasts to adjust.

From the beginning of pregnancy, the breasts become more tender and enlarged. The areola around the nipple gets darker and tiny little fleshy protuberances sometimes appear. You could start gentle massages in the early months to keep the skin supple and avoid stretch marks. This should be done regularly in the last months. Further along in the pregnancy there may even be slight leaks from the nipples as the mammary glands are preparing to produce milk. Breasts swell the most during the first and last months of pregnancy and you may feel the need for the support of a stronger bra if they become very enlarged.

If the nipples are protruding it will be easier to breast-feed. Try producing a little liquid to get the feel of it. If the nipples are inverted, flat or small it is essential to prepare them by drawing them out between the thumb and index finger during the last months of pregnancy. Do it for a short time after the exercise period. The nipples should become more elastic and better prepared for the baby to suck.

MEDICATION

All medications—aspirin, tranquilizers, antacids, sleeping pills, cough medicines, nasal sprays (these are the most frequently used drugs)—have drawbacks. They affect your own ability to reestablish a natural balance, and they will probably be absorbed by the placenta and fetus. Most drugs contain elements that may not be beneficial to a growing embryo. Few drugs have been definitely linked with birth defects, but all are considered hazardous at any time during pregnancy.

To absorb unnecessary or unproven medication is to take a serious risk. Remember thalidomide?

Pregnancy is not an illness, but as the body's metabolism changes, certain transformations may (or may not) bring some discomfort. The most common ailments are nausea, indigestion, constipation, and/or swelling of the hands, ankles and feet. These could be caused by the enlarged uterus squeezing the digestive system and blood vessels or by an imbalance in nutrition. Before taking any medication, you should see if these minor ailments can be corrected through your daily food intake. You can also try the basic medicinal herbs (see page 55), nature's own curatives. To counteract nausea, a daily intake of 5mg each of B_1 and B_6 is recommended, as well as brewer's yeast and other natural sources of B vitamins such as yogurt. You can also reduce or eliminate nausea by taking frequent small snacks of protein-rich foods, especially in the mornings. Try keeping a bowl of unsalted nuts by your bedside, for instance, to munch on before you get up for the day.

Of course if a problem persists, your doctor may prescribe suitable medication. Discuss with him/her what the medication contains and any possible side effects that may occur. Prenatal vitamins are always a good idea because women often change their eating habits as pregnancy advances. The baby takes from the mother everything it needs to grow, and this may cause the mother to feel certain cravings, a need for certain foods. It is not the baby that suffers; it is usually the mother who will be weakened if she does not take proper care of herself. The baby, being a parasite, will draw as much as it needs. Your need for iron, calcium and vitamins is increased and should be supplemented with proper amounts prescribed by a competent medical authority. If you are eating good, wholesome, unprocessed food in enough quantity, chances are you will not need to take extra vitamins.

There has been a lot of controversy over the need for folic acid. Some physicians feel that if there is a folic acid deficiency, premature labor may occur. However, even in women with marked folic anemia the baby is not affected.

DRUGS AND ALCOHOL

Most substances absorbed by a pregnant woman seep through the placenta and reach the baby. This includes harmful chemicals, caffeine, saccharin, alcohol, tobacco, marijuana and narcotics. All of these substances may be harmful to the growing fetus.

Most of the damage caused by drugs occurs during the first four months of pregnancy, while the cells are being formed and the structure of the new person is developing. At this time the baby's growth can be affected and damage can occur. In the later months, even limited use of drugs can cause minor complications, both for the baby and for your delivery. The problem is that most women, even though they may know of their pregnancy during the early months, do not realize the extent of damage that can be caused by drugs. This is especially true in these first months when you do not really feel or look pregnant. Yet, it cannot be overemphasized that these are the most crucial months in your baby's formation.

Any amount of alcohol can be dangerous to your baby. A woman who drinks heavily during pregnancy stands about a 50 percent chance of giving birth to a baby with fetal alcohol syndrome, which is characterized by low birth weight, facial abnormalities and irreversible mental impairments. But research shows that even moderate amounts of social drinking can cause signs of fetal alcohol syndrome in your baby, and can increase the risk of miscarriage. There is no known safe level of alcohol consumption in pregnancy. Any alcohol consumed by you will be experienced by your baby, and will remain in his system for an extended period of time. But we do know that the most harmful forms of alcohol consumption in pregnancy are "binging"—even if it only happens once—and habitual drinking—even one or two drinks a day. It's hard to refuse a glass of wine or beer when you're having a meal with friends—if it's an occasional pleasure, enjoy it. But if it becomes a regular habit, if you find yourself feeling even a little bit tipsy, if enjoyment turns into anxiety, then it's time to stop.

Many women find cigarette smoking less pleasurable during pregnancy, especially if they are having problems with nausea. If you are a smoker, this is the easiest time to quit. You will never have a better reason—your own baby's health. Women who smoke in pregnancy give birth to smaller, less advanced babies, and run a greater risk of miscarriage and stillborn birth. It has been proven that the effects of cigarette smoking in pregnancy are directly related to the number of cigarettes smoked per day, and that giving up or cutting down on smoking as late as the fourth month of pregnancy can minimize the harmful effects of this drug on the fetus.

If you occasionally smoke marijuana, you probably think of it as a gentle and relaxing drug. However, its effects on the fetus are not yet known; we only know that it does enter the fetus's system where it accumulates and lingers for days. Strong marijuana can sap your energy and induce paranoia, beside attacking your supplies of vitamins C and B_{12}. If it gets you high, you should know better than to impose a continuous lethargy on your baby.

People taking narcotics are not only harming the baby but they are weakening themselves. It's one thing to wreck yourself, why impose it on your baby? And consider the reality of caring for and supporting your newborn babe when most of your energy and money is spent supporting your habit. If you want to have a healthy baby, give it a clean start. Heroin addiction tends to cause small, lightweight babies. The smaller the weight at birth, the greater the hazards to the baby. In addition, the newborn has to go through withdrawal from whatever drug its mother was addicted to (morphine, heroin, methadone, Demerol, etc.). It is a violent, sickening and often fatal process.

Cocaine might not seem as serious a drug as heroin, but it is as strongly addictive in a subtle, insidious way. Regular cocaine use also has a destructive effect on your general health, partly by inhibiting the body's ability to absorb nutrients in food—nutrients that are vital to you in pregnancy. Effects of cocaine on the baby are neurologically damaging. Babies of cocaine addicts have been observed to be jittery, have tremulous movements with a lot of tiny strokes registered to the brain. Don't gamble with your baby's development.

People who abuse barbiturates (Nembutal, Seconal) are putting their babies in extreme danger. Instead of withdrawal symptoms starting immediately, they take seven to nine days to begin. This means that if the baby was born in a hospital, it will no longer be under the care of the medical staff in the nursery. There is nothing to counteract barbiturate withdrawal. A baby withdrawing from heroin can at least be given phenobarbital to ease the symptoms. Cocaine, amphetamines, angel dust, freebasing, laughing gas, downs...pass them all up; otherwise your baby will pay for your abuse for the rest of its life.

LSD has been observed to cause chromosome breakdown in the mother. It is a very powerful chemical. It is such a strong experience that it is bound to affect the baby in some way. You would not want it forced on you, so don't force it on your child.

ENVIRONMENTAL POLLUTANTS

Every day, in our homes and at work, we may breathe, touch and eat toxic substances that can be absorbed by the fetus. Many women are especially sensitive in pregnancy to the smell of chemicals and gases. Perhaps this is a biological signal to help us protect the vulnerable development of the fetus. It is hard to avoid the car fumes and industrial pollution of the city, but there is no better time than during these months to become aware of whatever you regularly inhale, rub on your face or body, dip your hands in, eat, touch. If you would hesitate to expose a small baby to it, you should protect the fetus from it as well.

Wherever you live, look into the quality of the air and water in your general environment. Fumes and wastes from industrial and chemical plants are among the most serious causes of stillborn births and major birth defects. In some parts of the world, the increasing incidence of babies born without brains has been attributed to severe pollution from very high levels of carbon monoxide and sulfur dioxide in the air. If you live in an area where there are known problems with chemical waste, be sure your water is free from chemical seepage. Drink bottled water.

Women employed in certain occupations are exposed daily to substances that can harm the fetus. The most commonly known risks exist for women working with plastics, dyes, textiles, or in dentistry, laboratories and agriculture. If you work with chemicals, gases or metals, you should find out the names of the substances involved and talk with your doctor about potential hazards to the fetus. Constant and excessive noise, heat and vibrations can also have harmful effects on a fetus.

In general, try to avoid chemicals in cleaners, soaps, creams and foods. If you have a choice of products, pick the ones with the most gentle and natural ingredients. In addition, watch out for these toxins, especially in your job or home, where you might be regularly exposed to them:

- X rays throughout your pregnancy.
- Frequent exposure to anything that emits radiation—microwave ovens, video display terminals. Little is known about the effects of routine ultrasound and doptone, which emit low levels of radiation.
- Chemical fumes from glues, strong cleaners, paints, etc.
- Insecticides, including roach sprays.
- Cigarette fumes.
- Nitrate/nitrite cured meats and foods containing MSG, additives, artificial colorings and preservatives.
- Quinine in large quantities.
- Canned tuna fish which contains mercury, and should not be eaten more than once a week. Also watch for the soldered edges of cans—mainly sardine—that are closed with lead.
- Fresh water fish, especially striped bass, because of PCB polluted rivers.
- Raw or undercooked meats and fish. They can transmit a microorganism which causes a disease called toxoplasmosis. Sick cats and cat litter can also transmit toxoplasmosis.
- Exposure to infections such as measles, chicken pox, hepatitis and German measles (Rubella), herpes and venereal disease, which can be damaging to the fetus.

Cleanliness

Each person has a different idea of what it means to keep clean. To some, it means showering morning and night; to others it is a daily bath or a bath every two days. It depends on what your body demands and how your skin reacts to being washed.

During pregnancy it is important to keep clean as naturally as possible. Avoid being influenced by chemical companies trying to sell their products. In reality you need very little to keep you clean: a good mild soap, Castile shampoo, a bristle toothbrush, toothpowder or ordinary toothpaste, a natural bristle hairbrush and scissors.

The external genital area particularly should be washed daily with soap and water. Gently cleanse over and inside all the folds, as it is a sensitive area. Avoid douches and all chemicals around the vagina as they may upset the delicate mechanism that cleanses it automatically. When wiping yourself after a bowel movement, the most hygienic method is front to back.

Being fresh and clean really makes you feel alert.

Herbs

Plants have the property to attract from the earth nutritive matter, vitamins, and minerals that are essential to living. A small percentage of these plants contain curative properties which, if chosen knowingly and prepared with care, can be fully effective.

Herbal medicines had been forgotten for a while. Phytotherapy, or the art of healing with plants, appears to many people today as a very esoteric science, but curing minor illness with plants can be simple and beneficial.

Our grandparents knew all these remedies without ever having studied botany or medicine. The recipes were passed down from generation to generation. Herbal medicine in fact goes as far back as the refined Greek and Egyptian civilizations.

Herbs, roots and bark can help us. This does not mean you should not consult a doctor when in pain. Chemically-based medication can be a blessing when the need to find a remedy in an emergency and in quantity is imperative. However, there is no one miracle drug and a chemical that cures one part of the body may cause side effects in other parts. For mild disturbances such as digestive difficulties, sleeplessness, constipation, tension, etc., herbal teas can be as effective as chemicals and less taxing on the organism. They are also far safer for the growing fetus than most commercial medications. And, you may really appreciate a basic herbal remedy in place of sitting for hours in a doctor's office waiting for advice on curing mild nausea.

Great caution should be taken with certain herbs during pregnancy and lactation. Do not ingest the following herbs during pregnancy: goldenseal, senna or other strong laxative herbs, aloe, pennyroyal (except in small quantities as part of commercial preparations, or in the last six weeks of pregnancy), mugwort, ginseng, mistletoe, strong chamomile or mint teas in the first three months of pregnancy, cottonroot bark, osha, black and blue cohosh in quantities larger than 1 cup. Most of these herbs can either stimulate the uterus causing premature contractions, or endanger the fetus by diminishing the supply of blood or oxygen to the uterus.

Preparation. Herbal tea is best prepared in an enamel pan. If elements (seeds, roots, bark) have to be simmered, use a pan with a lid to avoid the loss of volatile essences and precious oils. Otherwise, proceed as for regular tea. Pour boiling water on the dried plant and let it sit for five to ten minutes.

Avoid adding white sugar. If the herb tea tastes bitter, sweeten it with untreated honey. If the smell needs to be altered, squeeze in a few lemon drops. Drink it very hot in little gulps. Take it three times a day:

Water mint

once in the morning on an empty stomach, another full cup in the early afternoon and the last one before going to sleep. Use these remedies when needed at a particular time or daily as a prolonged treatment.

Latin names of herbs are given along with the English name so that when acquiring the herb from a botanical garden or a shop in any country (see Resources), there will be no confusion.

HERBS TO REMEDY NAUSEA

Peppermint *(Mentha piperita).* Mint and spearmint have been popular plants throughout Europe, North Africa, the Middle East and North America for a long time. They grow everywhere and are easily recognizable by their strong menthol smell. In the form of a weak tea or alcohol they have many uses. One is the treatment of nervous vomiting. A warm cup of mint tea will settle the stomach. It is also taken as a digestive and a stimulant but may keep a sensitive person awake at night.

Hop *(Humulus lupulus).* The same plant that gives beer its bitter flavor is also a tranquilizer or sedative. The plant itself is very ephemeral. Prepared as a concentrated extract, the fresh female hop cones have been recommended for centuries to cure nausea. A few drops of the tincture in a cup of hot water acts as a calming agent.

Chamomile *(Matricaria* or *anthemis nobilis).* Chamomile, also known in English as scented mayhew, is a tiny yellow flower that has a strong fragrance. It has the power to relieve many ailments, especially those generated in the womb and the stomach. If you are prone to vomiting, brew a weak tea of the dried flowers in the morning. It will also relieve intestinal gas.

Balm *(Melissa officinalis).* Balm is characterized by its lemony smell. It contains powerful ingredients with the same properties as the above herbs.

Ginger *(Zingiber officinale)* can help cure nausea. Ginger is available as a root, ground or in gelatin capsules.

Marjoram (a cooking herb), **Peach tree leaves** and *Anise seeds.* These plants can also help in the relief of nausea.

HERBS THAT AID DIGESTION

Garden Thyme *(Thymus vulgaris).*   A cup of tea made with a teaspoonful of this sweet-smelling cooking herb is a great stomach settler. Use it in place of Indian or Chinese tea, which have a tendency to overstimulate the heart.

Tilleul (small leaf lime) *(Tilia cordata).*   Use the leaves and flower. Lime-tilleul is taken after the evening meal to settle the stomach and to induce a restful night of sleep. If taken in heavy doses, it will make you perspire (as will sage and chamomile). It activates the production of bile and is highly recommended in cases of indigestion, heartburn and liver problems.

Rosemary, Vervain, Chamomile and *Mint* are also good for digestion. They are easily obtainable by the bagful from an herbalist, natural food store or in the spice rack at the nearest supermarket. The only difference is that the supermarket herbs may not be as carefully dried and picked from chemically free gardens as those fresh from an herbalist or natural food store. During the first three months of pregnancy, mint and chamomile should be brewed in small quantities as a very weak tea, since they may overstimulate the uterus.

Cumin, Coriander, Fennel and *Anise* are seeds that can be used for the same effect. They each have a particularly fine aroma and are also used to flavor various types of food.

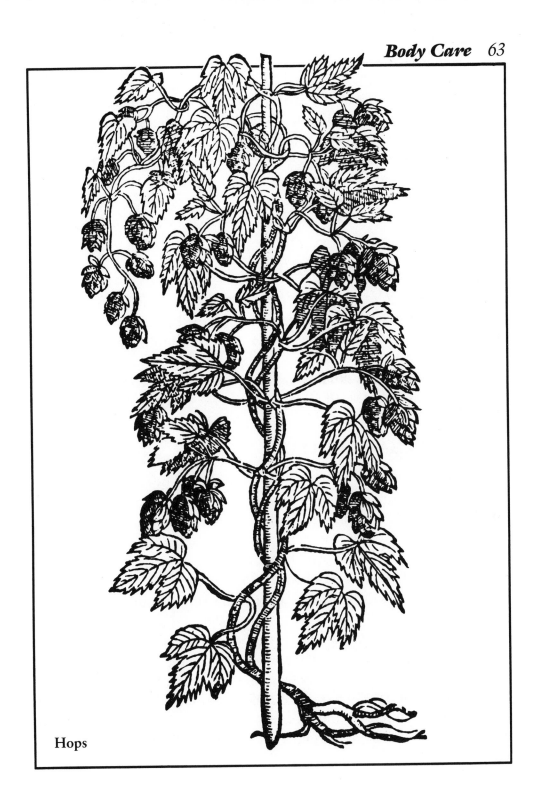

Hops

For immediate relief of heartburn chew on a lemon peel, on a fresh mint leaf or drink a glass of milk. Or to prevent indigestion, try drinking ginger tea fifteen minutes before meals. It is made by steeping ⅛ teaspoon of ginger in a cup of boiling water, then adding a squeeze of lemon. But most of all, consider the foods you have been eating! Watch out for the starches (pastry, white bread, cookies), overrefined sugar and grease in fried foods. These can really be treacherous during pregnancy.

HERBS TO INVITE SLEEP

Valerian (*Valeriana officinalis*).   The valerian root is the most powerful herb to induce sleep, but the smell is really foul. You can add mint or lemon. Valerian in large doses can cause headaches.

Chamomile, Vervain, Hop, Tilleul, Marjoram and *Balm,* already mentioned, are also used effectively to induce sleep.

HERBS TO EASE BIRTH

Red Raspberry (*Rubus stringosus*).   The leaves of this plant are best known for promoting a relaxed delivery and as an astringent. They are also beneficial in pregnancy as a uterine toner.

Spikenard (*Aralia racemosa*).   The spikenard root is known as a blood purifier. It is very effective if taken daily in combination with red raspberry leaves during the last six weeks of pregnancy.

Lobelia (*Lobelia inflata*).   Lobelia, also called Indian Tobacco or pukeweed, is a very powerful seed and plant. It is used by the American Indians. Place 1 level teaspoon in 1 cup of boiling water and allow to stand for 15 minutes. Take 1 to 3 teaspoonfuls a day at the onset of contractions. It has the unique ability of acting both as a relaxant and as a stimulant. This tea should only be handled by people who are familiar with herbs and dosages as an excess may induce strong vomiting. Use with great caution.

Spearmint* and *Peppermint teas are widely used during labor in Spanish cultures since they provide energy and help you to retain needed fluids.

HERBS TO HELP HEALING AFTER GIVING BIRTH

***Comfrey* (*Symphytum officinale*).** The root and foliage of this plant are very helpful in healing wounds. A poultice made of fresh crushed leaves laid on a cut or tear will help the edges to blend together and heal faster. A great tonic is a daily drink of comfrey and alfalfa mixed with any fruit juice.

***Goat's Rue* (*Galega officinalis*).** Flower and seed.

***Juniper* (*Juniperus communis*).** Fruit and bark. A gentle stimulant.

***Shepherd's Purse* (*Capsella bursa-pastoris*).** Plant. Excellent if you are prone to hemorrhage.

***Squaw Vine* (*Mitchella repens*).** Plant. Similar to blue cohosh.

Remember that one person's treat is often another person's poison, so we strongly advise caution in the use of the more powerful herbs.

HERBS TO FACILITATE LACTATION

***Borage* (*Borago officinalis*).** The seeds and leaves of borage

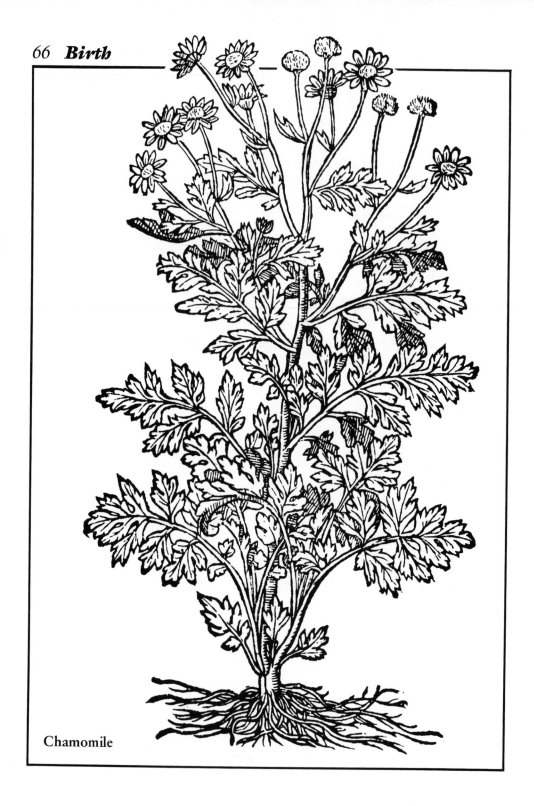

Chamomile

are rich in potassium and calcium which influence the glandular system. A tea made with the seeds and leaves should help to increase the mother's milk. If picked fresh from the garden, the leaves can be steamed and eaten like spinach.

Fennel *(Foeniculum officinalis).* Brewing the seeds and leaves of fennel can be traced all the way back to ancient Egypt. The seeds boiled with barley is a helpful and stimulating drink for nursing mothers.

Anise *(Pimpinella anisum).* An oil is extracted from the seeds of anise and, because of the high concentration of anethol, it acts as a gland stimulator. It should always be highly diluted, a few drops in hot water blended with a little lemon. Besides helping the milk flow, it is very refreshing. Anise is commonly drunk as a liqueur and used to flavor pastries.

Basil and **Cumin,** common spices for food, also possess elements to help increase maternal milk.

Women who are breast-feeding should be aware that most herbs enter the milk supply and may affect the baby. Herbs with astringent properties, such as yarrow, should be avoided since they tend to curdle the milk.

Foods

Your baby grows from the food you eat and the liquids you drink. Being healthy starts right in the womb; it is a lifelong process, but it is never too late to start eating with care and discrimination. The sooner a woman understands her basic nutritional needs, the foods that suit her personality, life-style and environment, the easier all aspects of life become.

How do we know which foods are the best ones to eat during pregnancy? Everyone has different tastes and eating habits but the necessary nutrients are the same for all of us.

Often likes and dislikes change when you are pregnant, which makes nutritional advice particularly important as your tastes change. Pregnancy is often associated with cravings and binges, and those binges can wreak havoc on your digestive system and your figure in the long run. There has to be discipline in the choice and amount of food ingested, otherwise the results of giving in to overindulgence can eventually be harmful.

When you are pregnant and you have binged for a few days you cannot start dieting, as you might have before pregnancy. It would be harmful to the fetus to fast, as it would lower your blood sugar and affect your mood.

The proper balance to aim for is to consume foods low in fat and high in complex carbohydrates, such as vegetables, legumes, fruits and grains. As for liquid intake, it is best to avoid coffee, soft drinks and most of all, alcohol. For beneficial replacement drink lots of mineral water and unsweetened fruit juices.

For optimum health remember that fresh food is better than frozen food and frozen food better than canned. Fresh foods are recommended because they contain ingredients that go to work for you. The intake of processed foods must be limited as they are high in fat and a great deal of their nutritional qualities has been stripped and tampered with during the processing and packaging procedures. Overly refined foods must be avoided as they are devoid of fiber and essential nutrients. Chemical additives, added to prevent foods from spoiling, pile up and linger inside the body, not knowing what to do or where to go as they have no digestive or nutritional value.

Your body will tell you if you are choosing the right foods by the way it reacts. If the food agrees with you, you will feel alert and energetic, and your bowel movements will come easily. Conversely, the body will make it hard to eliminate or it will rid itself of incompatible foods through diarrhea or vomiting. Digestive discomfort is often due to the stomach or intestines being pressed by the expanding uterus; but it is also due to a disagreement with the foods you are eating. Heartburn may be caused by indulging in greasy, fried foods or too much sugar and refined starch. Gas is the result of poor food combinations or improper cooking techniques. If pimples appear, your system may be telling you it needs a rest from heavy foods; it is eliminating undesirables in all directions other than the proper channels. Drink a large glass of fresh squeezed lemonade, and dine on a large mixed salad. Pregnancy and breast-feeding put additional demands on your body and it is up to you to establish a proper balance with quality food and fresh products. Remember to include in your daily diet a variety of vegetables, legumes, fruits and whole-grain products. For good sources of protein choose fish, poultry, lean meat and low-fat dairy products. By following these principles you don't have to be an expert to figure out how to get the necessary proteins, minerals, fats, vitamins and carbohydrates into your daily food intake. All you need is curiosity and the desire for you and your baby to be optimally healthy. To remind you of the good foods available, some suggestions are offered along with a few basic recipes.

PROTEINS

Proteins are most important to the growth of mother and baby. The esential amino acids they provide help in the maintenance and repair of body tissues. They play an essential part in building the baby's internal organs such as the heart and the brain. Proteins promote good skin, shiny hair, strong nails. The other important function of proteins is for the formation of hormones and milk during lactation. Excess intake may turn to fat.

lean steak & hamburgers
stews
chili con carne
boiled beef
shish kebab

bean sprout salad
lentil soup
green pea purée
sweet & sour tofu
black-eyed peas
green peas sautéed with bacon
green peas & almonds
rice & beans
millet
lamb couscous
barley soup
whole wheat pancakes
kasha
oat waffles

steamed fish with low sodium
    soy sauce
shrimp with cashews
steamed sole
broiled salmon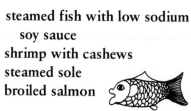

Lemon Chicken: Juice of 4
    lemons mixed with crushed
    garlic clove, 1 grated onion,
    s&p, olive oil, cumin. Sauté
    the pieces of chicken in oil,
    then place in baking dish with
    lemon sauce. Cover and sim-
    mer for one hour. Moisten the
    chicken pieces from time to
    time with the sauce.

cheese & nut quiche
yogurt soup
lamb & yogurt
tomato & yogurt cocktail
peanut butter
low-fat milk
spinach pie
hummus
sunflower seeds in salads

FATS

Fats are divided into two categories—animal (saturated) and vegetable (polyunsaturated). They supply energy in concentrated form, but also have other important functions in our bodies. The polyunsaturated fatty acids are found in vegetable oils, grains and fish. The saturated fatty acids are in butter, bacon, lard, meat, whole milk and cream. In order to keep blood cholesterol within a healthy range, limit consumption of liver, kidneys, egg yolks and custards. These foods are particularly high in cholesterol.

Salad dressing that will last for a while. In a glass bottle (1 quart) put half of a chopped onion, 2 garlic cloves, a sprig of thyme, s&p, ⅓ vinegar, ⅔ olive oil. Shake and use. It will taste better every day.

margarine, lemon & parsley sauce
  on new potatoes
hollandaise sauce on broccoli
grilled salmon
avocado salad

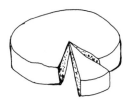

baked apples
  with walnuts
    & raisins
grated carrot salad
almond milk

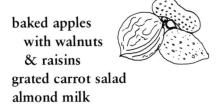

Egg Custard: Blend 4 eggs, ½ cup sugar, pinch of salt, pour slowly into hot quart of milk. Stir until sugar has dissolved. Pour it all in saucepan. Heat on medium fire stirring constantly until it coats spoon, add vanilla or almond extract, stir. Serve hot or cold.

low-fat cheeses
mixed nuts

codfish
salmon
sturgeon

CARBOHYDRATES

Carbohydrates help substain and invigorate the body, providing heat and vitality. Their properties contribute to good digestion. Complex carbohydrates are the unrefined, unprocessed nutrients that can be found in the basic foods such as whole grains, fruits, vegetables and legumes.

Refined carbohydrates come in the form of refined sugar (pastries), white flour and polished rice, which are deficient in vitamins, minerals and fiber. Carbohydrates are needed for all body functions and muscle exertion.

baked potatoes
sweet potato pie
shepherd's pie
sautéed potatoes
   with onions
mashed potatoes
corn on
   the cob
polenta
popcorn
tortillas
carrot & onion
   soup
cold gazpacho
minestrone
chicken soup with
   rice & vegetables

spaghetti with tomato sauce
   with ricotta
lasagne
whole wheat pasta primavera

Rice Pudding:
   Blend 1 cup of cooked rice, 3
beaten egg yolks, raisins, 2 cups of low-fat milk,
½ cup unrefined sugar, a pinch of salt, lemon rind.
Grease baking dish. Put in medium oven for 25
minutes. Remove & top with
2 stiff egg whites mixed with
sugar and lemon juice.
Return to 300° oven until
brown. Eat hot or cold.

fruit has its own sugar
banana whip
mashed bananas
   with honey
fruit salad

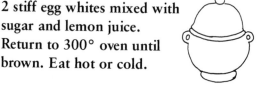

MINERALS

Minerals act as regulators in our bodies making certain the nervous system is well balanced. Of all the minerals found in the body, seventeen elements are basic to nutrition. Minerals work in combination to strengthen the skeletal structure. They are important for hormone production and essential to teeth, nerve cells, bones, tissue and blood. The seven macronutrients present in higher amounts are calcium (a pregnant woman automatically absorbs it and needs more in her diet), chlorine, magnesium, phosphorus, sodium, potassium and sulfur. Iodine and iron are also in extra demand during pregnancy. Minerals are contained in a balanced diet; they can be supplemented if needed.

whole wheat bread
pumpernickel
pita bread
chappatis (from India)
Irish soda bread
bread mixed with molasses

fruit compote
bread with sultanas
   (small seedless grapes)
breakfast cereals with raisins
muesli or granola soaked
   overnight in orange juice
fruit salad topped with honey
stuffed cabbage with soaked
   cereals, seedless raisins &
   shredded liver
bulgur wheat mint salad

Skewered Liver:
   Marinate meat in lemon, tarragon
   & cider. Roll in flour, s&p. Place
   liver between mushroom, onion,
   bacon, and tomato on skewer.
   Brush with oil & grill.

mushroom & spinach salad,
seawater fish
ratatouille

VITAMINS

Vitamins work on the body at the cell level; they are necessary for cell growth, and in promoting cell regeneration. Vitamins are organic substances derived from the plants and animals that we eat. They can be consumed in our foods or in supplements made from natural and synthetic sources. Vitamins and minerals are often interdependent on each other. Professional advice should be followed when taking vitamin supplements, because some such as A and D are toxic in high doses.

fruit juices
sliced orange salad with mint leaves

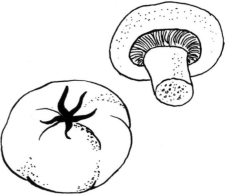

sliced tomatoes & mozzarella
   with basil
spinach salad
   with hard-boiled eggs, tuna, olives

FIBER

Fiber, or roughage, is a plant component that the body cannot digest. Fiber is found in fruits, vegetables, leaves and in the outer layer of legumes, grains, seeds and nuts. Fiber in its passage through the intestinal tract helps the elimination process in many ways.

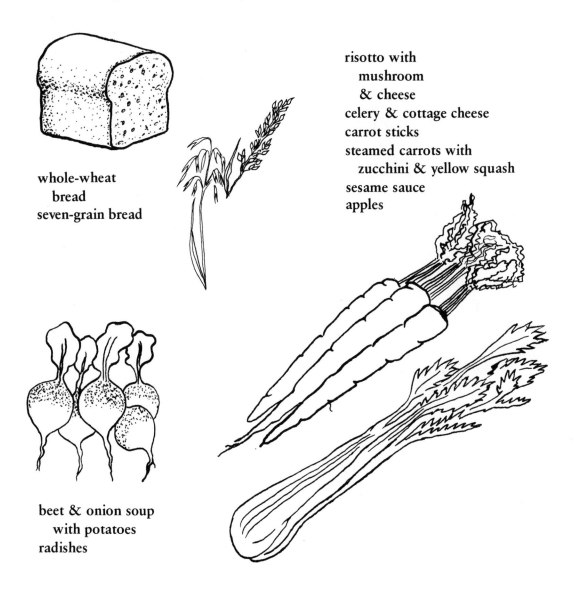

whole-wheat
  bread
seven-grain bread

risotto with
  mushroom
  & cheese
celery & cottage cheese
carrot sticks
steamed carrots with
  zucchini & yellow squash
sesame sauce
apples

beet & onion soup
  with potatoes
radishes

Clothing

There is nothing like the feel of good fabric against the skin to keep you in a good mood throughout the day. Simplicity is the password for the last months of pregnancy when you have to alter your way of dressing. Look for easy-to-wear shapes that offer comfort. Wear separates that are in the same range of tones, the kind of clothes that can be combined with each other for day and evening. Add personal style with a piece of jewelry, softness with a scarf, a touch of humor with a hat.

As pregnancy advances, your moods can change from one moment to the next due to the change in your metabolism and because your shape is changing. By the fifth month your choice of clothing narrows considerably. This does not mean you have to rush out and buy maternity clothes, even though there are now some very fashionable mother-to-be clothes around. Use your imagination! Look in your closet. Chances are that you have quite a few pieces of clothing you haven't worn which will now be perfect. Give them the last go around.

If you have the time and enjoy making clothes, use the drawings in these pages as suggestions.

Please yourself first when getting dressed and it will make all the difference in the way you carry yourself.

Shoes. Sneakers, flat shoes or broad base low-heeled boots make much more sense than high-heeled shoes, which strain the legs and back.

Stockings. Support pantyhose can help if your job includes standing for long hours. According to studies, they are supposed to relieve the compression on the veins and ease the circulation. Pantyhose designed for pregnant women can be found in maternity clothing stores, but they can be expensive so many women buy queen-size panty hose.

Underwear. As the breasts enlarge, you may need to wear a different kind of bra to help the muscles carry the new weight. On the other hand, without the pull of a bra sometimes the skin breathes better, and the pectoral muscles can get strong given the proper exercise. Of course, an athletic bra is essential for active exercise and mild sports.

The most comfortable panties are the stretch or cotton bikini type as they fit right under the belly. The waist-high underpants tend to put pressure on the middle of the abdomen due to the elastic. Another consideration is not to wear any underwear. It feels comfortable, particularly under longer dresses and skirts, if you wear a slip.

Girdles and maternity corsets, except in rare cases, are more cumbersome than helpful.

Pants. The jeans you have been wearing all along will do fine, as long as they are not too tight. Remove the zipper or buttons when you cannot fasten the pants anymore and replace with a wide piece of elastic cut in the shape of a pointed triangle. Drawstring pajama shapes adjust easily and always look good for evening when made in satin or silklike fabrics. Another comfortable pair of pants are the low-slung, long bloomer type, like sweatpants. They can be found in cotton knit or blended fabrics. Look for the ones with drawstrings—you can always insert a wide band of elastic instead if you do not want the knot bumps. Oversize painters' overalls, suspended from the shoulders, can be found in corduroy for the winter and cotton for the summer in a great variety of colors.

Dresses and Suits. A low-waisted jumper-dress can go right through the seasons. Worn with a shirt at home the jumper can go to the office with a loose jacket added on top, or it can be a comfortable sun dress by itself in the summer. For evening, loose dresses made of crepe, silk, rayon and other flowing materials give you the most ease and elegance.

Tops. For all seasons a large size shirt is usually loose enough to leave room for a growing baby. When the abdomen really starts to bulge, an oversize shirt worn over maternity tights or warm leggings in the fall,

or a large shirt over wool or stretch knit pants gives you all the room you need. The large shirt can be worn after the baby is born for nursing—it is easily unfastened. A shirtdress, with pockets, can be breezy in the summer or snug if belted loosely under the belly. Extra-large tee shirts feel good as nightdresses, or under big V-neck sweaters, jackets and open neck shirts.

Skirts. These can be found with dropped waist and adjustable front fastenings. The wrap-over skirt allows for a smart look at work, in the middle months, but thereafter an elasticized or shirred waist is more comfortable.

Coats. Men's jackets are usually large enough to accommodate a growing belly. Loosely fitted coats and raingear are wide enough to wear throughout your pregnancy. Armholes should not be too narrow; coats with raglan sleeves are easiest to get in and out of. When going out at night, wrap yourself in a large shawl. The same shawl can be used as a blanket to take a nap anywhere at any time.

Colors. Indulge in soft pastels and floral patterns when at home. Black, dark and gray colors that might be worn at work are better set off with a note of bright primary color for vivaciousness.

Common and Outrageous Fears

Basically, we are all the same. We may appear strong, indifferent or confident but we all have a certain amount of apprehension when confronted with an unknown situation. This is particularly true if the change involves physical alteration of our usual state. We all have fears concerning childbirth. It's neither abnormal nor weird to be fearful. Throughout history pregnancy has been termed "confinement," which is disagreeably synonymous with detention and seclusion. As for birth, it is often associated with pain and a hard time. For centuries, women have been told horrifying stories of unbearable pain and suffering. These fears may have been instilled in us from our own families—from our mothers, grandmothers, aunts and relatives—in hushed conversations not meant for children's ears. And later on, we are told more stories until our imagination begins to overcome our reason. No wonder many women are scared to have a baby! But, we know better today. Modern research and inquiry show that the majority of births occur without problems.

It is better to face and talk about our fears rather than avoiding, ignoring or keeping them locked up inside. Talking to other mothers, midwives and physicians is always helpful. Not being in the same high emotional frequency, they can rationalize and clarify some of your fears. Childbirth education centers are familiar with the intricacies of pregnancy and motherhood and may be able to offer you different points of view. Women's centers, now springing up in most cities, are also valuable places to go, talk and inquire.

Fear stops us from functioning well physically. A positive attitude makes for better health.

PREGNANCY = GROWING
BIRTH = CHANGE

The first and foremost fear is of physical pain and mental suffering.

It is now well established that if you have prepared carefully and are in good health, there is less suffering involved in pregnancy and childbirth. There is no denying that everyday life brings its daily share of disappointments but the interesting part is to overcome them with one's own resources rather than sinking deeper into despair. If giving birth does become painful because of various physical incompatibilities, and they cannot be overcome mentally, medical science has devised fast ways to relieve suffering.

Equally strong is the fear that the baby will be born with some form of handicap or deformity.

It's a universal thought: Possibly every pregnant woman has recurring visions of giving birth to a handicapped child. Often this is associated with a feeling of guilt: "It will happen to me because I have done a bad deed in my life and this is my punishment." So little is known concerning the causes of birth deformities. It is absurd to blame oneself if all good care has been taken. Statistics show that almost ninety-five percent of all babies are born normal; 4 percent are born with diseases, and only 2½ to 3 percent of full-term babies are born with physical or mental defects. Some of these deformities, such as cleft palate, are minor and can be surgically repaired within the first few months of life. We are taking certain risks when we become pregnant but there is no use torturing ourselves mentally for nine months. We know it is a slight possibility, a matter of fate to be dealt with if and when it happens. We are not alone in this world. There are other people who have had such experiences and, along with specialists, have started groups, centers and magazines to help each other.

Women who have had a miscarriage will naturally fear having another one. There is no wrongdoing in losing a baby. Most of the time it cannot be prevented. It is a particularly trying time if it has taken the woman a long time to get pregnant. It is sad and frustrating to be so suddenly without the expected child. But there will be new cycles, new seeds, new eggs to come. Besides, procreation doesn't have to come from your body exclusively. There are many children waiting to be adopted.

The fear of death—mother's death, baby's death—is another common fear. Mother's death in childbirth is so rare nowadays that it has become a remote possibility. Our time to die can come at any moment and there is nothing one can do to change fate. However, it is incredibly difficult to deal with the death of a baby one has been carrying intimately for so long. It is a shock. Knowing in advance that it can happen may help prepare for such an eventuality, although it's not a comforting thought. Talking to women to whom this has happened gives a better understanding that there can be subsequent children born and raised without repeated trauma.

The fear of raising a child presents a problem to many women. It is a twenty-year responsibility to raise a child, and, since we now have a choice, we should consider this carefully before we get pregnant. The responsibility is to provide for the child, possibly entirely if we decide to live apart from the father or if we become widowed or divorced. It's nothing fearful; it means loving, working, playing and finding out what help is available to do it best.

Other common fears include:

Fear of looking fat, of not getting back in shape afterwards; fearing that the man in your life will lose interest and patience; fear of not being able to get hold of the doctor or midwife or not getting to the hospital in time; fear of not knowing enough, not having practiced enough for an unmedicated childbirth.

Fear of changes; fear of being out of control; fear of isolation, of not being part of the dancing crowd anymore; fear of losing friends.

Fear of being pushed, rushed, crushed if living in a big city. Fear of environment.

Oh! so many fears, and there are so many more kept hidden, hurting whoever is suppressing them. Make it lighter for yourself.

Air those gnawing feelings and find the positive mental attitude to balance out the negative input.

Choices

**Birth is not one act
it is a process
—Erich Fromm**

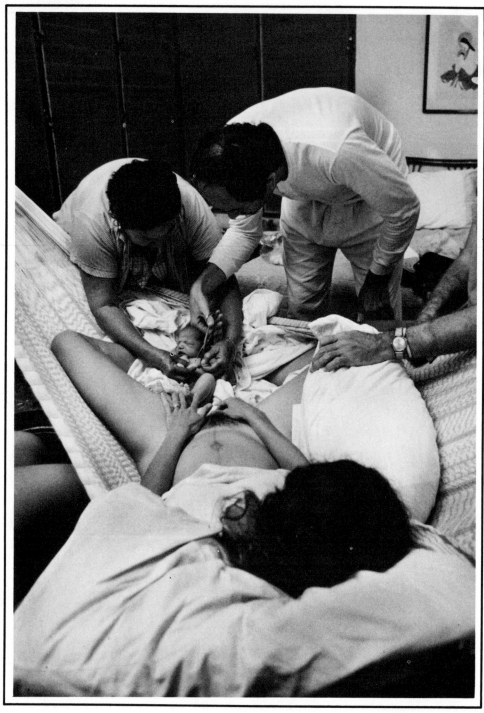

When a child is expected, a great deal of thinking goes into "the idea" of having a baby: health, food, air, rest, love, clothes, preparations for the day of birth. Equally important is your choice of method, location and the amount of medical help you will use to give birth. This chapter outlines the methods and choices available to you. Also, possible complications that you should be aware of during pregnancy, labor and birth are briefly described.

Birth Attendants

Once your pregnancy test has been positively confirmed, you will need to choose a doctor or a midwife who will provide you with prenatal and postpartum care, and who will attend your baby's birth.

You should look for someone with whom you feel comfortable, and whose experience and views on childbirth come close to your own hopes and needs. Ask for recommendations from your friends who have recently given birth.

DOCTORS

Doctors deliver babies in hospitals with which they are affiliated. You should feel comfortable with the doctor, and with the hospital's rules and routines. A few doctors have transformed their offices into out-of-hospital birth centers; some will attend home births. Obstetricians are trained to deal with the many complications of childbirth, but they may vary widely in their handling of normal births.

Find out if your doctor delivers babies. If not, ask him/her to recommend someone who does do maternity work. Or, call the medical society or local hospitals in your county for a listing of obstetricians or doctors who deliver babies in your area. Find out if the doctor practices obstetrics or just gynecology and if he/she has his/her own practice or is part of a group practice. In a group practice you cannot be sure which doctor will deliver your baby.

MIDWIVES

Midwifery is the ancient skill of physically and emotionally helping women take care of their bodies and give birth. A midwife does this by instructing, reassuring and comforting you during pregnancy and labor, and finally by "catching" the baby.

Certified nurse-midwives (CNMs) are specially trained to handle normal births, and to detect and evaluate complications, which may need referral, in pregnancy and labor. Midwives make limited use of drugs and sophisticated medical equipment, relying instead on the pregnant woman's natural rhythms and her ability to work with her own body.

CNMs practice in the midwifery services of hospitals, in birth centers, and in private and group practices dealing with home births. CNMs working in out-of-hospital settings should have medical backup. You can find a midwife by contacting your local chapter of the International Association of Parents and Professionals for Safe Alternatives in Childbirth (NAPSAC), International Childbirth Education Association (ICEA), La Leche League (see Resources), or by checking with the midwifery service of a nearby hospital. The American College of Nurse-Midwives (see Resources) can send you a list of such hospitals, and can tell you about any birth centers, private and group practices in your area.

Lay midwives generally attend only home births. They often have several years of midwifery experience, but are not qualified as nurse-midwives and may lack nursing expertise. Some states have made it illegal for lay midwives to attend births. Whether or not this is the case in your state, the choice of a lay midwife for home birth entails a certain amount of risk and responsibility, since there is no guarantee that she is competent at recognizing or handling unexpected problems in labor.

There should be no hesitation, at any stage during pregnancy, to try another doctor or midwife if the parents feel ill at ease with their first choice. There are many kind and competent medical people who believe that birthtime is a very special experience for the mother and father.

These are the people who will answer the plainest or weirdest of questions in detail, with patience, knowledge, experience and compassion. These are also the ones who do not keep you stupidly waiting in a sterile room. Of course there are always unexpected delays, but to wait over half-an-hour without previous warning is really an abuse.

The more informed a person is about internal development during pregnancy, the more fascinating the whole adventure becomes. Ask questions without fear, look at films, photos and diagrams until the mechanism is clearly understood. Remember, you are paying for these services.

Where to Have Your Baby

Basically, the place to have a baby is either at the hospital, in a birth center or at home. (Birth sometimes occurs in between these places, but that's hardly a choice!)

HOSPITAL

These places have a high concentration of trained medical help, medications and equipment that may be needed in case of difficulty or an emergency. Some also have neonatal intensive care units. Some hospitals have one or more birthing or labor rooms—homelike alternatives to the traditional delivery room—for parents who can expect a normal birth. These are often linked to the hospital's midwifery service, but can also be used by obstetricians. Use of the birthing room often depends on whether or not it's vacant when you need it, and in many hospitals you will still be subject to most of the routine procedures of the delivery room.

It is essential that you visit the hospital beforehand where your doctor is affiliated in order to become familiar with the unusual environment, the admittance procedure, the location of the entrance and the registration formalities.

• Visit the labor room. Will you have an individual room or do you have to share?

• Become acquainted with the delivery bed in a birthing room.

• Familiarize yourself with the delivery room, even if you are hoping to use the birthing room. Look around, ask for the overhead lights to be turned on as they will be on D-Day. It is impractical to try out the delivery table since it has to be kept ready and sterile for a potential birth, but know what to expect.

• Visit the maternity ward. There are either rooms with several beds and a glassed-in nursery for the babies or private rooms where you can usually have your baby room-in with you. Facilities vary (according to the individual's financial situation, unfortunately). Talk to the admissions office and nurses about timetables, food, visiting hours. Can your other children visit? Can you feed your baby between scheduled feedings?

• Does the hospital have an early discharge policy, allowing you to go home after twelve hours if all is well?

• Will your baby's father or other support person be allowed into the delivery room, or into the operating room if you need a cesarean section?

The more information gathered beforehand about the hospital procedure, the more you can relax and concentrate, knowing without apprehension what is to be expected.

Hospital Routines. A hospital birth often involves certain routine procedures. These generally include:

• Mini-prepping on admission—the woman's perineal region is shaved or clipped, and perhaps she is given an enema. The enema might make the contractions stronger. The father or support person is usually excluded from the prepping room.

• Fasting—the woman is not allowed to eat or drink during labor in case she should need general anesthesia.

• Intravenous (IV) drip during labor—a glucose solution is fed continuously through a narrow tube into a vein in the arm. The solution helps maintain energy while fasting, and the IV keeps a vein open in case of emergency.

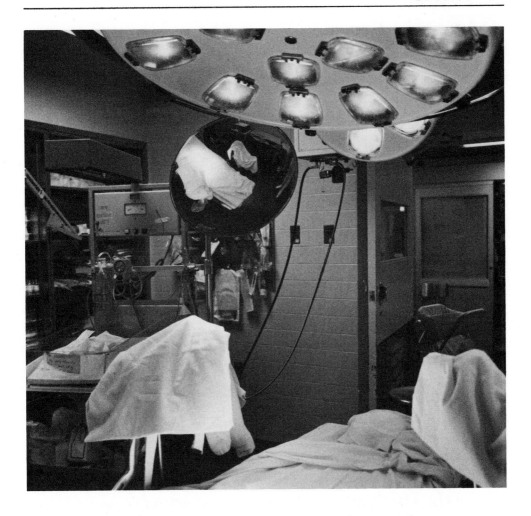

- Electronic fetal monitoring during all or part of labor.
- Use of stirrups, and sometimes wrist straps, during delivery.
- Episiotomy for the first baby.
- Unless there is rooming-in, routine separation of parents and baby during a recovery period of anything from one to twenty-four hours after delivery. The baby is taken to a special nursery. Many hospitals now allow the mother, father and baby a half hour together immediately following delivery. After the observation period, the baby will be brought to the mother every four hours for feeding, except at night, unless special arrangements are made.

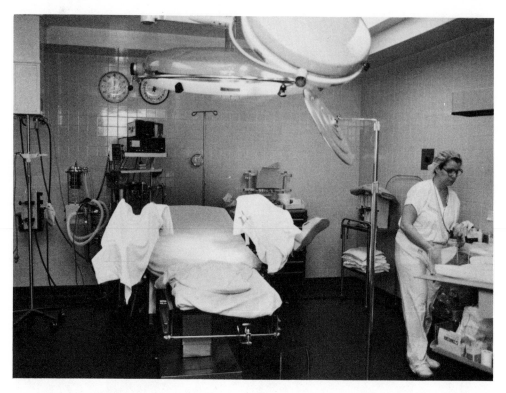

Discuss these routines with your doctor—he/she may be able to make some exceptions. You may be able to avoid many routine procedures if you give birth in a hospital birthing room.

Early Discharge. Many hospitals now offer an early discharge, or short stay, option, allowing healthy mothers and babies to return home twelve to twenty-four hours after birth.

Many mothers are anxious to return to the familiar comforts of their own homes, especially if they have to share a hospital room, and if visiting times for the family are limited. Some mothers find it difficult to breast-feed their babies in the strange hospital environment. You may long to introduce your new baby to his or her home, and to the special world you have created, whether it's a pretty quilt in a basket or a colorful room.

If you are hoping for a short hospital stay, you will have to arrange it

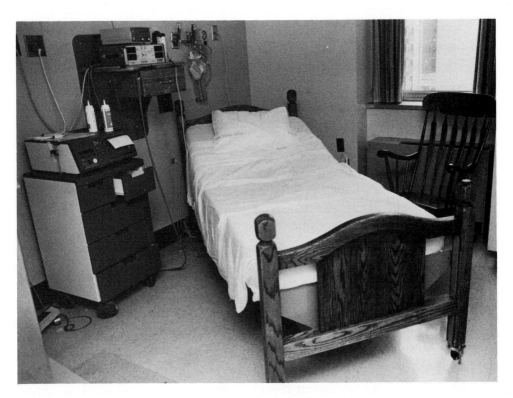

with your doctor and the hospital, and you will need to plan in advance for:

• Full-time help at home for at least the first three to five days. Your husband, mother, friend—anyone you feel relaxed with—will have to care for you and help you care for the baby. He or she will also have to take care of the house, meals and older children. You and the baby will want to do nothing but rest and grow close to each other. It is especially important to build up your strength, and therefore your milk supply, if you plan to breast-feed.

• A pediatrician's visit, preferably in your home, at least once in the first three days after your return.

• Parents should be thoroughly informed about newborn care so that they can recognize signs of distress, particularly the subtle indications of newborn jaundice. Talk to your doctor or pediatrician, or find out if an early discharge class is available at the hospital.

Some hospitals will go out of their way to make their clients, the new parents, feel good about giving birth in their midst. They may offer such options as a celebration dinner for the couple; social and informative events for mothers-to-be; topical classes on early discharge, vaginal birth after cesarean (V-BAC), etc., and special classes for siblings and grandparents; child care classes for both parents, sometimes available on closed circuit television in the mother's own room; postpartum clubs and support groups; child care telephone hotlines for the first weeks at home; ritual circumcision of the newborn. A few hospitals offer the possibility of preadmitting; allow siblings to see and touch the newborn; admit siblings and additional friends or support persons into birthing rooms.

HOSPITAL COSTS

The steep fees involved in hospital birth continue to escalate, as doctors and hospitals are faced with ever-increasing costs and malpractice insurance rates. Even if one chooses to use the resident obstetrician, the hospital costs will add up; your room and food, plus the nursery for the baby who is charged from the moment of birth, will start at about $400 per day (more for a semiprivate or private room). A four-day stay for the mother (labor plus three days) and three days for the baby will cost at least $1,500. The delivery, and any medications, lab tests or emergency services for you and/or the baby will be extra—anesthesia, including epidural, is a particularly expensive procedure. Some hospitals offer a three-day package, including labor and delivery, starting at around $2,500. With a cesarean-section the cost goes up by about $1,000. Part of these costs are reimbursable if you have medical insurance. Remember that some hospitals will ask for a hefty deposit if you have no insurance coverage and that hospitals, like hotels, have check-in times so if you arrive in labor at, say, 11:30 A.M. and check-in is at noon, you'll be charged for that extra day. Since room and board account for such a large portion of the cost of hospital delivery, early discharge plans can obviously save much of the expense.

If you choose to have a hospital delivery with a private doctor providing pre- and postnatal care and delivery, you'll have to pay a separate doctor's fee, starting at about $2,000 for a regular delivery and $3,000 plus extra for any tests for a high-risk delivery. In-hospital delivery by a hospital midwifery service will cost about $1,500 plus the regular hospital fees.

BIRTH CENTERS

Birth centers, sometimes called childbearing centers, are designed to deal with normal births in a homelike environment, such as a converted house or professional suite. These centers are usually staffed by certified nurse-midwives, who work as a team with consulting obstetricians and with you and your family. Birth centers are founded on the belief that birth should be a family experience, and that the midwife's role is to help you have a healthy pregnancy and a safe and satisfying delivery.

Birth centers provide prenatal and postpartum care and a midwife-attended birth in a comfortable labor suite. Most birth center programs include childbirth education classes, classes for children who want to attend the birth and postpartum support groups. The maximum stay at all centers is between twelve and twenty-four hours after the birth.

If you are hoping for something special in your birth experience—acupuncture, music or a video camera, birth by candlelight, friends or children by your side—then a birth center is the place most likely to accommodate you besides your own home.

Birth centers have basic emergency equipment and drugs. The midwife will perform an episiotomy if necessary, and sew a tear. She can give minimal doses of pain-killing drugs if really needed. Birth centers do not generally offer ultrasound, electronic fetal monitoring, pitocin-induced labor or any other of the more medical or technological procedures available in hospitals. Birth centers follow the "high touch" approach of home birth, rather than the "high-tech" approach of hospital birth.

When you arrive at the center in labor, there will be no admission procedure, and no routine "prepping." You will be encouraged to move

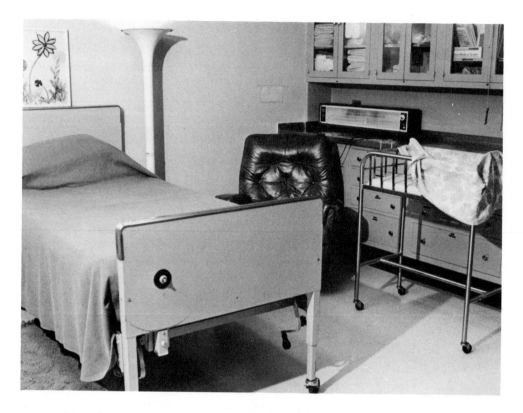

around in labor as long as you are able; to take a walk, prepare a snack in the kitchenette, take a tub bath or shower, read or watch television in the family room. You should take a tour of the labor suite during one of your prenatal visits, since it is usually separated from the already familiar prenatal areas of the center. During your prenatal visits you should also try to see every midwife at least once, since you will not know which one will be on duty to attend the birth.

The birth itself takes place in a comfortable bedroom. Your midwife will help you to find the birthing position that works best for you. After the birth your baby will be examined at your bedside by the nurse-midwife or a consultant pediatrician and will stay with you and your partner, in your room, until you go home.

The freedom to take charge of your own pregnancy, birth and newborn child brings certain responsibilities. You will be expected to learn about pregnancy, birth and newborn care in a series of eight to ten childbirth classes; to attend all routine exams, check your own weight and urine and keep your own chart; to tune into your body and maintain your health. Your baby's father or other support partner must attend the birth, and should prepare with you at classes. Since you must leave the center soon after the birth, you also have to arrange for help at home and a pediatrician's visit during the first three days after your return.

Eligibility. Most birth centers require that you enroll by the twenty-second week of your pregnancy, and before enrolling you will have to attend an orientation that explains the benefits and risks involved in birthing at the center.

Although birth centers have proved to be at least as safe as hospitals, for normal birth, you should seriously and honestly examine your feelings about out-of-hospital birth—it is believed that anxiety may contribute to long labors. But if you feel confident about the center and your ability to give birth, your next step is to schedule a first prenatal visit, which will include a full medical exam with the center's consultant physician, and a thorough review of your family medical history. The purpose of this visit is to screen out women who are statistically at risk in a birth center program. This includes women over forty (for a first birth) or forty-five, women who have had a previous cesarean, are carrying twins, or have certain chronic medical problems. In some centers the initial screening takes place over the first two visits. The fee for the physician exam is non-refundable.

On subsequent prenatal visits you will see a nurse-midwife who will continue to watch for complications in your pregnancy, work with you to try and overcome problems through diet and exercise, refer you to the consultant physician if necessary and support you in your transfer to hospital care if required during pregnancy or labor. About twenty percent of women enrolled in birth centers are transferred out of the program before, during and sometimes after labor (mainly before), because centers have to evaluate your risk status on a broad statistical, rather than an individual, basis. Even if you are not able to give birth at a center in which you are enrolled, you may still be able to use it for prenatal care and childbirth education, or just for information and support.

Choosing a Birth Center.   You can find out if a birth center exists in your area by checking the listing under "Birth Centers" in the Yellow Pages, by contacting the National Association of Childbearing Centers (NACC), NAPSAC, or your local chapter of the La Leche League or ICEA (see Resources). Many states now license birth centers according to safety guidelines set up by the American Public Health Association (APHA). These guidelines state that centers should not offer surgical procedures, that labor should not be induced or stimulated by pitocin, and that pain control "should depend primarily on close emotional support and adequate preparation for the birth experience." Follow-up care should be a part of the program, and an ambulance contract should be maintained.

If your state does not license birth centers, you can contact NACC, which certifies centers that meet its own high safety standards.

Birth Center Costs.   Birth center programs cost between $500 and $2,000, depending mainly on location and services included in the program. Nonprofit centers tend to be less expensive and to offer more services than centers that run for profit. Most centers have install-ment payment plans, and centers in low-income areas will often let you do barter work in exchange for all or part of the fee. If you have to transfer out of a birth center program for any reason, fees for care not yet received will be refunded.

Coverage of birth center costs depends on your insurer, your plan, arrangements made by the center, and the state in which it is located. Many private and employee health plans reimburse the full birth center cost; some even offer cash incentives. Some plans only reimburse for care in licensed centers or in centers meeting the APHA guidelines. Medicaid pays costs for some birth centers in some states.

The NACC are working for better insurance coverage of birth center fees. Contact them if you have questions about your coverage or com-plaints about a claim.

HOME BIRTH

In the bedroom, bathroom or special place where the mother feels most comfortable, home can be the most pleasant place to give birth. This is true only, however, if you are 100 percent healthy and positive about this decision.

Home is as safe a place as any for normal birth, as long as you have an experienced attendant, a doctor or nurse-midwife who likes delivering babies at home and who, after examining the mother's and fetus's development closely in the last few months, has declared them fit for home delivery.

Midwives attend home births more frequently than doctors. In either case in urban areas you will probably be required to attend a series of eight to ten classes geared for home birth and newborn care. You should make arrangements early for a pediatrician to check your baby within three to five days after the birth, and you must be sure that you will have proper help at home for at least the first three days. It is sometimes your responsibility to register your baby's birth and to obtain a birth certificate.

It is a good idea for the parents to have an extra adult in the home on the day of birth, a close friend or relative who can answer the telephone, change a lightbulb, take the dog for a walk while the father is helping the laboring woman or actually delivering his baby under the midwife's supervision. If children expect to attend, make sure they are well prepared for all the unusual sights and sounds of birth. The parents can do this job best, but the films and slides shown in sibling preparation classes are also useful. You will need to have someone on hand whose sole responsibility it is to care for the children. They will almost certainly grow restless before it's all over; they may feel disturbed and want to leave.

You will not have to do very much to prepare your home for birth. You will need a warm, well-aired room (68°F. or 19°C.), a bed, not too soft (waterbeds are fine for labor but not for birthing), at least six towels, several sheets of plastic to layer between bedsheets, and a gooseneck or table lamp. It is a good idea to prepare nests around the house—even if your "house" is a one-room studio—so that you can change position and environment during labor. Your doctor or midwife may give you a small list of household supplies (such as garbage bags and juice) and he/she will bring the rest, including basic emergency equipment.

In your home, you can give birth, relax and celebrate in your own time; there are no schedules, no changes of shift. Your doctor or midwife can find somewhere comfortable to sit and wait, unobtrusively if you need privacy. Over the months he/she has come to know you well, and can help you and your partner now in talking out the anxieties that sometimes surface during labor.

After the birth your doctor or midwife will stay with you for two to four hours, examine and weigh your newborn. After this he/she will be on twenty-four-hour call and will probably come back to your home on

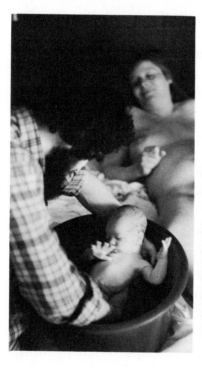

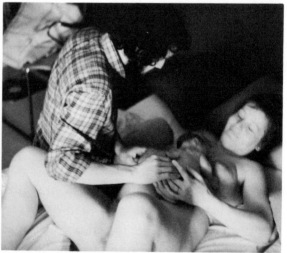

the second day after the birth, and again for postpartum exams.

The doctor or midwife's fee for home birth (including prenatal and postpartum care) varies greatly and can be anything from $900 to $1,500. The cost of classes, if required, is extra. Some home birth attendants ask for an initial nonrefundable downpayment of about twenty percent of the total fee, a sure way of making you face any doubts you may have about home birth.

Giving birth at home means you and the ones close to you are in charge of the ceremony. There are no routines, no formalities, no set codes of behavior to observe. Your calmness sets the tone. If you are looking for a doctor or midwife to deliver your baby at home, contact The National Association of Parents and Professionals for Safe Alternatives in Childbirth (NAPSAC).

Methods

Childbirth is a natural event that has the same basic elements for everyone. What makes the difference in birth experiences is the way one approaches and prepares for the adventure and what happens along the journey.

It's a good idea to find out, well before midpregnancy, what kinds of help for self-training and medical techniques are available. Then you can choose the right method for yourself. Once you have chosen a method of giving birth that suits your character, continue researching it in different books, by having conversations at women's centers, and by talking with friends and doctors. Remember that there are no rules saying you cannot change your decision at any time.

The following information concerning the use of drugs and surgical techniques is not meant to frighten. We only want to help you familiarize yourself with the different possibilities available. There are many variations for each of the techniques mentioned. We will outline the most widely practiced methods and make notes of less popular ones.

TESTS DURING PREGNANCY

There are many devices, most of them relatively new, which can be used to test the well-being of the fetus. You may or may not be offered these tests, depending on your individual doctor or midwife and the condition of your pregnancy. Discuss them with your doctor or midwife.

Ultrasound. Ultrasound is often used to create a sound picture (called a sonogram) of the uterus and its contents; the fetus, placenta and amniotic fluid. Before taking this simple and painless test, you will be asked to drink large quantities of water to create a clearer picture. Your bladder will feel uncomfortably full, but the test lasts only a few minutes. The mother lies down on an examination table, her belly is covered with a cool gel or oil so the microphonelike device glides easily over the abdomen when applied by the doctor or technician. This device emits high-frequency sound waves, which are directed toward the mother's uterus, where they echo back off the surfaces of organs, placenta and fetus. The echoing waves are then transmitted to the screen of a video monitor, enabling you to see the shadowy outlines of your baby, its beating heart, movements and the intrauterine environment in which it is growing. You can request a photograph of the sonogram.

Many doctors use ultrasound routinely in the first two trimesters of pregnancy to establish more accurately a woman's due date. There is, however, growing concern over such routine use of ultrasound. No harmful effects on mother or fetus have yet been seen, but the U.S. Food and Drug Administration says that it is too early to prove that ultrasound, used indiscriminately, is safe.

In high-risk and problem pregnancies ultrasound has been revolutionary. It is used diagnostically when a woman is spotting or bleeding, when ectopic pregnancy is suspected, or to confirm multiple births. It is also used to locate the placenta, to determine fetal growth and well-being and to indicate the best time for delivery in a potentially dangerous situation.

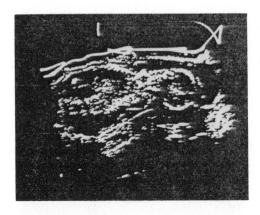

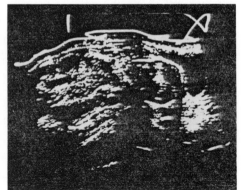

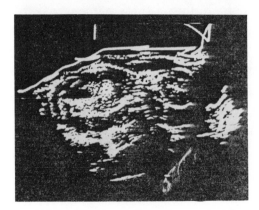

Sonar waves, projected onto a screen, detecting position of baby in mother's womb.

Amniocentesis. In amniocentesis, a small amount of amniotic fluid is withdrawn from the uterus to test for genetic defects and other problems. The procedure is performed between the sixteenth and eighteenth weeks of pregnancy. A local anesthetic is given in the abdomen. Then a long, thin needle is inserted through the abdomen and into the uterus, during which time you may feel slight uterine contractions. Ultrasound is used to guide the needle to the proper location, away from the fetus and placenta, into the area containing the most amount of amniotic fluid. The amniotic fluid withdrawn by the needle is then sent for culture and analysis; results take about three to four weeks.

Amniocentesis is used for genetic testing in cases where a history of genetic abnormality exists in either the mother's or the father's family, or if the woman is thirty-five years of age or older. Amniocentesis can detect about two hundred problems, but generally tests are only made for neural tube defects such as spina bifida and chromosomal abnormalities such as Down's syndrome and Tay-Sachs disease. It can be a very reassuring test if you have anxieties about your fetus's development—in fact, 95 percent of test results from amniocentesis are negative.

Amniocentesis can also be used to test the maturity of the baby's lungs as a guide to determining the right time for a cesarean delivery. It will also tell you the sex of your baby, but it should never be used solely for this purpose. Though in skilled hands it is a safe and 99.5 percent accurate test, there are risks involved, including a 0.05 percent risk of spontaneous abortion, damage to the placenta, or infection. In unskilled hands the risks are much greater, so you should check into the record of the obstetrician or prenatal diagnostic center offering the test.

Before going ahead with the test, you should also have a clear idea of what you plan to do should the test be positive. For this reason genetic counseling is done prior to the amniocentesis. The timing of the test generally allows for the possiblity of abortion. Some parents who have decided against abortion take the test anyway in order to prepare, practically and emotionally, for the future.

Nonstress Test.   The nonstress test uses ultrasound to determine the well-being of the fetus, if a pregnancy goes too far beyond the due date, or if problems such as diabetes arise. This is a reliable, drug-free test which enables the doctor to decide whether or not it is really necessary to induce labor.

In a nonstress test the mother is hooked up to a monitor and the baby's heart rate is taken by ultrasound. The baby is then encouraged to move in response to the mother's movements, and the heart rate is taken again. If there is an acceleration of at least fifteen beats for a few seconds, the test is "reactive" and the baby can be pronounced safe for a few more days while you wait for labor to begin naturally. You should be sure to eat before this test since the reading can be affected by low blood sugar. If the reading is insufficient, a stress test will be given.

Stress Test. In the stress test, previously called the Oxytocin Challenge Test (OTC), the mother is hooked up to an intravenous drip on a bedside stand and also to a fetal heart monitor. An infusion of synthetic oxytocin is fed slowly, through a thin tube, into a vein in the mother's arm. If this infusion causes three uterine contractions within ten minutes for a full half hour, and if with each contraction there is an acceleration of the baby's heartbeat, the baby is not in distress and can be left in utero for another week. If, however, the heart rate responds abnormally to the stress of contractions, it might be necessary to induce labor or to have a cesarean, since an abnormal fetal response to contractions often means that the baby is under stress.

The mother can sometimes cause her uterus to contract by stimulating her own nipples, which in turn releases a secretion of the hormone prostaglandin into her bloodstream. Your doctor may be willing to let you try this as a way of avoiding the oxytocin infusion.

Fetal Heart Monitor. The fetal heart monitor is an electronic device using ultrasound to detect fetal distress during labor, by keeping track of the baby's heartbeat as it responds to the mother's contractions. Use of the monitor is mandatory in most hospital delivery rooms and some hospital birthing rooms.

There are two ways of electronically monitoring the fetus, external and internal. The external is used more frequently, especially in early labor. A cool gel is rubbed over the mother's abdomen, onto which are strapped a wide and loose belt with two disklike electrodes. One records the baby's heartbeat, the other records the mother's uterine contractions. The pressure of the straps can cause a little discomfort and you have to stay in bed while you are hooked up, which may slow your labor. The electrodes are hooked up to a beeping printout device by your bedside, which the medical staff checks regularly. The sound from the monitor can help you to anticipate and prepare for a contraction, but it can also be quite a distraction, especially for your labor partner. If the sound is a nuisance, the volume can be turned off, but the monitor will continue to record and print out the necessary data. If the monitor shows that the fetus is reacting abnormally to the mother's uterine contractions, the doctor will probably want to get the baby out as fast as possible, perhaps by cesarean. Unfortunately, the external monitor's indication of fetal distress can be inaccurate, recording the mother's heartbeat by mistake and causing a commotion of flashing warning lights. However, if fetal distress is indicated, a fetal scalp blood sample can be taken to give an extremely accurate reading of the baby's condition. Between 50 and 90 percent of infants, tested in this way after distress was indicated by the monitor, are found to be in no danger.

For a more accurate reading, the internal monitor may be used, but only if the membranes have been ruptured either naturally or by the doctor. A small tube filled with fluid is put through the vagina and cervical opening into your uterus, and a small wire is placed into the baby's scalp (or buttock, in a breech presentation). These electrodes are then hooked up for printout. As with the external monitor, a fetal scalp blood sample can be taken to confirm the reading.

If you need, or want to use, either the internal or external monitor, try not to let it inhibit your movement too much. Change position every fifteen or twenty minutes, and avoid lying on your back since this decreases your baby's oxygen supply and can in itself lead to fetal distress. You will have much more freedom of movement with the external monitor. Electronic monitoring is used in varying degrees, depending on who is delivering the baby, on the hospital, and on the mother's risk status. Its primary use is in high-risk pregnancies and in induced labor, but most doctors and hospitals use it routinely as a precaution against malpractice lawsuits.

INITIALLY WITHOUT MEDICINE

To begin with, you could simply "let it happen!" and, in most cases, the baby would be born by itself. About 95 percent of all births happen without complications. However, every birth should be professionally attended in case of unexpected complications.

Breathing and Exercises. These are the basic elements involved in what is termed "natural childbirth" or "painless childbirth" (which should more aptly be defined as *prepared childbirth*). Conducted mostly by a professional physiotherapist (teacher), the classes draw from the findings of humanist Dr. Grantly Dick-Read (who wrote *Natural Childbirth* and *Childbirth Without Fear*) and the psychoprophylactic (meaning mind-health preventive) teachings developed by the Russians Pavlov and Nicoläiev, in the forties. It concentrates on physical and mental relaxation and on conditioning reflexes with self-induced signals. These signals are applied during uterine contractions from the beginning of labor through birth until the expulsion of the placenta. Variations such as the popular Lamaze Method can be practiced either at the hospital's antenatal classes or in private institutions. They usually start six weeks before the baby's due date, but for full benefit, exercises should really start around the fifth month. Changes in the anatomy are also clearly explained with colorful diagrams during the course. Some yoga professors also teach prenatal relaxation through deep breathing and stretching exercises that have proven to be very effective for easing labor and childbirth. Trying any of these methods does not rule out the use of medicine if the mother finds she eventually needs it.

Hypnosis. It is not a widely used method anymore but since Franz Mesmer made it popular in the eighteenth century, way before the invention of anesthesia, a few thousand childbirths have been directed under hypnosis. Any willing person can be hypnotized. It is best to practice and be under the influence of a hypnotist with whom one feels completely at ease. Hypnosis is based on gradually bringing out from subconscious levels a psychic strength to overcome built-in fears that have been acquired through the years. This is done through the power of repeated suggestion. Subconscious fears are replaced with the knowledge that the body can be commanded at will by either an expert or, subsequently, by oneself.

It takes quite a while to achieve the complete state of hypnosis. Myths have been perpetrated that hypnosis is not recommended for pregnant women with psychiatric problems and that once a hypnotic trance has been entered it may take a while to come out of it. However, an experienced hypnotist assures us that it is not so.

PARTIAL USE OF DRUGS

One of the main reasons for preparing thoroughly for birth is to enjoy the experience instead of fearing it and to be able to utilize the body's full potential instead of numbing it with drugs. But, birth is not an endurance test, and there are times when sedation is comforting and partial anesthetics are really helpful.

During labor, a woman may find the going too rough and she can ask for a medication to take the edge off the pain. In many hospital delivery rooms, pain-relieving drugs are offered routinely and repeatedly—you can refuse or accept them. There are various drugs that will help without knocking you out altogether. The problem with drugs is that any drug given to you will pass across the placenta and may affect the baby and you. Take this into consideration when accepting or asking for medication. Also, some drugs interfere with the mother's ability to concentrate on breathing or relaxation techniques. Others lead, almost inevitably, to the need for stronger drugs, or to procedures such as electronic monitoring.

Before asking for or accepting medication, ask yourself what other methods you could use to ease the discomfort or help yourself relax. Walking around, changing position in bed, emptying your bladder, or taking a warm shower will sometimes help. If you realize that you are close to the birth itself, you might be able to get by without drugs—the hardest part of labor is often the last hour. If you have a choice of medication, try to use the one which will interfere the least with your ability to push the baby out. You have the right to a complete explana-

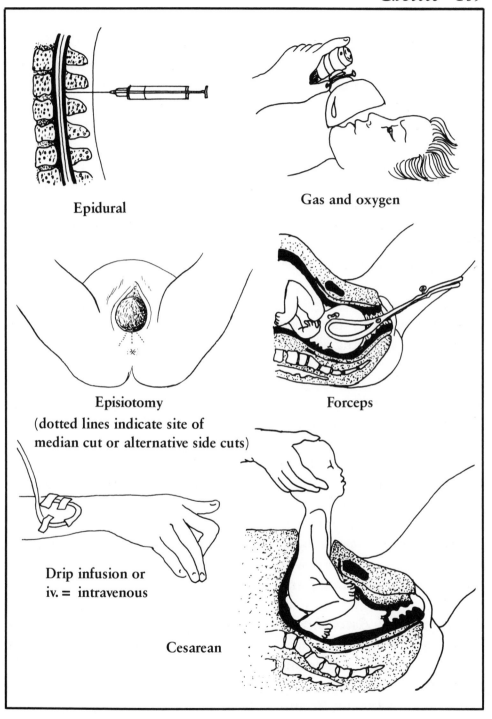

Epidural

Gas and oxygen

Episiotomy
(dotted lines indicate site of
median cut or alternative side cuts)

Forceps

Drip infusion or
iv. = intravenous

Cesarean

tion from your doctor or nurse of the risks, benefits and effects of any drug or procedure offered. This is called "informed consent." These eventualities should be discussed during prenatal visits.

If you are giving birth at home, remember that most of these drugs cannot be administered at your bedside. Many of them are not available at birth centers.

Tranquilizers are the mildest form of medication. In moderate doses the drawbacks from tranquilizers are nominal, and they can help relax the tension brought on by the strangeness of contractions, without causing drowsiness. Some well-known prescribed tranquilizers are Librium, Sparine, Equanil and Miltown.

Analgesics relax the muscles, reduce pain and may produce euphoria. Demerol, the analgesic most frequently prescribed in labor, is considered a safe drug—its effects can be reversed within a minute with an antidote.

Barbiturates, also known as sedatives or sleeping medication, include Seconal and Nembutal. Sedatives can relieve anxiety and bring on sleep.

Barbiturates and analgesics may both slow down the breathing and reactions of the mother as well as the fetus. The effects can be long-lasting in the newborn (sometimes up to a week or more), especially if taken in the last two to three hours before birth. If the calming effects of a barbiturate or analgesic wear off in the final stages of labor, you may find it impossible to deal with contractions, and will probably need a repeat dose, or something stronger.

Regional Anesthesia is a numbing of a particular area of the body. There are various ways to anesthetize an isolated section where tension concentrates. Regional anesthesia is also used to numb the perineum for episiotomy. If a regional anesthetic is used, you will also have to be hooked up to an electronic fetal monitor since blood and oxygen supply to the baby may be diminished.

Epidural is a regional anesthesia using a drip-injection of Xylocaine in the lower part of the back. The needle doesn't go into the spine. Rather, it goes into a thin layer of fibrous tissues through which passes a network of nerves. If the injection is successful, which it is most of the time, the pelvic area will be numbed almost immediately and there should be none of the sensation brought on by contraction and expansion. The body is numbed from the waist down. A catheter is usually inserted into the epidural cavity and attached to a syringe, for additional doses of medication. It is an expensive service and can only be performed by a skilled anesthetist or anesthesiologist. An electronic fetal monitor must also be used.

The mother can still participate, but only as instructed by the doctor or support person, because she cannot feel anything when the time comes for pushing. The anesthetic can slow down contractions, so pitocin stimulation may become neccessary. Stirrups must be used, and the doctor may have to use low forceps and perform an episiotomy to extract the baby. The side effects of the epidural itself are said to be minimal for the mother. She may develop some soreness in her back or a headache. The procedure has been known to cause a mild transitory slowing of the fetal heart and dropping of the mother's blood pressure.

Gas and Oxygen are relatively simple means to relieve painful second stage contractions. Gas is inhaled from a mask; usually it is nitrous oxide (laughing gas) mixed with oxygen, or Trilene by itself which comes through a tube from a compression tank. It is quite safe for a mother and infant. In certain hospitals, the laboring woman can choose to use the mask at her convenience, putting it over her mouth and nose to inhale the gas. The effect it produces temporarily is a certain euphoria which erases pain. If too much is drawn (nitrous oxide and oxygen) it can make the person laugh uncontrollably and feel pretty high.

Ether and chloroform are not used much any more as they often cause vomiting and aspiration, leading to further complications. Gas is an essential element in emergencies when there is no time to wait for the delicate task of locating the correct injection area, and in the delivery of twins. The uterus will sometimes begin to contract after the first baby is

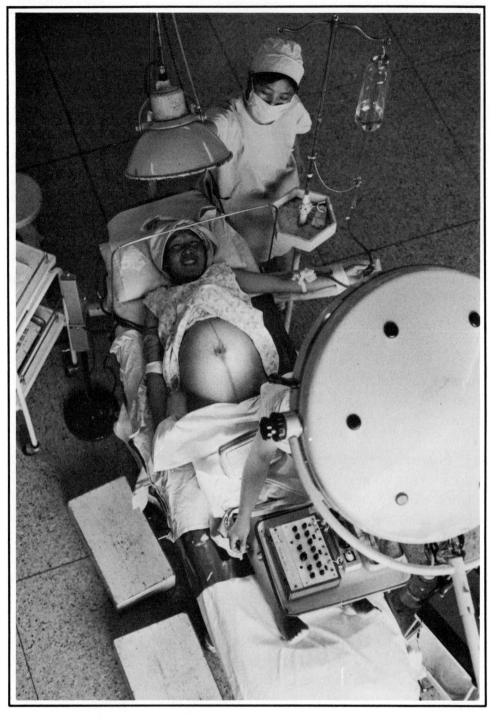

born, and gas is then used for uterine relaxation, facilitating delivery of the second child.

GENERAL ANESTHESIA

As women begin to understand the birth process and seek to participate fully in its every phase, there are fewer demands for complete anesthetization. General anesthesia, or the medical way of suspending sensation and consciousness, is brought on by gas inhalation (cyclopropane) and/or injections (Pentothal and curare). It is sometimes used in cases of cesarean section or other complications. It has to be administered by an anesthetist and is used only when really justified.

ACUPUNCTURE

For women who cannot tolerate and/or have a dangerous reaction to the drugs necessary for a general anesthesia, another possibility is slowly emerging: the centuries-old art and science of acupuncture. This ancient Chinese method, dating back as far as 2500 BC, is used for curing and for therapeutic anesthesia. Specific areas of the body are treated by inserting very fine needles in some of the 365 defined spots situated on the skin surface along the meridians (channels) which are mapped out from head to toe. In ancient times, the needles were made of gold or silver but today they are made mainly from steel.

The insertion of needles has a stimulating or equalizing effect. They reestablish a harmonious balance within the nerves (or of yin and yang), according to the fundamental Chinese law of evolution and the eternal permutation of nature.

Lately, the practice of acupuncture has resurfaced. Western doctors have a newfound interest in its application for various operations and as an anesthetic in various fields such as obstetrics.

In May of 1973, a thirty-year-old woman from Washington, D.C., gave birth to a healthy infant boy through cesarean section using acupuncture as the only pain-killer during the operation. She had had two previous cesareans, which had left her feeling doped up for days from the anesthetics. This time she didn't need a medicinal pain-killer during and for two days after surgery. For acupuncture to succeed, there has to be an appreciation and proper attitude on the part of the patient. This cesarean, performed by Dr. Oscar I. Dodek, Jr., with acupuncture administered by Dr. Shalom A. Albert, is believed to be the first one in the United States.

In Europe, acupuncture has been performed by two anesthetist-acupuncturists for three cesarean operations. The French team of doctors was headed by Professor Roccia and Dr. Marcel Niboyet; the operation was performed once in Turin, Italy, and twice in Saint Joseph's Hospital in Marseille, France. In China, this method has been used extensively for thousands of deliveries. At least one doctor in the United States has been looking into the use of acupuncture to induce labor, a treatment that has shown a 70 percent success rate in China and Sri Lanka. Acupuncture can also be used for normal deliveries to relax certain areas of the body.

Since western medicine guarantees safe results through anesthetics and there have not been extensive studies done in the West concerning the advantages of acupuncture, the widespread general use of the procedure is not likely to occur very soon. However, this does not mean that the art of acupuncture should be regarded as remote or frightening. Acupuncture could become a precious tool, in the hands of specialists, to prevent pain for people who have adverse reactions to synthetic pain-killers.

Possible Complications During Pregnancy

As children, one of the most fascinating things to do was to peek into the forbidden medical books high on the shelf in our parents' library. We read about all the weird diseases, getting quite frightened by the accompanying color photographs. Holding our breath, we would quickly close the book three or four pages later, feeling all those strange conditions creeping up on us all at once. It feels a little similar reading specialized medical books during pregnancy. Suddenly, the exceptions, the rare cases, almost become the rule. It is quite an absurd way of thinking if we bear in mind that 95 percent of all pregnancies in the United States terminate with normal birth.

To be prepared for the most common problems, we have outlined the possible complications of pregnancy: anemia, toxemia (preeclampsia, edema), bleeding, abortion, Rh factor, ectopic pregnancy, placenta previa, breech presentation. There are many in-depth books covering the medical explanations. For further information see the bibliography at the end of this book.

With your help, the doctor or midwife will be able to diagnose and treat these conditions early enough so that they will not be a problem at birth. However, a home birth is not recommended in cases of bleeding, toxemia and placenta previa.

Anemia. Anemia is a deficiency in the hemoglobin, the number of red blood cells, or the volume of blood. Anemia may develop during pregnancy in women who are not prone to it at other times in their lives. This is because of the additional volume of blood being circulated through the body and the increased demand of iron by the baby.

Anemia can be prevented or reversed simply by eating the right foods and taking iron tablets. If you are taking extra iron and are not really in an anemic state, your body will establish a block to stop the absorption, and the most inconvenience it can cause, if such is the case, is constipation.

Toxemia. In the early days of obstetrics, toxemia was thought to be a condition caused by an intoxication running through the whole body. Hence, the name *toxemia* was given to the condition. Doctors now believe that it is caused by inadequate protein in the diet. It may occur after the twenty-fourth week of pregnancy except in the cases of twins and abnormal developments. The symptoms are: the blood pressure goes up, there is protein in the urine, blurred vision and swelling of the face and hands. It can often be controlled by bed rest and proper nutrition.

For a first pregnancy it is also called preeclampsia which, at its worst and in very rare cases, can turn into eclampsia or coma and result in death. The incidences of death have been greatly reduced in the last fifteen years, but preeclampsia is still with us. It is common in first pregnancies that are unattended and unwanted, and for women with diabetes, kidney or heart disease. Other symptoms include rapid weight gain, accumulation of fluid in the face and hands, headaches and epigastric pain.

Edema. Puffiness around the eyes, swelling of the fingers and of the legs (especially upon arising in the morning, not after a long day of standing or walking, when such a manifestation of tiredness may show itself), are symptoms of edema, or swelling of the tissues, caused by fluid retention. With these signs may come severe headaches, dizziness, epigastric pains, persistent nausea.

How do you avoid it? Follow a healthy and varied diet, low in salt and free of carbonated beverages, which have a high content of sodium, the fluid-retentive mineral. Edema is still one of the causes of premature birth. If you suspect edema, get in touch with your doctor.

Vaginal Bleeding. Vaginal bleeding during pregnancy has different meanings according to which term of pregnancy you are in when it occurs:

1. First trimester bleeding is due to implantation (usually it is more like spotting) or to threatened abortion. A natural abortion or miscarriage (which is the rejection of the fetus by the body for a variety of causes) can be due to illness, shock, malformation, etc.

2. Second trimester vaginal bleeding can also be caused by the rejection of the fetus due to blood problems.

3. Third trimester bleeding is a more serious problem. It can mean the separation of the placenta before the onset of labor. This is something that happens in $1/85$ to $1/200$ pregnancies, known as abruptio placenta.

Bleeding may also be caused by toxemia. Usually the woman will go into labor prematurely. The real danger is to the baby, particularly if it is an internal hemorrhage. It is characterized by sharp pains in the abdominal regions and should be reported to your doctor as soon as possible.

Placenta Previa is another cause of bleeding in the last months which may be due to the abnormal site of placental implantation. Instead of being anchored high in the uterus near the fundus, it lies low near the cervix or even worse, over it. Heavy bleeding in the seventh month may be a warning. It could be followed by a hemorrhage of serious consequences. Placenta previa can be detected with ultrasound.

Ectopic pregnancy is when the embryo implants itself somewhere other than in the uterus such as in a fallopian tube or in the abdominal cavity. It is more common in women who use an IUD or have tubal damage from pelvic infections. It is difficult to detect by the symptoms. Vaginal bleeding may be the result of this ailment. Other symptoms include: rapid pulse, signs of fainting, piercing pains in the lower part of the abdomen and right shoulder pain. Consult with your doctor immediately as ectopic pregnancy usually requires prompt hospitalization and surgery. If suspected, it can be detected with ultrasound prior to rupture.

Rh Factor. Among the various tests conducted in early pregnancy, one is done to determine the Rh (rhesus) factor of the blood. If it is present, as a substance coating the blood cells, the blood is Rh positive, which is the case for most people.

If both you and the father are Rh negative none of your pregnancies will be affected. If his blood group is Rh positive and yours is Rh negative, it is possible that the baby will turn out to be an Rh positive.

The test is then repeated at the end of the second trimester to see if there is any rise in the Rh titer. If there is no rise in titer, a minidose of Rhogam is given to the mother. In this case your system may develop antibodies against the foreign blood spilling over in the bloodstream. During the next pregnancy these now permanent antibodies would be present and would break down some of the unborn baby's red blood cells, causing anemia. It is the reason, very often, for jaundiced infants, as the tiny liver is not yet ready to handle all the required processing and filtering. There are also certain nuclei in the brain that get jaundice and are the cause of permanent brain damage.

With an Rh positive mother, pregnancies will not be affected. If the mother is Rh negative, it will usually not cause any trouble in the first pregnancy. But, an injection of Rhogam within seventy-two hours following the birth of an Rh positive baby is given to protect an Rh negative mother.

If you have had an Rh conflict in your last pregnancy and no Rhogam (gammaglobulin) shot, an amniocentesis test can be performed during the new pregnancy to determine to what extent, if at all, the baby is affected. Sometimes labor may be induced as early as the thirty-fourth week of gestation if the fetus shows rapid anemic progression. A transfusion can be given to the baby while it is still in the womb. If the baby is born at term, a test is performed to find out its degree of anemia and, if needed, the baby's blood is exchanged with a donor's.

One Rhogam injection is also recommended in cases of pregnancy termination for the woman who is Rh negative.

Breech Presentation. By the beginning of the last month of pregnancy, most babies have settled into a head down, or vertex, position ready for birth. But some babies, for reasons not understood, position themselves with the feet or bottom down. This is known as a breech presentation, and it can cause problems at birthtime. Breech babies should not be delivered at home or in birthing centers.

If your baby becomes breech during the last month of pregnancy, your doctor may try to externally manipulate the baby in order to turn it around. However, since this procedure involves slight risks, and since the baby is likely to spin right back into a breech position, most doctors and midwives prefer not to force rotation. Instead, many doctors and midwives recommend an exercise that women have found effective for turning breech babies.

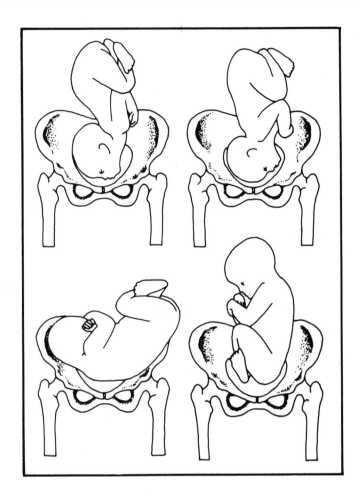

Labor and Birth

"Fear is in some way the chief pain producing agent in otherwise normal labor"
—Grantly Dick-Read, M.D.

Many months of physical and mental transformation have taken place and now the much-awaited baby is going to be born. Mysterious signals are being sent through your body and mind. Is this labor?

Scholars have debated for centuries over the correct interpretation of the Hebrew word in the Old Testament:

BE-ETZEV—IN SADNESS

from the fifteenth-century adaptation of the King James version of the bible. Still being read today, the passage reads "...Woman shall give birth in sadness." That is our heritage perpetrated through the centuries. Thanks a lot to the men who wrote it! In fact, however, the actual translation of the word can also mean "hard work." Birth is certainly one of the most strenuous physical efforts a woman may have to do in her lifetime but then there are some people who get excitement and pleasure from hard work. This conflict between fact and legend makes it difficult to describe the period of time before the actual birth—termed labor—to a woman who is having her first child.

No two people experience labor in exactly the same way, with the same intensity or duration. However, for women who are venturing into the unknown and having their first baby, we are going to attempt to describe the baby's motions, the rites of passage, the birthday of the new being. For the woman having another child we hope to add new insights into this fascinating phase of life.

We deal with the progression of a normal, prepared delivery. It will be brief because the next chapter is a series of interviews with mothers and fathers describing personal experiences and perceptions about pregnancy, labor and birth.

How do we know when labor begins?

It becomes a silent haunting question from the middle of pregnancy. But, in truth, the start of labor cannot be missed.

Towards the end of the ninth month (or ten lunar months) there will probably be warning signs. Contractions will sometimes be felt as strong menstrual cramps. It is only when contractions occur at regular intervals, with the rest period in between gradually getting shorter, that one can be sure it is real labor.

There are other signs which do not necessarily happen in sequence. One of these is that the baby's head settles in the pelvis. The mother may feel she can breathe easier as the pressure of the diaphragm is relieved as the baby moves down. Known as "lightening," this may happen weeks before D-Day. Also she may urinate more frequently since now the pressure is increased on the bladder. Another sign is an uncontrollable flow or trickle of liquid from the vagina, at which point her doctor or midwife should be called. This means the membrane of the sac surrounding the baby has ruptured and the amniotic fluid is running out. A late sign is "the show" or a thick mucous discharge tinged with blood from little broken vessels of the cervix as it begins to dilate.

It may take a few hours to a few days from "the show," or "bloody show," as it is sometimes termed, for rhythmic labor to start.

If you are having the baby at home, there is still plenty of time left to prepare a nest where you will give birth and to center your mind on what's happening to your body. If you are going to have your baby in a hospital, don't forget to take things that comfort you. Any of the following suggestions may brighten up a sterile environment, and help make labor more comfortable.

Smell: cologne, perfume, flowers or dried petals, bath oil or herbs.

Sight: colorful images, family snapshots, small statues, mobiles.

Touch: colorful scarf, sweater, socks and legwarmers for legs that get shaky in labor, lip balm, body cream, elastic or barrettes for hair, smooth stone, down pillow.

For the labor room and the days following birth bring a camera to record the birth (preferably with fast film to avoid the use of flash), small radio-tape recorder with music cassettes, earphones and a blank cassette to record the baby's first sounds, illustrated books, comic strips, note-books, pens, deck of playing cards or small games, puzzles. Hospitals provide food for the mother, but generally not for the father. He can use the hospital dining facilities or bring a snack along.

If you plan to have your baby in a birth center, you can take any of the above, though there is less need since your stay will be short. You should also bring nourishing snacks for yourself, the father and anyone else who plans to attend the birth. Snacks can be prepared in the center's kitchen facilities. Vegetable and fruit juices, yogurts, teas, honey, soups and light salads are good foods in labor. You can also bring a snack or bottle of champagne to celebrate the birth.

For the baby: infant cotton tee shirt, cotton receiving blankets, soft, light blanket (preferably wool or brushed cotton) or a tightly knit shawl. Bonnet, sweater, slippers and other going-home clothes for the baby, depending on the season. All baby clothes should be prewashed. Almond oil, baby hairbrush and diapers are also suggested. Many states now require the use of infant car seats. Check whether these are available in the hospital gift store, or if the hospital provides them on short-term loan.

RHYTHMS

During labor the body has a rhythm all its own. The woman and infant should dance along with it rather than resist. It is more powerful than painful. Birth is a different kind of sexual act, also done through the vagina. Oxytocin, the hormone released in the act of lovemaking, is also secreted while giving birth and nursing. The mind should direct the body so that it doesn't get tense when birth-pangs occur. It can really be

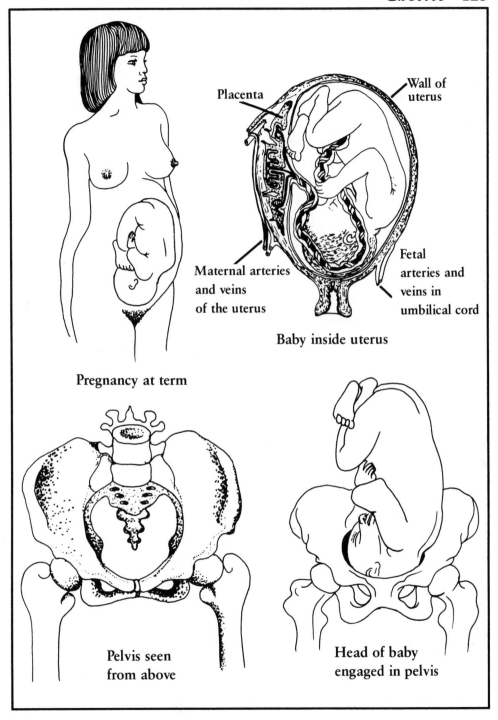

Pregnancy at term

Placenta

Wall of uterus

Maternal arteries and veins of the uterus

Fetal arteries and veins in umbilical cord

Baby inside uterus

Pelvis seen from above

Head of baby engaged in pelvis

fascinating to witness one's own body being taken over by BIRTH-FORCE. It is another dimension of sensations. Faced without fears, birth can be one of the highest moments in a woman's life. If you need warmth, reassurance, or feel out of sorts, don't feel shy about cuddling with your companion, husband or a friend.

When a pattern is established with regular contractions every ten minutes, the first stage of labor has begun. It is time to call the doctor or midwife and let them know. If you can stay on your feet, the force of gravity will help the cervix to dilate, speeding and easing your labor.

Upon arrival at the hospital, you will be directed to the preparation room after having registered at the admission desk, unless you have taken care of it beforehand. The mother and father will be comfortable now if they have previously visited the hospital and are familiar with the building and the procedures. In a birth center there is no admission procedure and no "prepping." You and your partner will be taken straight to the labor or family room, or your birthing room, perhaps after an initial internal exam.

In a hospital the medical staff will chart the mother's temperature, pulse, blood pressure and the fetal heart rate. The frequency of the contractions will be timed and a vaginal examination will be given. The routine varies with each establishment, but it is often part of the preparation to shave and clean the pubic area and to give an enema. These are unpleasant procedures but they do not hurt if done early in labor. Some hospitals are eliminating the shaving. In home birth and birth centers most women do not have their pubic hair shaven as it is found unnecessary. However, the area is kept very clean. Also, enemas are not usually given in home births and birth centers unless the woman is constipated. In most instances the body will empty itself during the course of labor. The pregnant woman is then taken to the labor room.

The contractions come and go. . . . Breathe deeply. . . . Walk around or rest. . . . Empty your bladder and bowels. . . . Doodle or doze in between contractions. . . . You may have hot flushes with perspiration. Ask for quietude or retreat to a calm area if too much is happening around you and you feel the need to concentrate.

The first stage of labor lasts from four to twelve hours. It varies with each person.

The cervix passage has been closed tight for nine months holding the child in the uterus. It will take a great deal of uterine contraction to open it up completely. The cervix flattens, stretches, begins to dilate (5 cm). The contractions are short. In early labor, they are often felt from low down in the back, slowly gaining ground through the body to the abdominal area. The rhythm gets tighter over the hours. By late labor, each contraction lasts forty-five seconds with an interval of three to five minutes in between.

No straining or pushing . . . No hanging on to a clock for the exact timing . . . Let your body be guided by its own rhythm and by your intuition. . . . Mother strength . . . Have confidence in yourself and trust the natural flow. . . . Let it happen. . . . Breathe slowly and deeply.

Deep Breathing (see page 40).   The contractions can hurt if you tense up. They become pains if you forget that most of the time your mind can cooperate with your body. It's an intense sensation to bring forth a child. Keep your mind on it. Calmness can help the muscles to relax. Lie down the way it feels best. Many women feel constricted by the narrow beds in the hospital labor room and say they should have brought along their own thin foam rubber exercise mattress to be able to sit or lie on the floor and have more room to move and stretch. Focus your eyes on an image inside or outside your head.

Along the way the contractions have become longer and sharper, each lasting forty-five seconds or longer with an interval of two or three minutes in between. The rhythm is not always that regular, it does not follow the hands of a watch. The contractions may even appear to override each other and breathing has to be adjusted accordingly. If the membranes have not ruptured yet, it may well happen at this stage. By now the cervix is about 8cm dilated and the baby's head is pushing through. The head could have become engaged a few weeks ago or it can happen after full dilatation. The intensity of the rumble as the head comes through the cervix can be overwhelming.

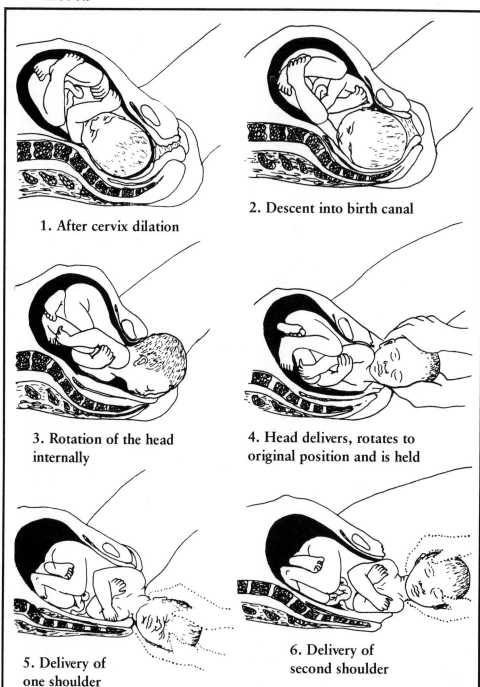

1. After cervix dilation

2. Descent into birth canal

3. Rotation of the head internally

4. Head delivers, rotates to original position and is held

5. Delivery of one shoulder

6. Delivery of second shoulder

It may leave you a little shaky. In the hospital, medicine will be offered time and again; we have noted the benefits and drawbacks. Take it or leave it.

The end of the first stage is quite an effort. You may be perspiring and shivering at the same time. It may even feel as if imaginary plugs have been pulled out of your body. The nose and the eyes may run. Some women vomit and others spend a lot of time on the toilet. It feels like a thunderstorm. It's draining but interesting to observe. As the contractions become more powerful it can get uncomfortable. Relieve your abdomen of the pressure with the breathing method you have learned or try shallow breathing.

Shallow Breathing (see page 40). Rest when the contraction is over. You probably will not feel like talking. Make yourself as comfortable as possible. Tuck pillows here and there. Wipe yourself cool with a wet handkerchief. If your mouth gets dry, suck on a wet cloth, sponge or ice chips. Kneel on all fours if it helps. Women from the Santa Cruz birth center in California have had wonderful experiences giving birth that way. Try a squatting position for a while. Don't feel inhibited ... leave that for another day.

Your companion could massage your back if it's pulling. Tell him/her where to apply the hands. He/she can help make the passage smoother.

In the hospital the father, coach or a friend can be in the labor room with you, but not all hospitals allow another person in the delivery room. Find out beforehand the rules and regulations of the establishment.

The baby's head is advancing through the tight pelvic bones. There is a certain resistance and the little head flexes, the chin touches the chest. As the head passes between the bones, it rotates a bit to accommodate the oblong shape of the pelvis and straightens up afterwards. The baby is in a transition stage between the uterus and the outside world. It is making its way through the vagina to the perineum. The first phase of labor has ended with full dilatation.

After being examined you are wheeled, or you may walk, to the delivery or birthing room. In your home environment you will find a position that is most comfortable for you. If you are lying down, have your back propped up, either held by your partner or with big cushions. It is considerably more difficult, and distressing for the baby, to give birth lying flat on your back. The doctor or midwife will examine you to see how tight the skin is around the perineum, and to establish the need for an episiotomy. You strain and feel the need to push. Sometimes, instead of breathing, voice expression, chanting, singing, sounds that are not necessarily words can be really satisfying. However, shallow or pant breathing relieves the pressure best in the long run.

The second stage of labor is beginning. It lasts about fifty minutes and should not exceed two hours. The baby's head begins to appear through the vulvar opening as it is pushed out by each successive contraction. When the contraction is over, the vulva closes a little and the head recedes less and less. The same process recurs, stretching the expanded vaginal muscles a little more with each new push. The skin becomes very taut, forming a mound around the shape of the head. When the vulva has encircled the largest diameter of the fetal head, it is known as "crowning." As the time to push comes, stay in tune with your body, which will tell you to change position often—when it hurts, when you feel stiff or discouraged. Try not to lie on your back, this is the hardest position for you and for the baby. Avoid positions that make you strain to push or that make your legs feel tense. Pay attention to your mouth. If your teeth are clenched or your lips are pursed, your whole body is probably tense. Relax your lips, let them part.

Think of your back as a gentle, flexible C-curve. Most upright or semiupright positions will encourage this curve, and will enable gravity to help your baby in its passage down the birth canal. Also, your perineum will stretch more easily, without tearing. Get down on all fours and rock your pelvis to and fro rhythmically. If you are lying down, have your partner sit behind you and prop you up into a semilying position. Or kneel down with your partner's knees as an arm rest. Lie on your side, with your top leg lifted and supported by your partner. (This is a good position when you have to resist the urge to push.)

Many women all over the world find the squatting position the most conducive to effective pushing in labor. Try squatting on the bed or floor—your partner can stand or kneel behind you, giving you underarm support, or you can use pillows or lean back against a wall or sturdy armchair. It can feel especially soothing to squat or semistand, supporting yourself by hanging trapezelike from a bed rail or high shelf. (This last position can encourage the baby to rotate if you are having back labor.) Squatting, kneeling or sitting in a knee-to-chest position, you will be able to see and touch your baby as it is being born.

Most of these positions can make labor easier for you, but harder for your birth attendant to control and monitor. A supportive attendant will work with you, moving monitoring and IV equipment as neccessary, kneeling down with you to catch your baby. But if your doctor is uneasy about delivering your baby in an unusual position, see if he will let you try out different positions until the head is almost crowning, and then help you into a more accessible position for the birth itself. Specially designed beds now in use in birthing rooms help the position situation.

A calmer period follows after this storm, and you can gather up your strength. At this point you probably feel tired but elated, finding the whole procedure weird. It's been quite a journey and there is still some way to go. The urge to push the baby out is strongly felt. When the contraction comes, you will breathe deeply and hold the last in-breath while bearing down. With all your strength, you grab your knees or the straps on the side of the table and press your feet on the leg holder.

The fetal heartbeat will be listened to in order to verify its regularity. During the second stage women often have cramps in the legs and feet due to alteration in the blood circulation. If it happens to you, move your legs around, ask a friend or the nurse to massage the area, strongly, for relief.

As the baby's head pushes on the perineum, concentrate on that area, remember the Kegel exercise and then try to relax those muscles. As the head struggles to emerge, the doctor may perform an episiotomy (a small incision of the perineum which will later be sewn up). The episiotomy prevents tearing which would cause a ragged edge, very hard

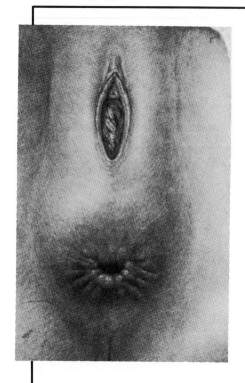

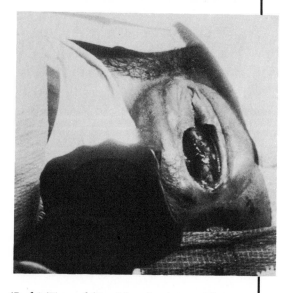

(Left) Top of head beginning to show at vulva
(Above) Head of baby crowning
(Below) Delivery of baby's head after external rotation

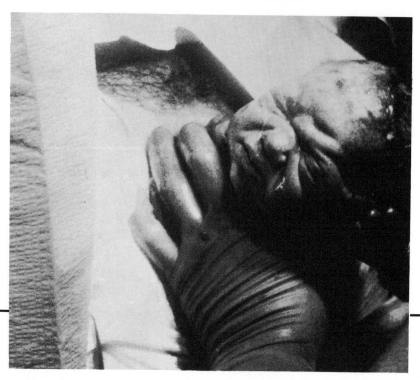

to sew together. The head is held in place and you may be asked to stop pushing just as the baby is ready to come out. This is to prevent the head from bursting out. PANT BREATHE in a fast manner; it will help to stop the pushing urge. Later, the labia separate and the head of the baby is born with its eyes and nose facing downward.

When you relax your pelvic floor and deliver your baby's head slowly, without pushing, the perineal tissue stretches slowly and is less likely to tear or require episiotomy. Before the head crowns, you can ask your birth attendant or partner to massage the outside and inside of the vaginal opening with a natural oil, which will soften the stretched tissue. He/she can also help by holding a hot compress—three washcloths soaked in very hot water and wrung—very firmly against your perineum, soothing and bringing needed blood to the area. The same hot compress or a gauze pad may be used to support the perineum from the time the head crowns, until after the shoulders and body are born. Relax, feel your baby as it slips slowly out into the world.

There is a slow external rotation of the head towards the thigh. The doctor holds the baby. The next contraction helps deliver the shoulders gently, and the rest of the body slides out, tugging along with it the umbilical cord. The baby gives a good cry. Mucus is drawn out of the nose and mouth if necessary and penicillin ointment or silver nitrate is put into each eye in order to prevent gonorrheal infection of the eyes which may have been picked up during the passage through the birth canal. The baby is still attached to the uterus and the placenta. When the blood has stopped pulsating through the cord, it is clamped or tied in two places, one close to the baby's abdomen and the other a little bit further up. It is severed with a sterile surgical scissors in between the two knots. In a birth center or home birth the father may cut the cord.

This is truly the most incredible moment! Suddenly, you see the person you have been carrying within you all this time. It is more than a surprise, it's a shock to find that there really is a new individual in the room and in your arms!

There is a tremendous feeling of boundless power in giving birth, but also of entire helplessness when you realize that without the father, midwife, doctor and friends, this moment of life could have been very different.

The child is born! There remains the placenta to be delivered which is the third stage of labor. Spontaneous mild contractions will bring out the remainder of the cord. The placenta is attached to the cord. No tugging or pulling. Most of the time, the placenta will slip out easily, anywhere from five to thirty minutes after the birth. The doctor will make sure that it is all in one piece as there should not be any part of it left within the uterus. Once the placenta is delivered, labor is over. If there has been an episiotomy, it is then sewn up.

This last stage requires minimal effort on your part: patience and pushing when the contractions come along, resting in between. There will be some bleeding from the rupture of the blood vessels as the placenta separates from the uterus. You may have held the little baby from the minute the shoulder was out or the baby may be given to you now. If the infant has a desire to suck from your breast, all the better as she/he will take in some of the colostrum. The milk will not come through yet, it takes a day or two, maybe three. The colostrum contains antibodies, vitamins and proteins that are meant for the newborn and can only be beneficial.

In the hospital, the infant gets cleaned, weighed, measured and foot-printed. Its reflexes are tested and an identification bracelet is put around its wrist. After the father, mother and baby have gotten acquainted and rejoiced, the baby is taken to the nursery for the next eight hours so that the mother can rest. It can be frustrating if the mother doesn't really feel tired. However, if the hospital has a rooming-in system, the baby can be with the mother all the time. If she was in the delivery room, the mother will be wheeled or walked back to her room and can lie back. In a birth center, the baby, who may already have been given a Le Boyer bath, is examined at your bedside by a pediatrician, and stays with you until you are ready to go home. Meanwhile, you can take a shower, have a celebratory snack or champagne or simply lie back and take it all in.

At home the baby is cleansed, but often the vernix, the buttery substance covering parts of the skin, is not removed. Instead, it is spread

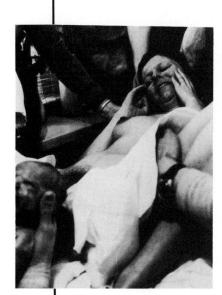

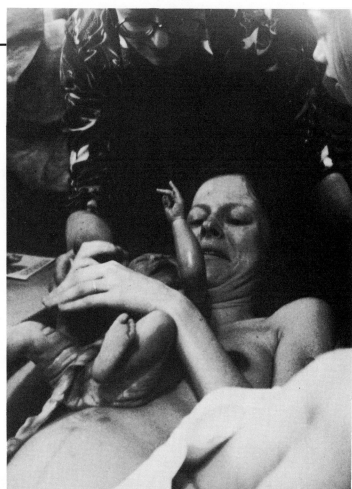

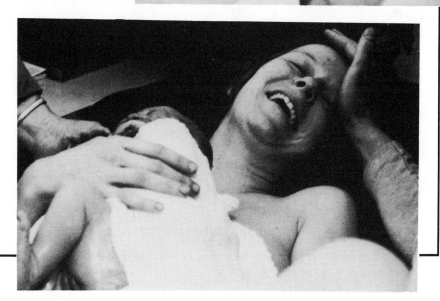

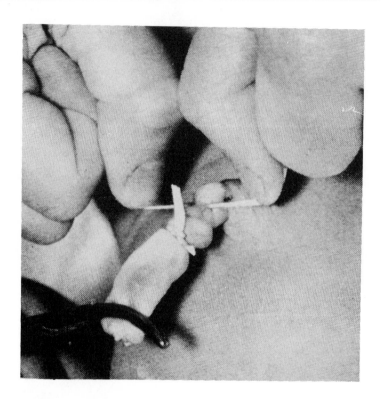

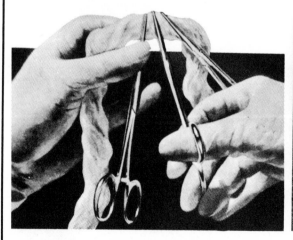
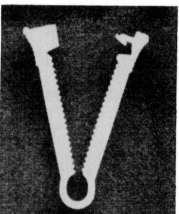

Various methods of severing the umbilical cord

around the tiny little body with the hands. The vernix sinks into the skin within the next twenty-four hours. It is believed to guard the skin against heat loss. The navel is well covered, the body is warmly wrapped and diapered. If the newborn cries hard a little warm water in a teaspoon may soothe. The crying may stop as soon as she/he is lying on the mother's abdomen, close to the beat of the heart, a familiar fetus-days sound. Once asleep, the baby can be gently moved if you want to change position or get up. The infant will rest best in an area where the light is not bright. The mother may do likewise. Rest. Take a shower with someone's help, have a light meal or just celebrate and rejoice.

POSSIBLE COMPLICATIONS DURING LABOR

Induction.   Induction is an artificial means of starting or speeding up (also called "augmentation") the process of labor at a chosen time, rather than letting the body begin by itself when it is fully ready. The physician can induce or speed up labor by breaking the bag of waters with a simple instrument inserted through the vagina and cervix. This procedure, called an amniotomy, can increase the chances of uterine infection, so the doctor will want to deliver the baby within twelve hours from the time the membranes have ruptured. The breaking of the membranes is sometimes performed midway through labor as a way of strengthening contractions.

Labor can also be induced, or stimulated, with an injection of pitocin, a synthetic form of the hormone oxytocin. It is injected into the vein through the intravenous drip (IV) and labor is continued by means of a constant drip of pitocin through a little tube (an intravenous catheter) into the middle of the arm or at the hand. The injection will induce labor only if the whole system is ready to give birth. Because the medication causes the womb to contract strongly and in a more regular pattern than it normally would, women generally find it hard to deal with pitocin-induced labor. Strong medication is nearly always required,

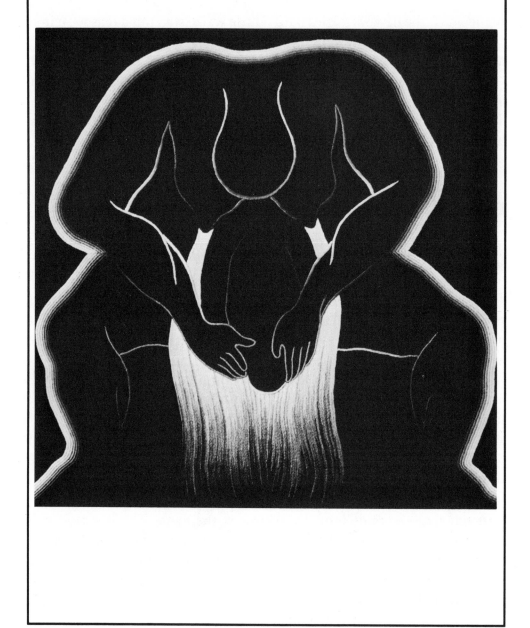

and the use of an electronic fetal monitor and IV are usually mandatory. Induction should not be done for the convenience of doctors or parents. A woman may be induced if she has diabetes or toxemia, if the membranes have ruptured and labor has not begun within a certain time period, if tests show that the baby's growth is affected by anemia, or if the baby is two weeks overdue and postmature. The postmaturity of an overdue baby can be checked by having a stress test or nonstress test, and with a sonogram that can indicate if there is adequate amniotic fluid in the sac.

There are various nonmedical ways that a woman who is ready to give birth can use to start labor. Manipulation of the nipples or gentle sexual intercourse (only if the membranes have not ruptured) can encourage the release of oxytocin into the bloodstream, causing the onset of normal contractions.

Forceps. Forceps are a metal instrument resembling two hollowed spoons joined together in the middle. This instrument is placed on the sides of the baby's head, like iron hands, to help out in a difficult situation such as exhaustion on the part of the mother or eclampsia or malpresentation. The forceps are usually used for these purposes, or after general or regional anesthesia.

Forceps can be used to protect the baby from excess pressure on its head, especially in the case of uncontrollable pushing by the mother. Or, they may be used to speed delivery if the infant has a low heartbeat; if the umbilical cord comes out before the head and endangers the baby's oxygen supply; if there is a premature separation of the placenta or if a breech extraction is necessary.

The name forceps rings a mean bell in most women's minds because, up until a few decades ago, they were used to reach way up, where the baby's head was still in a very tight place, and they often caused pain and damage. However, since those days, smaller and lighter instruments have been devised and forceps are now mostly used only in the lower parts when the head is showing. They sometimes leave traces on the baby's cheeks which should disappear in a day or two.

Anesthetics (general, spinal and epidural) and analgesics often interfere with the mother's desire to push and this may account for the necessity of using forceps.

Forceps have been used in the delivery of babies for many centuries. They were invented by Guillaume Chamberlain in the seventeenth century. Chamberlain passed his invention on to his sons who kept it a well-guarded family secret until the eighteenth century.

Cesarean Section.
Cesarean section is an obstetrical operation that delivers the infant through incisions in the abdominal and uterine walls. Legend has it that the name cesarean came from the law passed by the Emperor Julius Caesar, ordering that dying women have the operation during the last few weeks of pregnancy in the hopes of saving the child. In those days, in fact up until the sixteenth century, no woman was known to have survived the operation. Now, while cesarean is still a major surgical operation, it is one of the safest, thanks to modern obstetrics, performed almost always with success. About one in every five deliveries in the United States is a cesarean section.

There are various conditions that require a cesarean. It is necessary in cases of preeclampsia; infection due to prematurely ruptured membranes; when the pelvis is too narrow for the baby; when the placenta has detached from the uterine wall (abruptus), hangs down from the vagina (prolapse) or blocks the birth canal (previa). Most of these conditions are fairly rare. A cesarean is sometimes necessary in cases of difficult breech or malpresentation; twins; if labor does not progress because the cervix stops dilating or the contractions grow too weak; if the fetus is suffering distress; or if the mother has diabetes or toxemia. Many women who have had a previous cesarean are able to deliver vaginally. The increase in cesarean intervention over the past few years stems mainly from cases such as these, where the doctor and parents can choose between surgery or a potentially complicated vaginal birth. In these cases, discuss the necessity for cesarean with your doctor and get a second opinion if possible. If the need for cesarean is in doubt, it is a good idea to attempt a "trial labor." This means that you go into labor, and as long as there are no complications, labor and delivery progress. Not only does this significantly increase your chances of a vaginal birth, it is also good insurance that the baby is ready to be born, and that your own body is prepared physically and psychologically for motherhood. An elective cesarean section should never be performed more than ten to fourteen days before your due date.

Once the need for cesarean has been established, and you have agreed to it, you will be given the choice of general anesthesia, which puts you to sleep for the entire operation and has many aftereffects for both mother and baby, or an epidural, which totally numbs the lower part of your body, allowing you to experience the birth and to see and hold your baby as soon as it is born. The incision made may be low transverse (horizontal) or classical (vertical). The low transverse is done most frequently now and is the least likely to rupture during subsequent pregnancies.

Many hospitals now admit the father into the operating room, and his presence, his hand to hold, may help both parents avoid the disappointment that can follow when a woman must have a cesarean section. While the incision is being made, the father stands at the head of the table, while the nurse or anesthesiologist explains what is happening behind the screen that shields both parents from the operating field. Once the incision is made, the shield is removed, and father and mother can watch the birth. After the birth, you can ask to hold your baby, briefly, while you are being stitched up.

The postcesarean hospital stay is usually five to seven days. You will be encouraged to walk around after the first day to help ease the postoperation gas pains and avoid the formation of blood clots. You might feel nauseated and have abdominal pains from the sutures. The pain-killers offered to you after the numbness wears off will make you very drowsy. Don't resist sleep, it is what you need most at this time. In your waking hours, try to spend as much time as possible with your baby. Your birth experience has been intense. The physical and emotional tenderness that you and your newborn can give to each other will help you to heal. Remember, you gave birth by cesarean because you wanted to save your baby from distress or danger—it was not an easy way out.

You should arrange for help to be available when you return home, since you will continue to feel very tired for a few weeks. The incision should take about six weeks to heal. You will have to avoid heavy lifting and strenuous exercise for three months at least. To help regain your strength, find out about pre- and postcesarean exercises from a cesarean support group or childbirth education class.

Vaginal Birth After Cesarean (V-BAC).

With subsequent births, you may no longer have to undergo cesarean section just because a previous birth was by cesarean. Doctors used to worry that the uterine scar would separate during labor, but they are quickly discovering that with a little extra physical and mental preparation, V-BAC is quite safe if a low transverse incision is made. There is a 1 to 3 percent chance of uterine rupture, and if it does occur this is rarely an emergency. If the scar is going to separate, it generally does so before labor begins.

The better you feel about your body and your innate capacity to give birth, the more chance you will have of a successful V-BAC. Talk to women who have done it; look at statistics if it will help—the success of V-BAC is very well documented.

POSSIBLE COMPLICATIONS AT BIRTH

Premature Labor.

The fetus can be expelled by the body at any time during pregnancy. If expelled before the embryo reaches one pound (500 g), it is considered a miscarriage. By the time it weighs three pounds, it is already a premature infant. Born with a weight over 5½ pounds, it is considered a full-term baby. Most of the time the exact cause of prematurity is not known. Heavy tobacco smoking, inadequate nutrition and poor general health are recognized as important factors, and in certain cases prematurity can be traced to toxemia infection, twins, or the separation of the placenta. The admission of analgesic

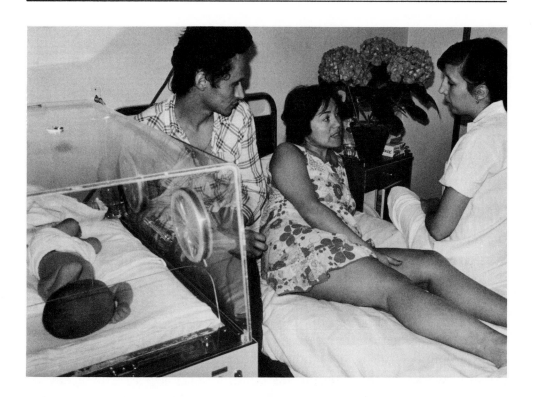

drugs in premature labor is restricted as much as possible to give the infant the maximum chance for survival. Some doctors prefer to deliver premature babies by cesarean to spare them the stress of a vaginal birth, while others use low forceps to speed up delivery.

The two days following the birth will determine the development of the premature infant. If the baby survives the first week, chances are good that it will be strong enough to carry on. Premature babies have to be kept under special observation until they reach their full maturity potential. Some hospitals have special neonatal intensive care units where the premature infant can be adequately cared for. All hospitals have incubators in which preemies are kept warm and protected from infection. In some hospitals with rooming-in, the incubator can be placed by your bedside. If the incubator is in the nursery, parents are encouraged to visit frequently and to participate in the care of the newborn until it is time to go home.

Very small babies may have to be fed by dropper or through a thin tube passed into the stomach. If this is the case, the mother who plans to breast-feed will be shown how to use an electric breast pump, so that her milk, which the baby needs as soon as it can be digested, can be fed by dropper, and so that she can establish her milk supply in preparation for the baby's readiness.

The incidence of prematurity has risen in recent years, but the survival rate of these infants has vastly increased due both to modern medicine and to a more tactile humane treatment of the premature infant. In Bogotá, Colombia, under the supervision of Dr. Edgar Rey at the San Juan de Dios Hospital, preemies as small as two pounds are kept snuggled warm against their mothers' breasts, under a blouse or sweater.

False and Slow Labor. Sometimes it appears as if labor is starting; there are contractions here and there, odd sensations in the back and lower abdomen. If they do not recur at regular intervals it is probably only a prelude for the real labor which will come in a few days or possibly weeks. If these sensations continue over a period of a day or more, it may be a case of slow labor due to the weakness of uterine contractions. If the labor is progressing, all that is needed is a lot of patience; but, if nothing much is happening, the doctor may recommend drip-infusion of pitocin to stimulate the strength and regularity of the contractions. Another cause for slow labor might be the disproportion in size between the mother's pelvis (either an odd shape or a small diameter) and the baby's head. If the head is large, it can take quite some time to go through the birth canal. In extreme cases of incompetent contractions or halt in the descent of the head, a cesarean section may have to be performed before any maternal or fetal complications set in.

Multiple Births. In about one in every eighty-five births, twins are delivered. Triplets, quadruplets, etc., are rarer still. Multiple pregnancy is to some extent an inherited tendency and occurs more frequently to women in their thirties. Fertility drugs also contribute to multiple births. Multiple pregnancy can be detected by ultrasound as early as the fourteenth week of pregnancy. By the twenty-eighth week it is usually possible for the doctor or midwife to feel more than one fetus through the abdomen.

Twins are relatively easy to deliver, but because there are slight risks of complication, birth should take place in a hospital. Premature labor is the main risk, so women carrying twins are generally advised to rest after the twenty-eighth week of pregnancy. As labor begins, the first baby is usually in a head down position. Contractions may stop for a while between deliveries. The second baby may be a breech presentation but can generally be delivered vaginally with the aid of low forceps and episiotomy.

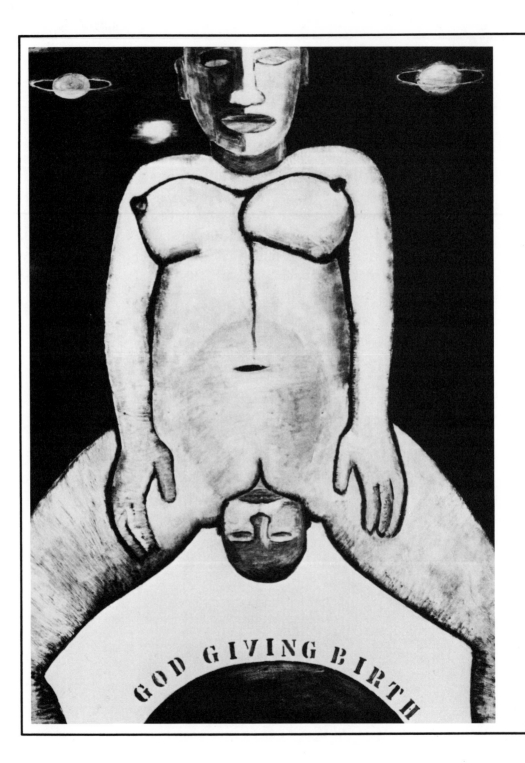

GOD GIVING BIRTH

Birth Experiences

BIRTH . . . INCARNATION

ANOTHER THING THAT PEOPLE
MUST SACRIFICE
IS THEIR SUFFERING.
NO ONE WHO HAS NOT
SACRIFICED HIS/HER SUFFERING
CAN WORK.
NOTHING CAN BE ATTAINED
WITHOUT SUFFERING
BUT AT THE SAME TIME
ONE MUST BEGIN BY
SACRIFICING SUFFERING.

—GURDJIEFF

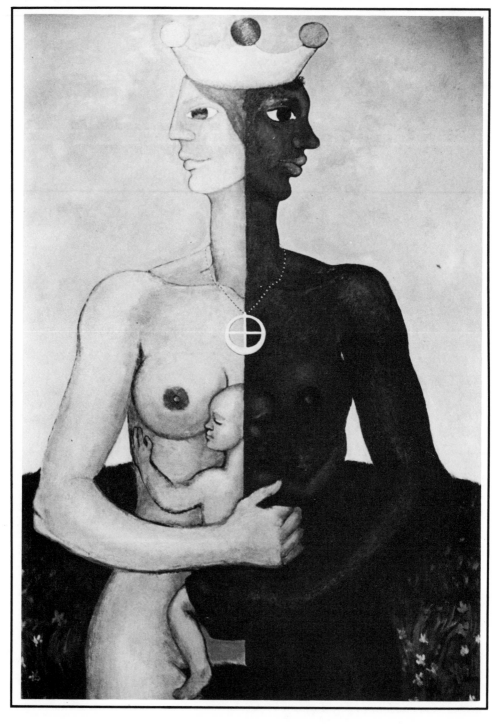

This chapter is a collection of birth stories as told by the mothers and fathers of newborn infants, and birth attendants, in the form of conversations, interviews, and letters. They tell which methods they chose for delivery and why, about their expectations, the development of labor and the experience of birth events, their moments of disappointment, joy and surprise.

Deedee Brigewater: Hospital delivery, prepared breathing, first child

Caterine Milinaire: Home birth, prepared childbirth, first child

Michel Odent: Director of Maternity at Pithiviers Hospital, France

Oona Napier: Hospital delivery, exercise preparation, first child

Lisa Lorelli: Hospital labor and delivery nurse

Ann Simon: A mother's view of nurse–midwifery

Maxime de La Falaise McKendry: Home birth with midwife, first child

Terry Davis: Hospital birthing room, second child

Gladys St. Louis: Hospital delivery, yoga exercise and breathing, fourth child

Connie Zalk: Hospital delivery by cesarean, artificial insemination, first child

Camilla Hoover: Hospital delivery, induced labor, second child

Jill Williamson: Hospital delivery, prepared childbirth with complications, first child

Zilina Luc: Giving birth in the fields, fifth child

Sandy Field: Certified nurse-midwife, home birth practice

Nancy Richardson: Home birth, third child

Mary Salter: Hospital delivery, cesarean, first child

Anna Pastoressa: Clinic delivery with midwife, first child

Lynn and Alan Fliegel: Clinic delivery by cesarean, second child

Joan Weiner: Home birth, stillborn, first child

Daisy Hess: Hospital delivery, Bradley method preparation, first child

Frederick Le Boyer: Doctor, author and filmmaker of works concerning the newborn

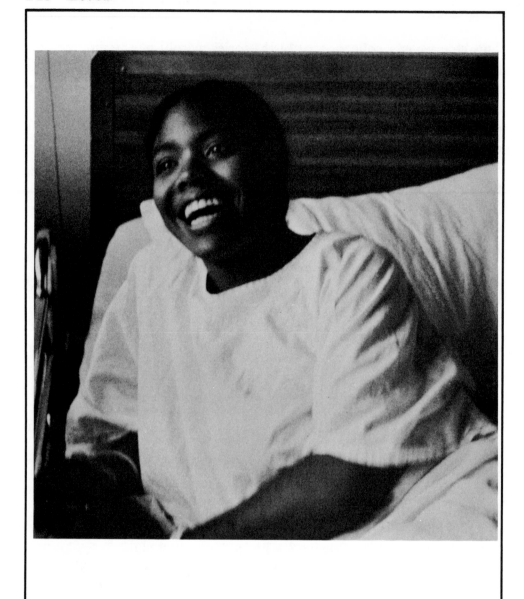

Deedee Brigewater
Hospital delivery, prepared breathing, first child

Caterine: When did you have your baby?

Deedee: Tulani, a girl, was born at 7:43 yesterday morning.

C: When did labor start?

D: The day before, at 3:00 in the afternoon, but it had started very gently in the morning around 8:00. But the last two hours before birth needed sheer hard concentration to stay on top of the contractions.

C: What sort of preparation did you follow before giving birth?

D: I went to prenatal classes. In a way, I feel I was not prepared enough or told enough about the enormous physical strength required to bring your child about in this world in the natural way. It's definitely the most colossal physical effort a woman will come across at one single moment during her lifetime. I kept on thinking, "Will I have enough strength to complete natural childbirth without drugs? Because I really want to see this baby, awake, from the first moment the head is out." I really concentrated on what was happening without panic and I knew that everything would be all right.

C: Was the father of the child with you?

D: No, Cecil is a musician and he was on tour. He arrived today and, let me tell you, I was only half myself during this birth episode. The father's presence is essential when it comes to emotional support. I know I would have been more relaxed had he been there, and also the energy circulated between him and me and the baby would have smoothed out a lot of tension. You see, in that hospital where I went I was placed in the labor room with another woman who was screaming and obviously did not know how to channel her fears. So it's kind of hard on you to hear these screams when you know you can avoid it and concentrate on breathing instead. My breathing turned to singing and that seemed to help us both.

It was a good thing I braided my hair before going to the hospital, I kept on having this compulsion to pull on it. It feels good to pull, squash, hug something, better someone . . . and I am sure it's meant to be the father of the child. You know, counter-strength . . . the alchemic vases . . . the strong partnership all the way.

C: What do you remember most about your visual surroundings as you were going through labor?

D: Blank walls, nurses, blank walls, blank ceiling! It was a very limited visual journey. It would be so great if they had flowers around and patterns on the ceilings and designs on the walls. It would be good to have a choice of either a blank room or a room like our world, you know, filled with images.

C: How was the delivery?

D: I followed the doctor's instructions. I concentrated hard because pushing the head out is really a big effort but it felt good. I was given an episiotomy. After the baby's head slipped out, it was sheer relief. And to see a baby being born from me was the most incredible event of my life! And then I got to hold the baby, but only for two minutes and it was taken away and only given to me today. That's a drag. The baby was taken to the nursery which is located directly across from the abortion rooms at Hillcrest General Hospital in Flushing, Queens. How much more insensitive can hospital planning get?

My next child I want to have at home with all my family there. I felt like cuddling up with my baby and was left exhilarated but in tears and frustrated from not being able to get to know my own child straight away. I know it's being done for your own good and rest, but two minutes after nine months of waiting is absurd.

C: Are there any special discoveries that you would like to tell a sister or remember particularly about giving birth?

D: The miraculous moment was when I started singing as a continuation of the breathing. I sing to earn my living and I sang to bring about this baby like I have never sung before. Imagine a labor room with singing women, what a chorus it would be! Singing was a great outlet for my emotions during pregnancy and at birth. It took the place of self-pity. So, when you are in doubt, keep on singing.

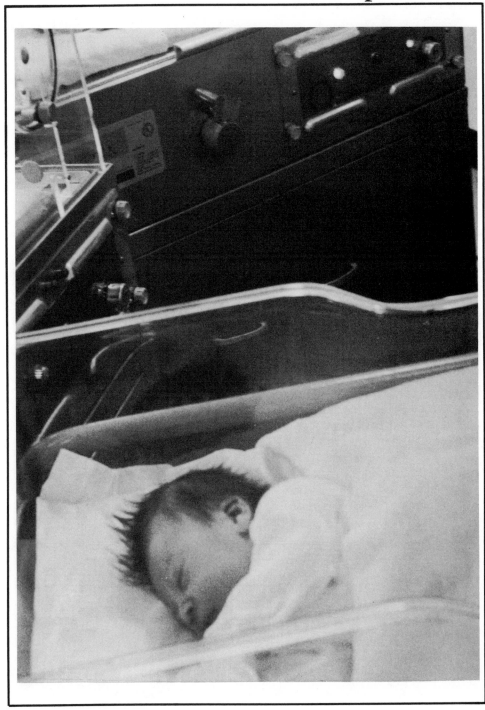

Caterine Milinaire
Home birth, prepared childbirth, first child

"May the magic of our baby's birth keep the smile eternally shining within us and around us."

What a strange fate humans have inflicted upon themselves: the fear of birth and the wish to be desensitized before witnessing the incredible bodyquake happening.

If one has been so traumatized through youth as to think childbirth is a painful experience, nature has provided nine full months of preparation. Time to think deeply about the new life. It's not too long. Time to adjust to body changes, time to breathe and stretch, time to get into healthy nutrition, time to erase antiquated concepts and figure out a personal code through intuition and common sense.

A NEW LIFE IS COMING. Children don't need us; we need them more than they need us. A child, the irresistible magic gift, the real bond, the total blend of two souls. The zero population growth movement is making us desperately aware of earth's critical overpopulation threat. It's time, more than ever, to be fully conscious of every phase of childing: conception in total ecstasy, pregnancy wished by both parents and carried through with thoughtful health care and the climax is birth! Birth is the greatest feast of joy, to be shared and helped with celebration by anyone who wishes to participate.

A slow evolution occurred in my mind from the time I decided to have a child until the sixth month of pregnancy. The more I went to see doctors and looked over hospitals, the more I became convinced that a home should be the place where the baby would be born. It became an obsession.

New York couldn't be the place. No air, no space, no peace, no rest. New York is a great playground but never a nest.

One day a friend talked about sunny Santa Fé in New Mexico. The same day another friend passed by telling us about the beautiful adobe house he bought in Santa Fé and about another one which was for rent. Everything began to fit. Oxygen for the baby, quiet rest, more time to be together in this sweet life meant to be enjoyed.

Once in Santa Fé I called the ASPO (American Society for Psychoprophylaxis in Obstetrics) who recommended two doctors. The first one I telephoned turned out to be extremely kind and calm. He and I convinced Mati, the baby's father, of the positiveness of home delivery. This new baby won't need liberating. It will be born free.

THE NINTH MONTH. Everyone is so impatient. The house is full of friends. Every day there is a new invention to induce the baby to show up. Syncopated chants, walks to the top of the mountain, painting the crib with good prospect symbols, long mineral baths at warm springs under the falling snow, drinking raw milk, reading the police emergency childbirth manual.

I am in no rush. I walk around proudly, tuning in to the other life moving along with mine. I laugh when we both feel so good I can run, dance and swim, knowing that the baby is enjoying all this from inside.

In the middle of the night the baby pressures me to get up, move around and get rid of the liquid squashing it. As if it were a TEACHER OF LIFE, the baby tells me: "Enough routine, get rid of your time habits, sleep at different hours, hear the night, see the dawn, feel yourself grow with me." I sleepwalk and sleeptalk with my baby.

Looking at me, self-declared fortune tellers announce without hesitation—a boy. Tarot card experts draw out "Male." And, when I am asked for a preference, "A boy? A girl?" I honestly don't care! Often at the end of my daily breathing exercises I would try very hard to center on sensing the sex of the baby but nothing was revealed. Instead, I would go off into the flames of the fire I had lit or the clouds behind the window. During the seventh month I had a dream of giving birth to a girl. She was lying next to me, a newborn. The next dream image was her at seven playing with angel Eleonore. Then she was my age, a twin sister sitting on a cloud. Last image was a mother figure, fading, while I was still in my 1971 present state, experiencing my daughter for the flash of half a century.

I AM READY—NO PANIC. I know the baby has to come out and will do so in its own time. Curious? Yes, extremely since I really can't figure out what the coming forth of this new life will do to me. Friends, experts, books, films, nothing is descriptive enough. It's *the* personal mind-body experience. Apprehension? No, I know it must be a joyous event, otherwise why would women keep on having more than one child? The Moroccan woman who mixed the henna for my hair last summer had thirteen children all around her and all were born at home. She was shining health and strength.

When is delivery day going to surprise me? One night on the road from Taos back to Santa Fé my body starts shaking, rumbles of an internal storm at the same moment that the car stalls, in the middle of a mountain climb. I lie down on the back seat preparing to have the baby in the car. Three or four contractions over the last half hour. The body was only tuning up.

A week later. I went to bed late, fluids start running down my legs, a little, no more. I fall asleep but awake in the middle of the night. A dream? Reality? Am I swimming in a warm pool? The rest of the liquid has been expulsed. Mild muscle contractions. A pull-let go motion. Of course nothing the way I had imagined. I feel an incredible urge to empty my body of all waste material; to be completely alone and figure out the strange spasms overtaking, with strength, my insides. Even though I had not planned consciously to confine myself, I lock myself in the bathroom. Everything was ready, at hand's reach, for the easiest development possible. The mandala Mati painted for me to focus on while out-breathing the contractions (Mati is a painter of intricate dreamscapes); a candle (it was still dark and I felt the bathroom light would be too bright); my favorite purple cotton tee shirt; two pillows and a foam mattress covered with batik.

As I am quickly gathering all of these essentials, Mati wakes up, moaning something about picking another night. He is tired and not ready for birth labor. My head is dazed but my body feels very strong. "Mati, please sleep. I don't need any help yet."

It's odd. I know it must be "the day" and I can't help feeling it's all a dream. Is it time already? So suddenly? Contractions come like waves, sometimes a gentle roll and at other times an enormous rush of energy bursting at the body's boundaries. The vibrant colors of Mati's painting in front of me open up into rotating depth dimensions in space. Doors of a mental-physical harmonious team, letting through a new force. Brightness forever on the baby's consciousness!

As I try to breathe the way I was taught, in the psychoprophylactic method, I slowly discover my own rhythm with each contraction: deeper, slower, inhaling and exhaling. In between I doze off, resting, dreaming, shaking loose.

THE DEEP SPRING CLEANING OF MY BODY IS OVER. Rid of food and liquid through every body orifice. As after an extended fast, there is a great feeling of lightness and I know instinctively nothing will be in the way at birthtime. Once again the natural body processing proves to take care of itself, with the benefit of faith.

Between deep breaths, I draw a hot bath, sending sandalwood fumes over the whole house. Doors are opening, hush, murmurs, dawn is on, daylight brings relief of night's dark corners. Brightness everywhere on a birthday. Little knocks on the bathroom door. My friend Barbara with an offering of chamomile tea and Mati softly smiling, coming to hold my hand. They want to call the doctor. I think it's too early. They telephone him anyway. Mati is massaging my back. I don't have to tell him where, he senses it. Hand strokes, riding over inside tensions with their strength and warmth. The doctor, gentle and friendly, steps into the bathroom. "How is it?" "Good, crazy, shaky, incredible!"

The baby is slowly entering the labyrinth. The bathroom is getting too small. It's cool in the house. I put on the purple cotton tee shirt barely covering my bottom (perfect for delivery) and it is loose and smooth against the skin. So important, the feel and touch of familiar clothes, if there have to be any during a major body mutation. In the large room I have to walk through, on the way to the bedroom, the friends, Barbara, Reno, Michael, Ramona and the doctor are all sitting close around the big table, speaking low. The preparation is over, I feel the baby coming.

BIRTH—WHAT A CEREMONY. I probably would have turned pale gray, having the baby at home in New York; but here in the space and clearness of Santa Fé it is a joyous feast. Encouraging friends all around, completely in tune with each of my explosions. They are coming quickly now. I am either sitting or kneeling on the bed which is a mattress on the floor. Mati grips me, vibrating, shaking the baby out from the back. Like a chant, my voice turns to music, inhaling, breathing out faster, to a pitch. Sounds of birth-raga. Barbara sits beside me, breathing to a concentrated rhythm, bringing me back to it whenever I go too fast. Michael is taking photographs, Ramona is holding Noah (Barbara's baby). I ask Reno to get the movie camera and the gun light. With one hand the doctor's wife fixes his sterilized mask and with the other holds her own baby. The doctor is sitting on the floor and I am opposite him at the edge of the bed, held tight by Mati's legs. The rumble inside me is so strong, I jump up a few times and start walking out of the door; not pain, but bursts of emotion. Incredibly intense sensation of the body being turned inside out. How sweet to see warm, friendly, surprised faces and colors all around the room rather than starched hospital white. Instead of anesthetics: music, sun and air. Instead of nurses: friends who have experienced a similar adventure. Barbara (twenty years old) who also had her baby at home three months ago, has tears in her eyes.

ALL INHIBITIONS ABOUT MY BODY ARE GONE. There is no shame, only an overwhelming openness. Being totally at ease with myself, becoming easy, as never before. I ask the doctor if I can put my feet up on his shoulders. How he was able to perform this way remains a mystery.

"Hold it, hold it, hold . . . Okay, now push that little baby out of you!"

Pushing, laughing, puffing, waiting, panting, squashing and pulling on Mati's hands with unknown force. My whole being impatiently expels the new life.

10:54 A.M. THE SUN IS FLOWING INSIDE THE BEDROOM, BLASTING WITH VITAL RAYS A NEW HEAD. Push . . . episiotomy incision with my consent. Totally painless, the perineum is numbed by the baby's pressure. Push . . . the top of the head is out to the mouth and already screams. A reality sound, voice rendering concrete a long-awaited child. What a blessing to be a woman! What a magical gift! I cannot remember a more extraordinary burst of happiness in my life. Rapidly, the rest of the tiny body slips out. Alive in front of us, a long and thin little person, moonstone color, kicking and yelling, still circuited to me by a pale blue umbilical cord. Thank you!

"How is it?"

"Good, forceful, supernatural!"

After removing the mucus from the baby's mouth and nose, David, the doctor, places the child on my stomach; still covered with vernix and sucking on my breast avidly. He then asks Mati to cut the cord.

"Please do it David," I ask. I have visions of falling into bottomless depth if Mati moves one inch away from me. One more push, the placenta, like a glorious piece of food, exits in one large mound. Reno, after filming every moment of the actual birth, takes the placenta to bury it in the garden, planting a tree on top of it. Local anesthetic injection. Three stitches.

Mati, totally exhilarated, still holding me from the back, asks after a while: "What sex is it?" I had completely forgotten to look. "A girl!" He beams, Mati loves to be surrounded by women.

David tells me to get up. I glide around the house with Baby Serafine in my arms. I can see my smile reflected on everyone. It goes from head to toe. They are wordless but not soundless. Wows and phews. Tears and laughter. We have all witnessed the most real and sacred of ceremonies—the rites of life.

I HAVE WHAT I HAVE GIVEN.

It's time we realize we don't have to perpetuate the fears and rules of our ancestors. Time for the individual to open up and be as it goes: lifefully.

It is now fifteen years later. . . . Serafine is a wonderful daughter, taller than me and wise beyond her years. As I reread my account of her birth I am amazed at the self-assurance and strength I expressed in the face of the unknown concerning the act of giving birth. But all things considered I would take the same route; I would choose again to give birth at home. I still feel strongly about the essential importance of not having been disturbed in any way from following my visceral maternal instincts. My personal intuitions were unhindered and free to run their course, allowing for a totally positive experience that let my body's impulses and functions follow their natural processes.

If I could afford to raise another child and give birth again, the only changes I would make would be to prepare the room better for the doctor or midwife so they could be more comfortable while the birth motions take their course. I would have a deep armchair, a low stool, a thermos full of something warm to drink, some food, picture books, perhaps music, just as if it was a party, and hope for the best.

I have often been asked if I would marry next time before deciding to get pregnant. I am now in the middle of my life, and I am still not convinced that the institution of marriage—as delineated by governments around the world—suits my free spirit. A form of spiritual blessing might feel appropriate. Those deliberations and reflections are subjects in themselves for a whole other book . . .

I asked Serafine last year if it bothered her that I chose not to get married?

"You mean that I am a bastard?" she replied. "Not at all because you and daddy, even though you separated, get along very well. I get to spend a lot of time with each one, and you both look after me in the best way you know; with a lot of love. I don't know any other kids in my class whose parents never married; I know many children with divorced moms and dads. In fact I am surprised there aren't more children around me with parents who have made your choice. It is not a big issue in my life. For us it seems to work just like that."

I was stunned! I had never thought of my own daughter as a bastard. In my eyes, and in the eyes of those who love her, she is not of inferior or dubious origins, or even illegitimate. She is a person, willed to life by loving, responsible parents—born just as children have been since the beginning of time, long before the invention of marriage.

At this point I look forward to being a grandmother and hope that if my daughter decides to have a child she has as great a moment at birth-time as I did.

Michel Odent

Doctor Michel Odent is a practicing surgeon and the director of the maternity unit at Pithiviers Hospital, Pithiviers, France. For the past twenty years his lectures and writings have influenced doctors, midwives and parents-to-be around the world.

Caterine: I would like to elaborate on your point of view. . . . As a doctor delivering babies, you say that the nature of your work is to facilitate women in the natural function of giving birth, and to help create an environment conducive to freedom of movement. It seems so obvious. Why is this not practiced in more hospitals?

Michel: It is easy to talk about freedom of movement, but freedom of movement is not enough. It is only possible when you have a feeling of intimacy, and in the context of our modern obstetrical units or huge modern hospitals, it's difficult to achieve this feeling of privacy. So in places where they say you are free—you can walk—women stay in bed because there are too many people around; they are not at home. Women don't feel at ease. They may have visited the hospital once, if at all. There are too many men around. For these and many other reasons women cannot have this feeling of privacy, and this word—privacy, intimacy—is the key to understanding what a woman needs on the day of birth.

C: You emphasize the importance of intuitive knowledge on the part of the woman in charge of bringing her child into the world. Yet many women feel scared of that moment. How can they obtain such confidence if they do not feel it instinctively?

M: We could help many women to exploit their own potentials much better than we generally do.

C: By "we" who do you mean?"

M: I mean people who counsel on childbirth, people whose role is to help women to give birth. But few people really help women to give birth. You know that the practice of the medical discipline we call obstetrics has never been focused on helping women give birth, but more on just controlling the process. That's why the medical man puts women on their backs, that's why we create midwifery schools so that the midwives are no longer mothers helping other mothers, but merely professionals who are being trained to control the process, and that is why doctors have developed the technology to control the process.

I'm thinking of people whose priority will be to help with the birth. What do you do when you have this priority? It's the same as what you do to help the mother-to-be to become more instinctive, to forget what she learned, or what she read in books; and in order to help her exploit her potential, we have to remember some very simple rules.

It's much easier, for example, when a woman feels strongly that she belongs to a human group, a human community, that she's not an animus. It's difficult in our society to feel this way. Many people go from one city to another, from continent to continent, one job to another, and so on, and the family is increasingly reduced to a nuclear or even a single parent family. For many reasons, few people can satisfy their fundamental human need for community.

We have to understand that on the day of birth, the active part of the brain is the primitive part of the brain. It's this part of the brain that has to secrete a lot of necessary hormones. Inhibitions can come from what we call the neocortex, the upper part of the brain, and when a woman is giving birth it's just a brain process, and we must not disturb the laboring woman when she is reducing the control exerted on herself by her upper brain, the neocortex.

This brings us back to the importance of very simple rules, for example, semidarkness or silence if she desires, because any kind of sensory stimulation stimulates the activity of the neocortex, reinforcing the inhibitions. When you talk too much, you are stimulating the brain. Privacy is also important, and a sense of privacy depends, on the whole, on what the room looks like, on who is present; generally I think, especially in our society, there are too many people present, even at a home birth.

C: Labor and birth are in part a sexual event, therefore an intimate moment. So what do you recommend to make that passage more relaxed and more comfortable?

M: More intimacy. Once more, that is a key word. But the problem is that the feeling of privacy, of intimacy, depends on the culture to which you belong.

Many modern women in our society hardly ever have this feeling of privacy—perhaps only in the bathroom! Whereas in a traditional society where women spend their entire lives together talking about their menstrual cycles, their private lives and so on, they can give birth together.

In our society it's very different. In the past ten to fifteen years, it has become common for fathers to be present at the birth. The baby's father is considered an intimate person, the most familiar person in the nuclear family. And perhaps it's been necessary in the context of our modern hospitals. But it's not always so simple. Of course some couples achieve a perfect privacy when they are together, if they have been living together for a long time, sharing emotions and odd circumstances—and in this case the presence of the baby's father may be positive.

But it may be different: Some men want to control the process, they want to give orders about how to breathe or which may be the best position. They want to be the coach, and in this case, labor often becomes long and difficult. We have found that the kind of man who can contribute most positively, most efficiently, is the man who wants to protect the laboring woman from the outside world, to protect her privacy.

The kind of intimacy many women need when they are giving birth is not exactly the kind of intimacy you have with a sexual partner. You know, when a woman comes close to giving birth, she often needs to defecate. It's not what you do in the presence of your sexual partner, but it's what you did in the presence of your mother as a child. When giving birth many women need the kind of privacy they had with their mothers, so they probably have more need of a mother figure. This figure is an experienced female presence, motherly, not too young,

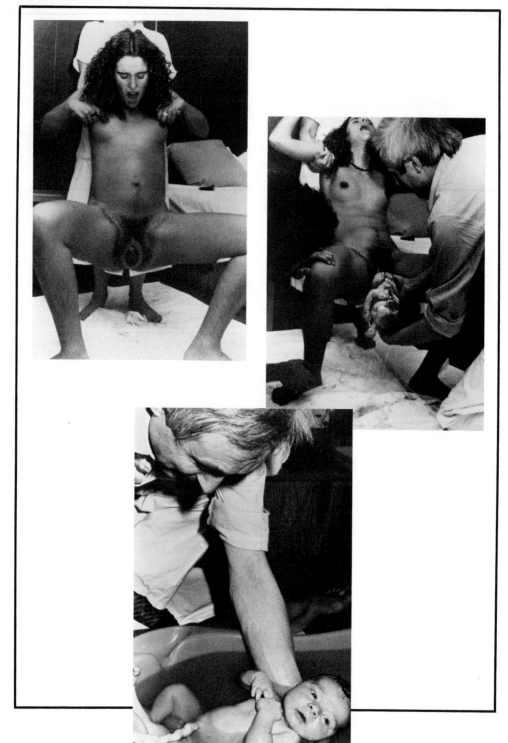

female . . . a midwife, and you know this was originally the role of the midwife, and midwifery is as old as mankind.

I think we are just rediscovering a fundamental human need. This is the key if we really want to find an alternative to common practice. If we want to rediscover that need we must take into account the private lives, the gender of the people who are present in the birthing room, and also privacy. But when we say that, we have to consider things that are basic to obstetrics. We have to start again.

C: You often talk of the affinity to warm water of mothers-to-be, and of labor being easier if a woman immerses herself. How do you explain it? Isn't it dangerous for the baby?

M: We cannot explain why a laboring woman is attracted by water. It's something we found, we observed, and it's something that has been well known in many other civilizations, where the birthing place was close to the river or to the sea.

Because many women have been attracted by the water, we have tried to use this attraction. First they can take a bath or shower. We built some small pools in the maternity ward, filled them with warm water, and we have found that when the first stage of labor is long and difficult, when the cervix is 5cm dilated with strong contractions, painful contractions, and the dilation is not going smoothly, the best way to break the vicious circle—and it's a vicious circle, because the mother is more and more anxious, labor is more and more difficult—is to allow the mother to relax in a pool full of warm water. Many women who enter the bath around 5cm reach complete dilation within an hour.

If it's longer, if it's not working in the water, it means that there is a serious complication. We have to be careful. Perhaps we need to do a cesarean. The water's a good test, but how it works is difficult to know. In certain cases we just say, let's go to the pool, we turn on the tap, we look at the nice blue water flowing and the baby is born before the pool is full.

It's not rational but there are some physiological explanations. The water is warm, and to give birth smoothly a woman must not secrete

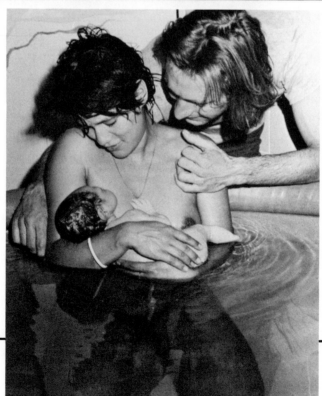

too high a level of adrenalin, which happens when the body is too cold or too hot. It's a way to break the vicious circle.

C: It relaxes the muscles.

M: Yes, that's possible, too, because it's warm water. The warmth might have a direct muscular stretching action. You know the tendons and fascias are made with gelatin, and the physical properties of gelatin depend on the temperature level.

It's possible that warm water will create a feeling of relaxation through direct muscular action. And also, it's a way of reducing other sensory stimulations so you have not only darkness, not only silence, but also you don't have to face gravity, you don't stimulate the vascular system or the inner part of the ear. In our daily life, all the time, we use a lot of energy to overcome gravity. But not in a warm pool.

It's another way of reducing sensory stimulation and the activity of the neocortex, and of making the woman more instinctive, more in touch with her primitive brain; this is always the most important thing to understand.

C: Don't you think the freedom to choose her own birth posture is important?

M: Only when a woman is at ease can she then find postures that will make her labor easier. Then she can be on all fours or she can squat. And when the action of the cervix is complete, when they feel the urge to push, most of the women need to leave the pool and go back to their birthing area.

In some cases, some women are so comfortable in the bath that at the last moment, when the baby is coming, they are so instinctive, that they are really in another state of consciousness. They feel, they know, that the baby can be born underwater. They feel it.

It's not our aim to have babies born in the water, but it happens now and then. We just have to understand that a newborn human baby is exactly like a dolphin, perfectly adapted to immersion. The first breath may be triggered by the first contact with the atmosphere, a certain difference in temperature.

Personally, I have assisted 120 births underwater. It's nothing compared with the thousands of women who have left the pool before the baby was born, compared with thousands of women who didn't go to the pool. But it's important to know that it's possible, because wherever women have the option of relaxing in a pool, an underwater birth will happen now and then. So we have to be ready to catch babies in the water.

C: And does that present a complicated procedure?

M: You draw the baby toward the surface, and when the baby has reached the surface, and is crying, shouting out, you then put the baby in the mother's arms.

C: So it's not dangerous in any way for the baby?

M: Underwater birth is not our aim, but it happens, and from our experience we can say that it is not dangerous.

C: How do you view the role of the midwife in restoring the mother to the central place at birthtime?

M: The midwife is the key person, and if we really want to find an alternative to obstetrics, we must remember that the midwife was originally a midwife among other mothers. When I say find alternatives to obstetrics, it means that we are reaching a time when we must no longer try to accuse obstetrics or accuse the obstetricians. And in finding alternatives we must be very radical because we have to reconsider what is basic in obstetrics, and especially what is the relationship between doctors and midwives.

In every place I know around the world where there are good midwives—authentic midwives and mothers who are really autonomous, who are really in charge of the laboring woman—these midwives know that there is a surgical team next door who can intervene or do a cesarean if necessary. In all these places, the statistics are incredibly good compared to those for mothers in hospitals without midwives; particularly the rate of cesareans and other interventions is very low.

That's why we need to change the relationship between doctors and midwives. What we need on the one hand is very experienced midwives, and on the other hand, surgical teams, doctors who would be at the service of midwives and the women instead of controlling them.

But you would need to change everything radically. You know that in the past, it's a long story, men have always tried to become involved in childbirth. It was originally an event among women. But men have tried in many ways to take over.

C: Why?

M: Why? It was a need for many men. Birth was mysterious, there was a time when women were goddesses, women could give birth by themselves, it was creative, mysterious. But men could not share this experience. They tried in many ways.

Take for instance Christian baptism. It may be considered a spiritual birth, given by the religious fathers; it was perhaps the first way for men to take over this process.

Then the doctors tried many ways to enter the place of confinement. You know that in the sixteenth century, in Germany, there was a doctor who was condemned to death and burnt alive because he had disguised himself as a woman to watch a birth. During the seventeenth century male doctors found a way to enter the place of confinement. They invented the forceps, they put women on their backs, and immediately the attitude was different. It was no longer a matter of helping a woman to give birth as midwives did, because she used her feminine intuition, her own experience. The priority became to control the process. That's why they made women lie on their backs, to control the process better. That's why they created midwifery schools, so that midwives would no longer be mothers, they became professionals, and there was a terrible struggle among doctors to control midwifery training.

Man's struggle for control became more and more an obvious priority. Now in the age of technology we're reaching an absurd point where many people feel that the more you control, the more you observe the event, the more you disturb it.

There has been another new phenomenon recently which concerns man/woman relationships. Even at the beginning of this century, at the time of home birth, the presence of the man was often tolerated, but he did not share in the whole experience. He was relegated to particular tasks, filling a basin with water and so on. But it's only in more recent times that women have wanted to have the baby's father present. It began with the time of concentration of births in huge hospitals, at a time when the nuclear family was taking over.

C: Don't you think within the impersonal context of the hospital the father's presence was reassurance for the mother?

M: Reassurance? It was a need to gain privacy. But we're now at a time when it doesn't seem so simple.

C: On the one hand you have the sexual couple, and on the other hand, you have the woman in her total intimacy.

M: It's possible that in ten or twenty years we'll understand that the introduction of the man, the baby's father, into the birthing place, is another way for the man to take over the process, another stage, another way.

C: An evolution.

M: We are reinforcing in our birthing places the nuclear family as a model: mother, father, baby. This sort of family cannot satisfy the needs of the newborn infant baby. It's difficult you know. The nuclear family doesn't satisfy the needs of the old people who are dying either. And it cannot satisfy the need of adults who need a larger community.

Another point, the title holder of *baby's father* is considered the ruler. It's normal, it's a necessity. And sure, women might dare to say that they would prefer the baby's father to go out into the garden when they are giving birth; on the other hand few men would dare to say that they want to leave the place, so it's a rule.

But perhaps you have to be careful. You have to think also of the problem of sexual attraction. Sexual attraction needs mystery. And now women are less and less mysterious. Men can enter the birthing place. They can see the baby being born. Women are no longer goddesses. There is nothing like mystery.

C: But maybe women don't want to be goddesses any more.

M: They don't want to be goddesses? We are in a male-dominated society. The role model is masculine. Women want to do the same job as men and so on.

We are in a time when many people have seen a normal birth, what they call natural childbirth, etc., with the baby's father present. I think that what is much more important than this whole question of midwives is to rediscover the *role* of the midwife and to understand that often, when the baby's father is really sharing the emotion, present and so on, the midwife's role is reduced to a technical one. The baby's father asks the midwife, how many centimeters is the cervix. And the midwife says, it's only a technical hole.

If we want to rediscover midwifery, we generally speaking have to rediscover man/woman relationships as a whole and in the birthing room. And also to rediscover how important the doctor/midwife relationship is and how in the past it was based on instinct and female intuition.

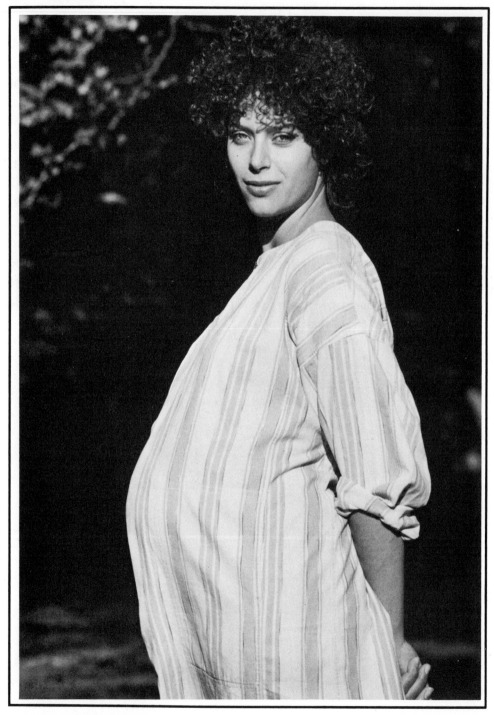

Oona Napier
Hospital delivery, exercise preparation, first child

Los Angeles, November 16

Dear Caterine:

Thanks for your letter. I am enclosing some information on the Cedars-Sinai maternity department. My husband Hugo and I went to visit it twice, once with the Lamaze teacher and once on a hospital tour. The visit with the Lamaze teacher was much more thorough. The teacher took us into the labor room and hooked me up to the fetal monitor so that the class would have an idea of what it looked and felt like. The hospital tour was brief and we barely got a chance to see the recovery rooms; the labor rooms were shown to us in photos. We were shown videos of a vaginal birth and a cesarean birth, which were clear and fascinating, then we had a lecture by the resident anesthesiologist.

We were very impressed by the hospital; it's very beautifully decorated with lovely paintings on the walls, no ghastly hospital smell, and the ABC room (by the look of the photo) is very warm and cozy looking. They provide a staff nurse to be with you throughout the labor and delivery. The recovery rooms are comfortable and have all the modern conveniences, e.g., shower, bathroom, color TV and a cot for the father if he wishes to room-in. The meals are cooked on the same floor and, according to one mom, are surprisingly good!

Have a good Thanksgiving.

Love, Oona

San Francisco, Thanksgiving Weekend

Dear Caterine:

I went to see Karil Daniels who is assembling a video tape on water birth, while I was in San Francisco. I took a friend of mine along and we sat through the video of one hour, totally enthralled. Here is a brief description of it:

It starts with a warning to future parents to approach only professional doctors who know how to deal with water birth. There are shots of babies and pregnant women and a short history of birth with midwives, then doctors and hospital. The narrator explains how the Lamaze and Le Boyer methods started. Charkovsky and Michel Odent are shown. All this is in cross-fading stills. Next there are interviews with women on the streets and what they thought of the idea of water birth. A doctor then answers their queries. He talks about the advantages and disadvantages of gentle birth. M. Odent then explains that he tried water to relax women while in labor. He said there is less possibility of tearing of the perineal tissues. A couple is introduced, M and B; they explain why they wanted a water birth, how they made sure that the water was clean and that she felt comfortable, light and warm. She advises finding a birth attendant who is sympathetic and supportive of the method. Next we saw the hospital in France where Michel Odent practices. There was a large tub that looks like a Jacuzzi. He encourages weekly group singing in pregnancy. He says "the right place to give birth is the right place to make love," which I thought very appropriate, too. He explains that the best time to go into the water is when the cervix is 5cm dilated. We then see two births underwater. Dr. Odent describes a birth in 1983 when a woman labored for forty-eight hours; when they finally put her in a bath she gave birth almost immediately afterward! Then we see the birth of M and B's child at home with family and friends, very hippified! The woman describes how the pain feels and how she is handling it by breathing. They move her to a bath and her husband is in the bath, too. Someone listens to the heartbeat. They let the baby come out in its own time. The birth seems quite slow. The baby stayed underwater for a long time before coming out into the air. At one point it is lying underwater with its feet still inside the mother's womb until she gives one last push and it slowly floats to the surface. They say there is no danger of it drowning as long as the placenta is still attached to the walls of the uterus. The baby supposedly can still breathe from the umbilical cord for as long as three or four minutes. We then go to Russia where we see Igor Charkovsky with young children training and playing in the water. The kids seem totally unafraid and play around like little water babies. We see newborns being breast-fed in the water and we watch him prepare pregnant women for water birth. We see women exercising with their babies. Apparently Charkovsky is not entirely popular in the Soviet Union. The Russians like what he is doing as far as exercising goes but don't quite approve of the water birth method.

I was very impressed by the way the baby comes out and doesn't seem to want to cry. They all looked so blissfully calm and happy. The mothers appeared much more in control of the situation.

It seems like a good method and I would choose it myself the second time around but not the first. From the film I gathered that only a small number of children have been born this way and so it would be a hard thing to find a place to do it!

Well, good-bye for now,
Oona

Hollywood, December 3

Dear Caterine:

Here is a short outline of our first Lamaze class:

It was a very small class held at the house of Sandra Son Jaffe. We were all asked to bring three pillows and a snack to each class. Hugo seemed very embarassed to go to these classes and I talked to some other ladies at my exercise class and they all report the same from their husbands, so I guess it's a normal occurrence. When we got out of the car to go into Sandra's house we could tell who was coming to the class because they were all carrying pillows (the pillow people, we called ourselves). The first class had only four other couples. She gave us a small physiology lesson to show us what a woman's body looks like as we go through the changes of pregnancy. Very useful for the men and it taught me a lot. Before that I didn't know the reasons for the chronic heartburn that I had been getting. Then we did some relaxation exercises where the woman lies down and the "coach" tells her to tense up a certain part of her body but keep everything else relaxed. We are supposed to practice these at home at least fifteen minutes a day. She talked for three hours about what to bring to the hospital, e.g., rolling pin and tennis balls (for massage), water spray bottle and lip gloss (for dehydration), music and tapes, a snack for the "coach," etc. She told us about posture and exercises for the back and breathing. I found it very helpful but must admit that the woman seemed a bit patronizing and too in love with her own voice so that by the end of the evening we really wanted to get out of there. One thing that I thought was a very good idea was that she had lots of files with birth reports from other mothers. All of them were different, from cesareans to ABC rooms, with or without drugs, at different hospitals and with varying lengths of labor. I found it fascinating to read through these reports and get an idea of the different types of birth. In each subsequent class we were taught a new breathing technique, starting with the slowest "slow rhythmic breathing" and ending up with fast "hee-hees," which are supposed to be used for the most painful part of labor. The "coach" is taught how to massage the woman in the case of back labor and is supposed to be in charge of reminding the woman to keep relaxed and breathe regularly. I think it has helped me tremendously, I certainly don't feel as anxious about the coming birth and feel that I can handle the pain much more easily now. Sandra did seem to know a lot about the hospital procedures and talked us through the whole admission to the hospital, up until the time when they give you the postpartum room—even how to secure the nice rooms with space for another bed for the "coach." This information was very clear and I thought it very useful because hospitals can be very intimidating places.

Last week she described what we would go through if we had to have a cesarean and for what reasons. Next Tuesday is our last class. We will also have some mothers come in with their babies next week and they will talk about their birth experiences.

Much love to your daughter Serafine.

Oona

Los Angeles, December 19

Dear Caterine:

I woke up and went to the gym: worked out, stretched and swam. Afterward Hugo and I did errands; on the way I felt really hot and claustrophobic. We put the air conditioning on in the car. When we got home I felt really weird—a bit nauseous; I thought it was because I hadn't eaten so I had a salad and a cup of peppermint tea. Then I felt as though my water had broken. I went to the toilet three times and changed sanitary pads and I called the doctor. I wasn't sure what it's supposed to feel like except that when I sat down or got up every once in a while I would feel warm liquid gushing out and I was unable to stop the flow. I couldn't believe that this was IT because I had been told that I would feel so nauseous that I wouldn't be able to eat and that I would have loose bowels, neither of which I had. Also, my due date was January 3. Around 4:00 P.M. I felt period pains but nothing very strong. Hugo made me a cup of tea and I waited for the doctor to call me back. I thought maybe it's going to happen today! Dr. Mandell called me back at 5:15. By now I was getting Hugo to time the cramps and they were very irregular, about one every five to six minutes and not too painful. Dr. Mandell said I could wait at home until the pains got so frequent and intense that I couldn't walk through them. I decided to make some mince pies while timing the contractions. Later I went to the bathroom and some clear slimy substance came out which I took to be my mucous plug.

At around 8:00 P.M. the mince pies were out of the oven and we went to the hospital. A friend, Jackie, was with us at the time and she helped to get our Lamaze bag together. Hugo packed coffee and meat loaf sandwiches and we left. We got to the hospital and I was examined by a nurse, undressed, put on a gown and strapped to a monitor. I was 2cm dilated and 70 percent effaced. At about 11:00 P.M. I accepted Nicentol because by this time I was really having a lot of pain. The nurse told me that it was a very mild pain-killer and that it would not stop the pain completely but just take the edge off it. At Lamaze classes I was told about the Nicentol, but I wasn't told that they could only give a minimum of four shots before the effect wears off and they would have to give something more powerful instead. I think if I had known that it would lead to an epidural I would have tried to hold out against the pain longer.

At the beginning I found the Nicentol really wonderful; it didn't actually stop the pain of the contractions but it made you feel as if you didn't care about it so much. After that I was so hooked on the "non-pain" of it that I accepted the offer of an epidural. The epidural really gave me the shakes. I couldn't stop my teeth from chattering for fifteen minutes! Dr. Mandell was there most of the night, checking on me to see that everything was all right. The epidural took ages to work, the tube had been placed at a wrong angle so my legs went numb but not my uterus. Finally after about an hour and a half I felt nothing and what a relief that was! I'm such a coward when it comes to pain. I was even able to sleep through some of the night, off and on. At around 8:00 A.M. my own doctor, Dr. Frankel, came in—he examined me and I was only 5cm dilated. They gave me pitocin to bring on more contractions and speed up the dilation. He also said I had a very small pelvis and it was going to be a tight squeeze. I was having contractions now every three minutes and at around 10:30 I was 10cm dilated.

I started to push; Dr. Frankel, the nurse and Hugo were helping me by holding my feet so I could push against them. I didn't feel anything down there so I had to rely on the monitor to tell me when a contraction was coming and then I pushed like mad. After an hour and a half I had come to a plus 2 station. The doctor said I would have two choices, either to keep on like that another two hours (and he didn't think I had the stamina) or he would take me into the delivery room and do a forceps delivery, which would slightly bruise the child but would get him out faster.

At this point I was so tired of pushing and impatient to get the baby out that I welcomed the doctor's suggestion. I was a little worried about how the baby would look but I trusted the doctor and knew that he wouldn't have suggested the forceps delivery unless it was absolutely safe.

They wheeled me into the delivery room; the place really gave me

the creeps. I had never been in a hospital before and I hated the bright
lights and the cold room. I didn't open my eyes for most of the time I was
in there. They gave me another epidural and then I pushed while Dr.
Frankel pulled with forceps and another doctor pushed on my stomach
while Hugo counted. It was horrible. I was screaming like crazy, I
thought I was going to be pulled onto the floor with each move. I nearly

lost my marbles! Finally after three extra big pushes they pulled the little baby out of me. He cried and bleated like a billy goat. (So did I.) He was very blue and battered around the head. Seven pounds and twenty inches long.

It was 11:48 A.M., December 20. Nobody told me about how I would feel afterward; it was almost as bad as the actual birth. I started to shake and vomit, my head was pounding and I felt incredibly sick. Apparently it is the result of the epidural anesthetic. They took me into another room and gave me some pain-killing shot, which made me sleep for a while. When I woke up I was in urgent need of a pee but couldn't go; I had a catheter put inside me which was agony but also a big relief. Later on I went to the postpartum hospital room where they cleaned me up and I could finally drink a glass of water! Boy was I thirsty! I still couldn't pee because my poor pelvis area was so completely swollen. I couldn't walk well because of the stitches. I felt like I had been put through a Moulinex. But on seeing little Leo Orlando Napier, it was all worthwhile. I am going to sleep now and will tell you about him later.

Lots of love,
Oona

Los Angeles, January 3

Dear Caterine:

Leo Orlando seems to have the most wonderful disposition. So far he has been very quiet and only cries when necessary. He does a lot of sleeping, doesn't suffer from colic and according to a lot of mother/ friends is extremely good compared to their children. I was a little shocked at his appearance when he first came out. He was all misshapen in the head and his face had a bit of palsy from the forceps so that one eye didn't open properly and he looked very bruised. After only a day his head was back to normal and he looked quite beautiful. The facial paralysis went away after about a week. Today, he looks perfectly fine, no signs of a difficult birth. He is sleeping a lot less, spends his mornings looking around at the world and sucking on his hand or a pacifier. He seems quite content to lie in his basket and stare at a black and white picture that I have put opposite him. He usually wakes every 3½ hours to eat and then sleeps again. It took two weeks for the umbilical cord to fall off. It took about the same time for the stitches to stop hurting me. I started to exercise the third day after the birth. When I got home I rented the Jane Fonda recovery tape and did that every day. Now I take turns with Hugo to go to the health club and am taking a regular exercise class there. At first it was a bit frightening to see how out of shape my body had become but slowly the stomach started to shrink back. Now I just look a bit pudgy. I still have to lose fifteen pounds but it doesn't show too much and I'm not too worried. I know it takes time and I don't want to go on a drastic diet since I'm breast-feeding.

The breast-feeding was a bit difficult at first. The first three days at the hospital I got very frustrated because Leo was so sleepy that he wasn't interested in food anyway and the nurses were trying to force it down him. I was worried because my nipples were slightly inverted. Finally about the fourth day when I had taken him home we both started to get the hang of it. Now he is feeding quite happily although he still tends to fall asleep after only one breast and refuses to wake up and take the other one; but he has gained 12 ounces in the past three weeks so I know that it is working!

Love to you and Serafine.
    Oona

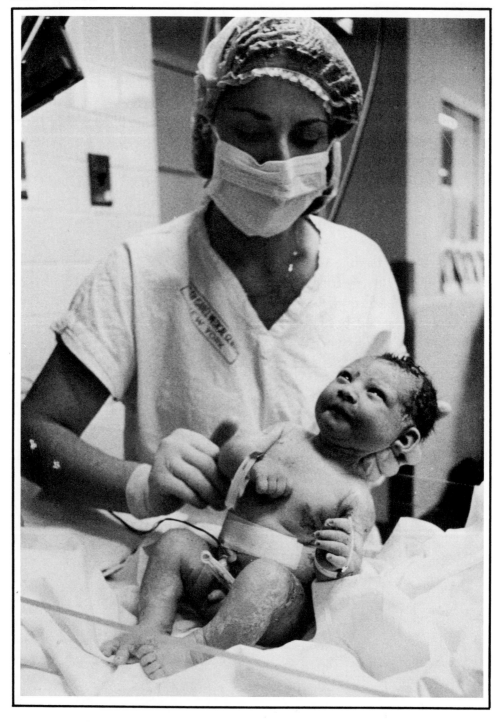

Lisa Lorelli
Hospital labor and delivery nurse

As a labor and delivery nurse working in the hospital system for twelve years, Lisa Lorelli has attended many births. Personally she has been responsible for assisting the deliveries of fifty babies.

Caterine: What do you consider the most important part of your work with the mother, with the parents-to-be?

Lisa: I see my main function as offering total support for the expectant couple and assistance to the physician or the midwife at the time of delivery. Involvement begins at the time of admission. I feel that the intimate contact must be established as a priority, so the expectant couple will feel they are in capable hands even before they become classified as a patient. Contact is established with something as simple as a greeting or exchange of names between contractions.

C: After much observation of the father and doctor's involvement at birth time, Michel Odent, the French doctor, questions their presence in many instances. He goes so far as to suggest that sometimes the mother giving birth can open up and let go better with only the presence of an experienced midwife. In other words, the presence of the father can inhibit the mother. What do you think of these ideas?

L: Parental involvement for both members of the expecting couple should revolve around them being classified as a couple. The father is very welcome in our setting, we are striving for maternity-centered childbirth, which would include fatherly involvement. We do everything to include the father; however, if they feel they cannot go any farther we take a supportive stance with them. But for the most part, they have trained in the Lamaze technique with their wives and we encourage them to do it together because it is such an intimate time in their lives, it is not a time to be separated.

C: Do you think a midwife or a labor and delivery nurse's ability is affected by the setting? For example, is your work more relaxed in the birthing room than in the traditional delivery room?

L: The birthing room atmosphere often lends itself to a more natural type of labor and delivery; however, in our unit we strive to make every room a birthing room. That includes just routine labor beds; often there is no need to transport the patient, we will help them to deliver in whatever position they are in at the time if the delivery is imminent. Therefore if the birthing room can be set up for an imminent delivery and used properly, it will give a very calm, restful atmosphere and most patients do come back and say they appreciate the fact that we did it this way.

C: Do you find that women giving birth these days are asking to do it in different positions, such as squatting, kneeling or standing and supported under the arms?

L: Most expectant couples today will have some form of Lamaze childbirth preparation, and most of these classes advocate delivery in any position other than lying traditionally on the back. A patient with this knowledge, and with a little support from her coach, will usually ask to sit in a rocking chair or ambulate or walk until she gets active. For me, the best position for delivery would be lying in a left lateral position. I advocate this position because the perineum will stretch nicely to accommodate the baby's head, and there are fewer vaginal tears. For laboring, we do advocate squatting or sitting upright, which will help advance the baby's position down the birth canal. The patients do ask for it and we do try to accommodate them.

C: Is there an increase in demand by parents over the last ten years for nurse-midwives?

L: Absolutely there is; it is quite popular in New York right now because what the midwives advocate for the patient is total comprehensive care. In that respect the midwife has seen the couple through the prenatal course, which is nine months, and they treat birth as a normal physiological process. The woman is not considered sick. The emphasis is on the normal; midwives do everything to advocate birth in a healthy, natural setting. Midwives are in demand at this point in time because people are going back to deliveries in a natural atmosphere, where the mother can be awake and breast-feed almost immediately, if she wants, and the father's close participation will make them feel like an integrated family as soon after the birth as possible.

C: What would you like to see improve in the hospital maternity system, in the birth room procedure for parents?

L: In general, you have to realize that obstetrics is an ever-changing concept. Family-centered maternity care is increasing and becoming the way that parents as consumers want it to be. I don't know what the future holds for them. I only know that, at present, we do try to give them a sense of participation and for the woman, a feeling that giving birth is a normal process. People who choose a hospital with birthing room facilities want the type of atmosphere where, if there is a problem, they will have immediate help there, yet if there's no problem, they will definitely be able to cope with the support of a nurse and/or a midwife.

C: Would you ever consider working at a birthing center or doing home deliveries at some point in your career?

L: Home delivieries, no, because after eleven years of nursing, I know exactly what can go wrong. I like to anticipate the best, but I do think of the worst at times, because I am the person who will be relied on, should something go wrong. I also have vast intensive care unit experience. I would think that my skills are good enough for a birthing room facility, and yet I would consider that only within a hospital context or setting.

C: I understand that after a full day at the hospital you take night classes. What is the next stage for you?

L: The next stage would probably be something like in-service development for my fellow employees. I would like to teach other nurses how to cope with expectant couples the way I've been doing for eleven years. The rewards are tremendous. I still get letters from the parents who allowed me to be with them during their birth. My nursing is an art.

C: Why wouldn't you become a full-fledged midwife?

L: I don't like the hours. The "on call" just wreaks havoc with your life.

C: On call means...

L: On call means every second or third night you are on for twenty-four hours, if you have five births in twenty-four hours, you do five births; if you have no births, you do no births. And this goes on and on. Most midwives with a complement of three in a practice will handle about thirty prenatal patients a month.

C: And after the twenty-four hours on call, how many hours are you off?

L: You're not off, you cover office hours and you do prenatal screening as well as normal gynecology.

C: In other words, the demands on a midwife are pretty heavy?

L: They're tiring, they're stressful, but if you ask any midwife they'll tell you it's worth it. They really are very gentle people and they love their work, as opposed to some attending physicians who come in and want the delivery as quickly as possible so they can do their other work.

C: Besides infinite patience, what quality do you think nurse-midwives should have?

L: The most important is a sense of compassion and empathy. I think you have to have a deep sensitivity to what someone is going through. I've been around it for so long that I know that if a mother says, she feels like pushing, and even if she's been examined and is only 2cm, I usually will believe her because it's her body; she knows it very well and I have no right to say this is not true. I think it's very unfair to treat the patient any other way. You have to be one of them and you have to respect their rights as individuals and not try to tell them what your labor and birth was like. You've got to see them as having a new experience and try and give them the most joyous one that they can possibly have.

C: How do you think the fetal monitoring and the automatic IV affect the relaxation of the mother and her ability to really relax her muscles?

L: Well, the intravenous is usually not automatic. It used to be, so you're correct in assuming that it was. Now, we wait until the patient shows signs of needing an intravenous and that includes severe dehydration where she's been up all night and possibly throwing up from being in labor.

C: Very often, hospitals don't allow people to drink.

L: That's right, but we give them ice chips and do encourage them to drink water to hydrate themselves in some way, because the mother can spike a temperature and the baby's heart rate will increase. So when we do an intravenous it's not prophylactic, it's because the mother does need one. As for fetal monitoring, we've come a long way from the notion that women need to be strapped down in labor. When we do use the fetal monitor we use it as an assessment tool to see how the labor is progressing. They show us an awful lot, more than just the baby's heart rate. They measure the frequency of contractions, not the intensity, but the frequency; the woman who's laboring usually closes her eyes when she's trying to relax and concentrates on the contractions. It's then the coach's responsibility to tell her when the contraction begins, peaks and comes down. In the long run if you would interview any of the mothers after their delivery they'll usually say that it was a valuable guide for them throughout their labor. They do assume whatever position they want with it; the external monitor will allow them to assume different positions and I find it a valuable and useful tool.

C: Early on in your studies did you know that you wanted to help deliver babies?

L: I knew when I did the obstetrical part of my nursing rotation that it was nice, it was fun, it was joyous, and I told myself that I'll be the best I can be at this particular skill. I watched senior people and I followed them. I worked with the midwives and picked up most of my information from them; for the rest I just listened to patients and developed my own skills.

C: Do you have any children yourself?

L: No, I don't, but I plan to in the future. I love my field and I only hope that I get someone as compassionate and nice as I am to support me in whatever capacity they can.

Ann Simon
A mother's view of nurse-midwifery

"Why not?" I asked myself as I considered the possibility of having a nurse-midwife deliver my second child. Through local publicity and the first-hand report of a friend, I had recently been hearing about the Maternal Health Service (Springfield, Ohio).

As I thought back on my experience with a private obstetrician during my first pregnancy, I realized that I certainly hadn't needed a highly trained specialist to conduct the routine prenatal examinations, or during that particular (unusually easy) delivery either. Let me make it clear that I was very satisfied with the obstetrician whom I saw during my first pregnancy, but by the time I was pregnant again he happened to be delivering at a different hospital which did not have some services I wanted. So, why not place myself in the care of nurse-midwives? There would be a doctor to double-check that the pregnancy was normal, and one of several specialists would be on call for delivery if any complications were to arise. I was satisfied that I would receive good quality medical care and I liked the idea of trying out something new. So I did.

As it turned out I was delighted with my decision. I had certainly concluded correctly that I would receive good medical care. But it wasn't until I entered the examining room on my first visit that I received a glimpse of what has turned out for me to be the real outstanding benefit of the program. There on the bulletin board above the desk were prominently and proudly displayed several dozen snapshots of newborn babies. I was delighted and astonished: the nurse-midwives had cared enough about these babies and their mothers to put their pictures up! The nurse-midwife entered the room, sat down comfortably, and asked if I had any questions. After discussing all my concerns, she usually had some information or suggestions of her own to add before asking me to lie down so she could examine me (gently, I might add). Revolutionary procedure. I always had to wait until after being examined in order to ask my doctor questions. I was left lying on my back to shout my inquiries to his retreating figure.

That the nurse-midwife volunteered information I didn't even ask about was even more amazing. I later learned she was following an informal agenda of topics to discuss at each visit if the patient hadn't already brought them up. The topics included general information that would satisfy the woman's natural curiosity about what is going on inside her body during pregnancy and what to expect during childbirth and her hospital stay. Instructions were also given about crucial aspects of maternal care, such as nutrition (with more individual attention than a list of foods passed out casually at the first visit), the importance of rest and naps, future plans for birth control, and the necessity for giving thought to organizing the home and meeting the needs of all members of the family at the time of the new baby's arrival. Incredible.

By the time I learned that I would be joined early in labor by a nurse-midwife who would remain present until the birth, I knew enough about the Maternal Health Service not to be surprised again. My husband and I were well prepared by our previous childbirth experience (and a refresher course) to work together to keep me comfortably participating during labor and delivery, and we were expecting to do it basically by ourselves. But the encouraging presence of the nurse-midwife made the job much easier and more enjoyable for us both. I was so confident of her sincere dedication to me as a person that I was able to relax and trust her absolutely. She interpreted the progress of labor much more accurately than we could have by ourselves, and she supported both of us— emotionally and physically—through a period of fatigue and discouragement. By the time she held up our new daughter for us to see, my husband and I felt a real bond of intimacy and gratitude to the woman who had assisted and joined us in the joy of giving birth.

The nurse-midwife regards pregnancy and childbirth as a real, living heartfelt experience, as well as a series of important physical signs and events scientifically to be observed and dealt with. She is concerned with the feelings and the life of the pregnant woman, as well as the condition of her uterus, blood pressure and related physical details. She regards the mother as a human being in the midst of one of the most exciting moments of her life, rather than a body to be manipulated through a series of procedures designed to promote optimum efficiency on the part of the doctor and the hospital staff.

Any woman who is regarded with such consistent respect and individual concern throughout pregnancy and childbirth could not avoid liking herself and her baby as a result. Given the choice of selecting obstetrical care again at any time in any place, I would go far out of my way to find a nurse-midwife if I possibly could. I enthusiastically encourage my friends to take advantage of the benefits I enjoyed so much, and I look forward to my own two daughters having the opportunity to do so some day.

As I anticipate the increasing participation by nurse-midwives in obstetrical care throughout the world in the future, two concerns come to mind. I think it should be made widely known that nurse-midwifery programs provide unique advantages of warm and comprehensive attention above and beyond meeting standards of medical excellence, so that women will be informed about the nature of care available to them if such a program is established in their community. Even more important, I hope that the established professions will share my conclusion that the nurse-midwife has far more to offer than an additional pair of arms and eyes to aid the busy obstetrician, and will incorporate the mother-centered attitudes and approach of nurse-midwifery into their own established office and hospital routines.

Maxime De La Falaise McKendry
Home birth with midwife, first child

We were all born in the same house in St. John's Wood, England. It was built for my father by his mother. He was already established as a portrait painter. It was an incredible house, like a country house in the middle of London: a garden on each side, huge kitchen and pantry, sitting rooms, bedrooms, studies, corridors. My mother was married in that house. She swears that no one ever knew she was pregnant except my father. She was very slim and wore floating dresses. One day in the middle of a luncheon party she suddenly left the room, went upstairs and gave birth to me.

At the time I was expecting Loulou, Alain and I were living in Paris. I was working for a magazine as a fashion editor, painting backgrounds, modeling, drawing fashion sketches and doing English translations of the captions. By the time I arrived in London, my mother had arranged everything in the house for the birth. The gamp (midwife) had already moved in. A huge woman, she gave me a book to read about other people's deliveries. But they were all tricky experiences, especially for women with ballet training like me. It told of their twisted muscles and narrow passages as the worst for giving birth. The gamp had also brought a mass of rubber tubes into the house. When I started to have birth pangs, I set fire to the medieval-looking rubber implements. It gave me a lot of satisfaction. I didn't know what they were meant to do but it relieved me knowing that they wouldn't be used on me. There was this acrid smell of burnt rubber all over the house and a little heap of black mess on the bathroom floor.

The gynecologist, who had been checking me out in the last days and was supposed to deliver the baby, was unavailable. He was playing golf. The midwife sent my husband to buy some ether.

First, I drew a hot bath and stayed in it with a book and a large dose of whiskey. The birth pangs were mild. I had brought my old French maid with me from Paris. She would come in the bathroom crying, "Oh! I never thought I would see Madame in such a state." Finally, very soaked, I got out of the bath, completely relaxed. Having been in the same state as the baby inside of me, I could sense it would just swim out. There was a portable table set up in the bathroom. I got up on it for the gamp to look at the dilation stage. Alain put a little bit of cotton wool with ether under my nose asking me at the same time to translate French captions. The pangs got stronger… "Ce petit chapeau divin en feutre de calais cache un petit nid ou un rouge-gorge tient des cerises dans le bec …cette adorable chasuble bleu rayé…"

I was lying on that table (it was padded with all sorts of pillows) feeling totally relaxed from the bath when the doctor arrived. I became really curious to see who would come out of me and got interested in the whole birth. They strapped me loosely to the table. I guess they were afraid I would fall off. I didn't have time to protest. In a half hour, after a lot of tam-tam like the beginning of a really good dance, Loulou was born. I didn't tear or need to be sliced, being so stretched from the hot water.

Even after the umbilical cord was cut, the spiritual connection was so strong. We shared the same bed. It was so important. Hospitals are not concerned with the spiritual side, they even hide your insides from you, for them it's garbage. I wanted to see it all, feel it all.

Alexis, my second child, was born in the hospital by induced birth. It was so boring waiting in this blank room. The induction seemed to spoil the whole natural rhythm of birth. I felt rather like a hen laying one of a million supermarket eggs. After the birth I was led to my room, he to the newborn ward. It all felt very abstract. Alexis only became real and personal after we had gone back home.

Terry Davis
Hospital birthing room, second child

Terry Davis's first baby was born prematurely in a hospital's surgical delivery room. The baby was immediately whisked away to a neonatal care unit. For the birth of her second child, Terry was determined to have a more intimate experience and she chose to deliver in a birthing room at another hospital. The pregnancy and labor proceeded normally, the birth experience was just as Terry and her husband, Andy, had wished.

Caterine: You have two young children and you were telling me that the first birth was not quite what you had expected. What happened?

Terry: Well, I wasn't fully prepared for one thing. I hadn't finished my Lamaze classes. The baby was five or six weeks early and I was totally taken by surprise.

I gave birth in a hospital in New Jersey, which was a horrible experience. I received very little support from the hospital's staff. I was also very angry because I didn't expect the pains to be as bad as they were. There was absolutely no privacy. There were a lot of people in the delivery room that I hadn't seen before. A mirror was hanging above the delivery table so I could see what was going on. Eventually there was a tremendous amount of blood and I thought I was hemorrhaging and dying and no one was telling me. At that point I didn't ask if anything was wrong so I don't think I really wanted to know for sure. Then out came this baby girl; the umbilical cord was cut immediately. The nurse scooped her up and put her on a table as all these tests were done on her. She was premature and they wanted to make sure she was okay.

C: How premature was she?

T: About five to six weeks; she weighed 4 pounds, 15 ounces. And she looked ugly, like a little plucked chicken. Then the pediatrician brought her over to me—and she was all wrapped up. I just looked at him and asked what do I do and he said, touch her. I took my finger and touched her face, and that was about it. They took her away to clean her up and begin monitoring her. It was very, very strange. There wasn't any of the immediate maternal affection I had expected. I was very upset about it. I was then wheeled into this closet-sized recovery room. At this point my husband went to see his parents and the baby, and actually I think I wanted to be alone, I was so depressed. I just rolled over, cried, said I'm a mommy and fell asleep for about ten or fifteen minutes.

C: What a strange experience for a first baby...

T: I didn't even hold the baby, I didn't really even see the baby until that evening, and she was born just before noon. I was so dazed. I didn't know what to ask for, didn't know that I really had the right to ask to see my baby.

C: How old were you then?

T: I was thirty. I was in a total state of shock. Unless I demanded or I asked for something, no one volunteered. It was a very awkward experience. I also had to leave the baby in the hospital when I went home because she was premature. It took me a long time to recover. I think I'm constantly working on my relationship with Sarah because we just got off on the wrong foot. She was a very colicky baby for four months.

C: In spite of all that... you wanted to have another child?

T: The second pregnancy was so very different from the first. With the first pregnancy I had marginal placenta previa, so I had problems with bleeding throughout, and I was bedridden when I wasn't working. The second one was a normal pregnancy. There were no problems after some initial spotting. At this point we had moved to New York. After I had had the pregnancy confirmed in New Jersey I started doctor hunting in New York and with that much more experience behind me, we started looking into different doctors and different hospitals and trying to find a good match. We checked several New York hospitals that were highly recommended. One was redoing their whole maternity unit and putting in birthing rooms. At another, several appointments were cancelled after I got there. I tried to look into the midwifery program at another hospital, but they never returned my call. So I felt that obviously this wasn't meant to be. I then met Joe Berger, a doctor at Beth Israel Hospital. I was very up front and very honest with him. I told him what my first birth experience had been like, and that this time I wanted to have my second child in a birthing room if all went well. Dr. Berger was very honest with me in saying that he did not necessarily agree with the birthing room, it wasn't his choice of delivery and, quite frankly, would avoid it. I went to see some other doctors, but there was a manner about Dr. Berger that I really liked. So I went back to him and asked him to consider a birthing room under optimum circumstances. He said that if I did not need an episiotomy he would consider it. I really thought that was as good as saying forget it. But I appreciated his willingness to consider it and I found him to be very sensitive throughout my pregnancy.

C: And how was the birth?

T: When I arrived at the hospital, the labor room was full. I thought oh no, it's gonna happen, I'm gonna have my baby in the hall! They brought me into the recovery room where there was a free spot. I had the place to myself, it really was a comedy of errors. Andy had brought me up and had gone back down to the car to get all the video equipment. He could not get the video equipment past security so he was stuck somewhere in the bowels of the hospital, trying to battle the guards. He came back up, saying, the hell with the video equipment and at that moment Dr. Berger shows up, saying, "So we're gonna have a baby!" Give me a break!

It was also the end of a shift and the nurses were not thrilled to see me. One of them came in and yelled at me because my insurance was under Terry instead of Theresa or Theresa instead of Terry; it was something very stupid. The last thing I needed right then was to be yelled at. And, luckily, with the change of shift in came Lisa who was fresh and awake.

C: A midwife?

T: I don't know if she was a midwife. In any case she was a nurse, and she was absolutely wonderful even though I was absolutely terrified.

Toward the end of my pregnancy, I told Dr. Berger I was really afraid that I wasn't going to be able to take the pain. He said if you need some drugs to get through the pain, that's okay. All you care about is that you're healthy and safe and the baby is safe.

I put all my faith in Lisa in terms of what she was telling me to do and I also put more faith in Andy this time.

At one point during labor I told Lisa I had to go to the bathroom. And I'm hooked to the intravenous now, I've got the fetal heart monitor wrapped around, so Lisa gets me up to go to the bathroom, try to picture this; she carries the IV, I've got the fetal machine slung over my shoulder, we go into this toilet which is even smaller than the labor room. I've got this toilet seat here and she's hung up on my IV and I've got this slung over my shoulder and I'm on the toilet with my head against Andy's belly and thank God I sat on the toilet, because I did indeed have a bowel movement. And she says, if you feel it pushing, push. So I did and I must have sat on the toilet for 15 minutes and pushed when I had the urge and Andy said to me later, you know, there I was thinking, here we are in a hospital, why are we going to have a baby on the toilet!

When I got to the hospital I was 7cm dilated, but the baby was still in a plus 3 position. Joe Berger told me afterward that he didn't really know whether I was going to be able to deliver vaginally, because he didn't know whether the baby was going to drop or not. I think that is probably why I pushed for as long as I did, close to an hour I think. She did indeed come down, but I attribute a lot of that to Lisa who tried her hardest to get me to change my position in bed, in back labor positions. It was just so uncomfortable but I was least uncomfortable being in a sitting position.

C: Because you didn't have enough room to move?

T: I don't know, I certainly didn't want to get up and move around, I just didn't feel like it. But Lisa did feel that if you can get a patient up and changing position, it helps the baby drop.

Well, Lisa is saying, Joe, she's a prime candidate for the birthing room, let's do it Joe, she can do it. And he's going, no no no. But she took him down and showed him the birthing room. He comes back, and says, come on, we're moving down the hall. Joe is holding me up, Lisa is holding the IV behind me, I've got my gown closed in the back and can barely walk, Andy is pulling up the rear with all the video equipment.

C: Do you think being in the birthing room made it easier for you than being in the standard delivery room?

T: It made it a much more intimate, personal atmosphere. It wasn't the sterile, cold, impersonal situation that I found the surgical operating room to be. It was just a little room where there was no one else but Andy, myself, the doctor and the nurse and then the baby. And we established a very intimate relationship. It was very loving, it was very warm, nobody was there out of duty, no students to invade my privacy. After the baby was born, nobody took her away, we were just able to be there, upward of an hour after, and I understood after that when Lisa said they like to get the babies down to the nursery within a certain amount of time after the birth, to get washed up, weighed and measured, etc.

C: So all in all it was a good experience . . . would you change anything around if you were to have another child?

T: I think I would consider going farther with it. With my first child I did not care who delivered me, I did not have a preference. Second time around, we did do it in the birthing room and things were okay. Third time around, I don't know, would I do it at home? I'm not sure about that. There are more and more birthing centers going up. I would probably consider a birthing center that was affiliated with a hospital. As to whether I want my daughter to be present, it would depend on how old she is. Birth freaked me out twice in a row, you know. I know it has freaked my husband out twice. I was going through a lot of pain. The first time he felt helpless, the second time he was helping me, it worked and he knew that. I'll have to play all that by ear.

Gladys St. Louis
Hospital delivery, yoga exercise and breathing, fourth child

Gladys: Vanilo is now six days old. I don't know if it's because I haven't had a baby in four years or because he has been benefiting from the breathing exercises and the vegetarian diet I have been following, but this baby seems so much calmer. He doesn't cry as often as the others did. Maybe because I am much calmer myself. For instance, now he is sleeping, he lies happily in his crib. It's not at all the same as the others, there is a difference.

Caterine: What method had you chosen to give birth to your other children?

G: When I was expecting my first child a friend gave me a book about natural childbirth by a French doctor, Jacques Gaillard, I think. I tried the exercises, not with regularity, but enough to get me through the first three births in a conscious state (but not exactly without anxieties). However, this time I went to Professor Cayemite, a teacher of Hatha Yoga, in my third month of pregnancy, as required, and started training with his breathing method and a few basic postures.

I think it helps. I have seen friends suffer needlessly for days because they were not prepared. You can control your own body with your breathing when the contraction happens and then the doctor knows when you are having a contraction. But, if you haven't any control over your body and you just twist and grimace without giving yourself a rest, it's difficult to figure out what's happening. And, if you don't know, how can you let the doctor know?

C: And how did the birth go with this child?

G: The day I felt ready I said to Professor Cayemite that I would see him tomorrow at the hospital. This time I didn't feel that what was going on was pain. It was more like something was in the making. I waited until 3:00 A.M. to go to the hospital. When I arrived, the doctor said I was 3cm dilated. I would feel the contraction coming and I would breathe slowly in rhythm and it would all go well. It may have been because I am now used to having babies, but it was more likely due to the breathing. No pain. A few minutes later I felt like pushing. I told the doctor. At 5:38 A.M. the baby came without great efforts or problems. It went so fast this time. Before, for the other births, there were many moments when I didn't know what to do with myself and I wished the process would speed up.

C: Were you given a local anesthetic?

G: What's that?

C: A drug that numbs part of your body against pain.

G: No, nothing medical except for the incision. I didn't want to take any of the herbal teas women here (in Haiti) usually absorb because I wanted to be able to evaluate the strength of the contractions and how the method works for it. I wanted to be able to tell the others first-hand if the breathing really works and how. With the herbal teas the sensations might have been covered up. But, for the incision which had to be sewn I still followed the traditional local custom of taking a bath of palma Christi leaves (ricin oil). The doctors don't approve of it. They say it's empirical, but it works for me and that's essential. I felt so much better afterwards. I think it's one of the good customs that has been passed on through the generations and I will recommend it to my daughter.

C: Did you have your other children in the hospital?

G: Yes, always in the hospital because I always consulted with a doctor and they want to deliver children in well-equipped hospitals. But going along with Professor Cayemite's method, I could have had the child at home if my husband had been prepared to receive the baby. I couldn't take the risk. He wouldn't have known what to do with the umbilical cord.

C: Isn't he interested?

G: He is. In fact, he wanted to go with me to the hospital and stay. He drove me there and the doctor told him it might be up to twelve hours till the baby came. I knew it would be any minute but we thought it was best if he went home. Anyway, the children had to be driven to school the next morning. A yoga teacher came by a few months ago and said that he had delivered his own baby. My husband told him that it was too bad that he couldn't have learned from him.

I do not intend to have any other children. People in Haiti have twelve to fifteen children but I think that four is more than enough. But, if I ever change my mind I will have the next one at home. I went to the hospital for fear of complications and because there is no one at home who knows how to receive the baby with basic first-hand knowledge. I would rather stay at home any time. It's cozier, you are more at ease. I don't much like going to the hospital. When I was there I spent a sleepless night thinking about my other children.

C: How long were you in the hospital?

G: Two days! I had the baby early Friday morning and I got out Sunday morning. There were no complications, the child was very healthy. A funny thing happened when I arrived at the hospital. One of the doctors asked me if I was calm and relaxed and I said yes and then he told me that my regular doctor was away for a couple of days. I guess he thought that that would worry me but all went very smoothly. It's really worthwhile to prepare for your baby!

C: How do you feed him?

G: I do mixed feedings. I do not have enough milk so I also give him formula. There is another thing I noticed with the other births. Two days after giving birth I always had fever. I was told that it was because of the coming of the milk. This time I did not have fever and the milk came easily.

However, I experienced something I cannot recommend. I was completely breast-feeding my second child and around the sixth month after I had her I was still not getting my period. In the early months I thought it was normal because of having a new baby. I know it does happen, but, when I went to see the doctor, he told me I was five months pregnant! I don't wish that on anyone. No sleeping at night with the new baby, tired during the day with the two of them. Oh! It was the most exhausting time of my life. But, anyway, I think that when you know how to breathe "well" a lot of things get easier.

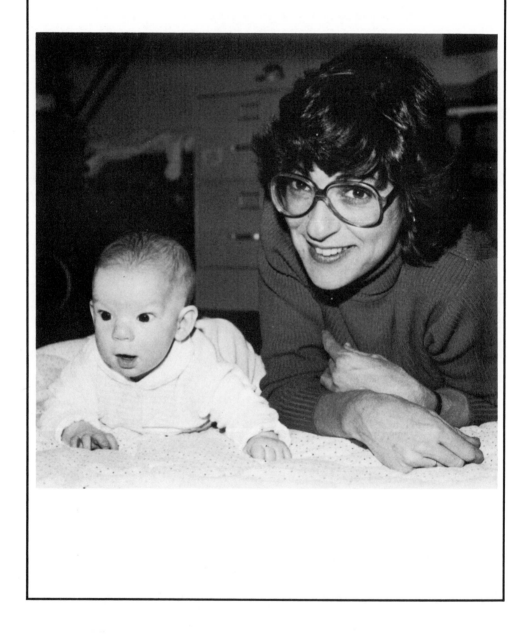

Connie Zalk

Hospital delivery by cesarean, artificial insemination, first child

After years of marriage Connie divorced a husband who did not want to have children. She was then artificially inseminated and gave birth to a boy, David, by cesarean section.

Caterine Milinaire: Can you tell me about the circumstances surrounding the birth of your son, David?

Connie Zalk: In 1978 during a routine exam my doctor, Joe Berger, discovered an edunculated fibroid tumor growing on a stem. Picture a tiny flower, like a tulip head with a long stem. Most fibroid tumors grow right on the wall of the uterus, as muscle fiber, but this one was free floating in the uterine cavity. And there was some concern . . . they didn't know what it was. Joe, my doctor, couldn't believe that I wasn't aware of it. I was operated on less than a week later. During surgery he discovered four small tumors, what he called seedlings, on the uterine wall that could become large fibroid tumors. I was thirty years old, married at the time, and felt this biological clock ticking, not only because I was getting older but also because I was told that here was a reason why I might not be able to have a child.

My husband and I ended the marriage about a year after the surgery. And although not having had a child contributed to it, that wasn't the direct cause of the divorce. He knew I wanted a child very much and he did not. And I kept saying that's okay, but it wasn't okay although I didn't realize that until much later.

Several years later during a routine exam, Joe found that the seedlings had blossomed; he looked at me and asked me if I still wanted to have children. I said yes and he replied that it's now or never. I went home and "never" just rang in my ears. In all honesty I was glad to have that push because I'm not sure I would have done it otherwise. I thought about it for six or eight months, I discussed it with my family, with my parents, not looking for permission but to say look, I want you to know this is something that I am considering. I thought about how I wanted to do it; and did I want to know the father. Joe and I talked about donors.

CM: By then you had selected to have artificial insemination?

CZ: I wasn't sure yet. I was interested in pursuing that idea just to know how it worked. There were a couple of possibilities. I could get married, I could back myself into a relationship, have a baby, not worry about it. And I ruled that out immediately. I would have preferred, if I had been married at the time, to do it very convention- ally and very traditionally. But the more I thought about it the more I realized I didn't want to know who the father was, I didn't want the emotional ties, I didn't want any potential legal battles on the horizon. That's when Joe and I talked about donors, where would we get the donor from, what choices did I have, how it would work in terms of the expenses, and I did a lot of research. That's how it started.

CM: What did you find in your research?

CZ: The first thing that I found was that there were a lot of doctors who wouldn't even consider doing artificial insemination on a single woman. They just feel that it's unethical.

CM: What's their main objection?

CZ: Only that they don't want to be responsible for potentially creating a problem down the road. But Joe immediately said that he would interview these people for me, he would do all the screening. Joe felt very strongly that he didn't want to use a sperm bank at that time, primarily because sperm banks provide frozen sperm. He feels that the chances of becoming pregnant are better with fresh sperm. And I liked the idea that he knew who the donor was. I trusted him more than I would trust some anonymous clinician. It also meant that, if I were ovulating during a weekend, he would be available and the donor could be available.

CM: That's a tricky proposition, isn't it?

CZ: I'll say. That particular summer when we started, I was calling Joe from Fire Island with my temperature readings, and I would say to him, should I come back to the city Saturday morning and he would say, yes I'll meet you in my office tomorrow morning. And then it was always, let me call the donor and I'll call you back. It was remarkable.

CM: So you had to try several times?

CZ: We tried over a year. We were inseminating either two or three times a month. I think after about six months when I didn't become pregnant I went for the first of a series of tests, a hysterosalpingogram. It turned out that I had one blocked tube, so half of those inseminations were wasted. Then we tried again, I guess either the ninth or tenth month that we were inseminating; a sonogram was used to determine whether I was ovulating on the side that was not blocked, and to see when the egg was going to rupture, and we hit it the first time.

CM: And you never met the father?

CZ: No.

CM: What would happen to the father, he would come and sit in another room?

CZ: The donors that Joe primarily uses are residents and interns at the hospital, he always had more than one. Joe Berger would call one of them and the specimen would be left at the hospital.

There is a story that I've told people and it's easy to laugh about it now, but it wasn't at the time. One day I happened to get out of work a little early and I was in Joe's office at around 5 P.M. I'm sitting in the waiting room and in walks a man; to say unattractive would be the understatement of the century. I described him to people as Quasimodo, with a terrible pockmarked face and very thick glasses, wearing a three-piece polyester suit, hunched over, and he waves to the receptionist behind the window and walks in the back. He was obviously known to these people, and I just panicked. In my mind this is the donor, this is the potential father of my baby. I broke out in a cold sweat. A while later this guy walks out and waves good-bye, and the next thing I knew Joe's receptionist is saying okay Connie, let's go. I couldn't get out of the chair. Joe came out and I was practically in tears; I couldn't get the words out and I finally explained what I had just seen. He just laughed; it was a messenger from one of the labs.

CM: How do you proceed once you have the egg just at the right time and the fertile live sperm?

CZ: It's as though it were just a routine gynecological exam. A speculum is used to open the vagina so that there is a clear shot at the cervix, the sperm is put into what looks like a syringe, injected, and then they tilt the table backward at a slight angle and you have to stay there quietly for about a half hour. Then you get up and get dressed and walk out and say, maybe I'm pregnant.

CM: Must be a weird feeling . . . ?

CZ: Totally weird, not to know who that person is.

CM: How did you feel when you finally conceived?

CZ: Scared. All of those years of thinking about it and all the planning—almost two years from the time that Joe told me I should think about doing it to when it happened. There were so many moments where I would ask myself, what am I doing? I was getting very mixed reactions from family and friends.

CM: You come from a traditional family?

CZ: Very traditional. On one hand everyone said, we understand why you want to do this, on the other hand they were all saying, how are you going to manage? And that was the same thing I kept asking myself. So I was frightened. I must say that in the planning of the whole concept I went to my boss at City Hall—I work for the mayor of the City of New York—and I was concerned about his image politically. I told my supervisor my plan and asked about potential problems for him or the mayor or for anyone else there. And he said, this is your life, you'll do what you want and don't worry about anybody else. That kind of support was and continues to be I think the most important thing that keeps me going. Actually he suggested that I bring the baby to work, if that would make it easier. Which I hadn't really thought of, and which I wound up doing.

CM: What a wonderful boss.

CZ: He's marvelous. Everyone I work with was rooting for me, but not some of my closest friends. One girl almost stopped talking to me over this.

CM: Because she was so shocked?

CZ: Shocked and . . . she thought it was totally crazy. I don't think anyone was willing to come out and say to me you're out of your mind, but it was obvious a lot of people felt that way.

CM: You have to be a really strong person to carry something like that through. Did you have to seek any psychological help at any point?

CZ: No I didn't. People have asked me that. I had been in therapy on and off for many years before and had talked through wanting to have a child. I was tempted to call the woman that I had been seeing to kind of check it out, but decided I didn't need to.

My sister-in-law is a psychologist and we spent a lot of time talking about it. It was my sister-in-law who helped me decide things like what would I put on the birth certificate for the father's name. I was told that I would be given a choice. I could put down artificial insemination by donor, or I could put down nothing, or I could put down a name. And I struggled with that. It was my sister-in-law who convinced me to leave the space empty because when this child applies for a passport at age seventeen or eighteen it will be no clerk's business that he was the result of an artificially inseminated donor. He can tell anybody anything he wants with a blank.

CM: How was the pregnancy?

CZ: It was very difficult. First of all I miscarried that first pregnancy. Classic eight week miscarriage.

CM: You must have been terribly disappointed?

CZ: I think Joe was more disappointed than I was. I was very disappointed. I had very mixed feelings about it. One one hand I was relieved to know that I could conceive because at that point I was thirty-six and had never conceived. And, as destroyed as I was, it was a very good test for me because it gave me one last time to ask, do you really want to do this. And I was grateful for that because I had no hesitation.

CM: So you had to go through the whole process once again?

CZ: Yes. The pregnancy was very difficult. I had been warned by Joe that the fibroids could get very big because of the hormonal changes, and sure enough they did. When I was about seven weeks pregnant in both pregnancies I was already in maternity clothes; when I was fifteen weeks pregnant I was getting big very fast and I wasn't gaining a lot of weight; so it wasn't baby weight; it was tumors.

When I went for my amniocentesis at sixteen weeks, the sonogram showed a mass next to the fetus that was 32cm (about 14 inches). I checked into the hospital the next day. Here I was 16 weeks pregnant, I looked like I was ready to deliver.

In fact Joe was going to try to remove the tumor and maintain the pregnancy. There was a possibility that the fetus wouldn't survive, that he wouldn't be able to remove the tumor or that I was going to wind up having a full hysterectomy right then and there. That was the most frightened I think I was. But mostly, the *never* was looming again. I was going to lose this baby and it was never going to be possible. I was admitted into the hospital the next day in the middle of the afternoon. The surgery was scheduled for early the next morning. I was scared to death, I was facing major surgery and all the other experiences that went with that. In the preceding twenty-four-hour period, Joe had gathered together from three or four different sources every sonogram that had been taken of me going back seven years, so he could try to figure out what it was. He went through the films with a couple of the radiologists that night. At about 10:00 P.M. they decided that it was just one of the fibroids gone nuts, and it wasn't a cancerous tumor, an ovarian cyst or anything else. So he decided not to operate. He called me at the hospital and told me to go home.

CM: You went on with the pregnancy?

CZ: Yes, and I was warned that I might run into some serious problems later on, at twenty or twenty-four weeks, but nothing that would be life-threatening.

CM: Did all that happen?

CZ: Yes. Although not as bad as I had imagined. Joe kept telling me that once we make it to twenty-six or twenty-eight weeks we're okay, so that's all I was going for. I knew that it was a healthy boy because of the amnio so that was a tremendous relief. And when we hit twenty-eight weeks, I was ready to go out and celebrate. Actually, Joe and I went out to dinner, and he said, you're fine now, anything could happen and there would be a viable baby.

We were doing fairly regular sonograms; at twenty-six weeks the radiologist in the hospital had said, you're just going to get bigger and bigger and either this baby is going to win out or this tumor is. The baby was winning so it was pretty incredible.

CM: All that must have cost you a lot of money.

CZ: Yes, it did. I had anticipated it. I had said that I wouldn't undertake this without having $20,000 in the bank, and I didn't start until that's what I had. If I was going to do this I was going to do this on my own.

CM: How did the actual birth go?

CZ: It was difficult. I was about five or six days overdue, and in some early nonstress testing it was beginning to look like there might be a problem. Joe decided he was going to induce. At this point I was ready, I had had it, it was enough. This was now October 31 and I said we're not inducing on Halloween, I will not have a Halloween baby. So I came back November 1.

We started inducing around 10:00 A.M.; by about 7:00 P.M. nothing was really going on. Joe asked my permission to go home for dinner and I said he could go. Before he left he broke the water. . . and it turned out that the water was filled with meconium, which is a really bad sign. Joe had at that point made a decision to let me go another hour, and if I wasn't completely dilated we were going for a section. Since I had been warned before I got pregnant that a cesarean was likely because of the tumors, I was almost prepared for it. Labor started to get serious at around 8:00 P.M.

At around 9:30 the decision was made to do a section, and I was wheeled into the operating room. I kept saying to them, set up the mirror, I want to watch, but Joe said, Connie this is going to be very messy, this is not going to be just a simple section. So he was a little tense, my sister-in-law was not allowed to be in the operating room.

CM: You were by yourself?

CZ: Larry the anesthesiologist, who had been with me all night, was holding my hand, and I had Joe, and the other nurses who were around, who I really trusted. I was watching in the reflection of the lights. Joe makes the first incision, and I hear him say, "Oh my God, you have tumors growing on top of tumors." I don't know how he pulled it off, because the anesthesiologist later said to me he had never seen such a difficult cesarean delivery because of the tumors. The baby was born and was completely covered with meconium, he wouldn't even let me see him. I remember Joe saying, aspirate the baby.

They stitched me up and I went into a recovery room. I kept asking to see the baby and no one would let me see him.

CM: You must have been very worried that there was something wrong with the baby.

CZ: I was very scared. Larry, the anesthesiologist, kept saying he's fine, he's just very messy, they're going to clean him up and they'll bring him to you, which is what they did. I saw him only for a couple of seconds and I don't really even remember.

CM: How long did you stay in the hospital after the birth?

CZ: He was born on a Thursday night, and I was released Tuesday.

CM: Five days later.

CZ: I can't say enough about the hospital, the people were so nice. I think I was actually released a day earlier than usual because Joe saw I was anxious to get home and get settled.

CM: Could you have done it without the help of your parents?

CZ: There is no way that it could have been done without my family's help. While I was in the hospital my brother and a cousin moved all the baby furniture in for me.

CM: Did you miss having your husband around at that point?

CZ: I didn't miss having a husband around. I missed not having someone who could do those things for me. So Diane the baby nurse did them.

CM: Did you think you missed having a daddy for your child?

CZ: No, not at all. My brother and sister-in-law were visiting me in the hospital; we had a bit of an argument with the hospital staff, because by the rules there is unlimited visiting for fathers. In the end we made arrangements with the head nurse for my sister-in-law to be "the daddy" for the records, so that she could be there when all the other daddys were, like at feeding times.

CM: What a funny world . . .

CZ: Yes. The house was filled with people during those first three weeks.

CM: That must have been tiring.

CZ: I was exhausted and in retrospect it was a mistake. You see, I run the mayor's office of operations. My title is controller and director of administration. I am a director and supervisor of fourteen, and the office has a hundred people. I had a staff meeting at home when David was about six days old. I was on the phone constantly to the office.

When David was around three weeks old I started thinking about going in to the office. We went to visit; I wanted to show him off and there were a lot of people around who were anxious to see him. But having made that trip with him and seeing that it wasn't so hard to get him packed up and out of the house, I think that prompted me to say, if I wanted to I could do that.

When he was almost five weeks old I went in to work with him. The office had been completely equipped. I had a carriage there and a crib, a bookcase with diapers and clothes, and now I have a playpen, things like that. Everyone had been told that I would be there when I could and if I wasn't there I'd be home and reachable, and I was going to try a couple of days a week. I took it real easy. The advantage of the office, and it sounds terrible when I say this, is that I think the anxiety that a lot of mothers experience comes from being overwhelmed by the constant demands of an infant. In the office there were twenty people who would have done anything to relieve me and they did. If I needed to go into a meeting somebody would take him. If I was just having a very difficult day or I was very tired (I have a bed in my office), someone else would take him and I would take a nap.

CM: Surely you must have come across some traditional people who disapproved of some of your ways.

CZ: No one ever said it to me directly, but some people were saying terrible things to my secretary.

CM: That's something you have to contend with?

CZ: Sure, and I had thought about it even before I conceived. My attitude in the end was, too bad. If it's a problem for them it is their problem! But this was not a secret, everybody knew the plan and part of that was very conscious on my part, so there wouldn't be the gossiping and the speculation and, if people had a problem with it, let them work it out early.

CM: Do you think not having to deal with a man leaves you with more free time?

CZ: It never really entered into it. It would have been allright. Interestingly enough, the woman who lives directly across the hall is in a very traditional marriage, her baby is seven and one-half weeks older than David, and I was watching the differences between us. And I seemed to be coping much better than she.

CM: You can make all the decisions...

CZ: Exactly, she was coming to me and complaining that her husband doesn't understand when she's saying she needs time alone, and he doesn't... and I would close my door afterward and be so glad not to have to deal with that...

I kept waiting, and I still wait I guess, for the moment when I wake up and I say what have I done? And it hasn't happened.

CM: How are you going to cope when your child asks for his father?

CZ: I'm not sure. I have thought about it. There has been a lot written and this is no longer so new and so unique. There is a group in New York called Single Mothers by Choice. And while I've not been particularly active with them, I do see them as a resource: how do they deal with it, how do they recommend that it be dealt with. Essentially, the commitment that I have made is that I will be honest with him. At what age you explain artificial insemination, I'm not sure, but fortunately for me there are a lot of women who have already been through it and have dealt successfully with that. But I will not lie to him.

CM: After going through all this do you think that you would want another child?

CZ: I definitely would want another one, whether or not I'll do it, I don't know. The thought of being able to pull off one was so remote when we started, that if somebody had said to me, three years ago, I'd be thinking about a second, I would have said no, there is no way, if I could only get one then that would certainly be enough. Today is the day that I went to talk to Joe about number two.

CM: What would you recommend for a woman who wants to go this route?

CZ: It's very personal and every case is different, and I don't think that most women could pull it off without emotional and financial backing.

CM: In other words David is possible because of a certain affluence and women being free to do it today. This wouldn't have been quite possible ten years ago?

CZ: Well it was done ten years ago, but I think it was done in a very different way.

CM: You would have had more to cope with emotionally.

CZ: There is no question about it. Maybe I'm putting too much emphasis on the financial aspect; what I feel really good about is that I have not asked my family for anything.

CM: In the end it all worked out?

CZ: It's been better than I ever would have expected. It has not changed my life drastically at all. I think it changes couples' lives much more drastically.

CM: So you feel if you had been in a couple situation it would have probably been more complicated?

CZ: From what I've seen in friends in couples, there is a really difficult time of adjustment when a baby is present and I haven't had that.

Camilla Hoover
Hospital delivery, induced labor, second child

Caterine Milinaire: Your new baby boy is two weeks old now, how did the birth go?

Camilla Hoover: Quickly, I had it induced.

CM: Were you aware of the different choices that you had?

CH: Yes, I know about natural childbirth and exercises. I heard about having babies induced eight years ago when I first came to America from Sweden. I thought it was a fabulous idea. My girlfriends all did it that way. For Herbert, my first baby, I was going to do it that way, but he came one month early so I didn't get a chance.

CM: Induced means that you choose the time of birth?

CH: Yes, you choose the time to bring on the labor with certain drugs. Usually, the doctor waits until your due date. Mine was February 5, my doctor came back the 29th of January. I went to see him and said, "I can't stand this anymore. I am getting fat and I am really impatient for this baby to be born." He said, "Let's examine you." I had had a few contractions already. They didn't mean anything, it was just the baby turning around and he said I was a little bit dilated. So I was really ready despite the fact that it was a week early. He said, "Do you want to have it this afternoon?" and I said, "No, I have a party tonight, but tomorrow will be fine." I went and had my hair done first and I went to Doctor's Hospital at five the next day. They wrote down all the information like age, address and then, up in the bedroom, I filled out another form. Then they took a blood test, blood pressure, listened to my heart and the nurses asked me what I was doing there! I guess they did not know I was going to have it induced. They asked my husband Bunker to leave and they started preparing me: an enema and a shave, but only halfway, just between the legs.

CM: How did you feel about that?

CH: It's embarrassing, but I am very ticklish so I was actually giggling.

CM: How did you feel about being administered an enema?

CH: That's nothing. It goes very fast and they are very professional. I was talking on the phone to a friend at the time. It didn't bother me the second time. Once you've had it done you know how it goes. They took me downstairs to a preparation room. I took my book along because I figured it would take awhile as the doctor hadn't arrived yet. A little while later they inserted a needle in my hand. It must have had different tiny little exits, like a hollow fork, because they kept on adding different solutions at the same time without ever removing anything. My hand was taped flat on a wooden plaque. They gave me glucose drops, it makes you stronger and helps you come around faster afterward. My husband was allowed in again. The doctor arrived a few minutes after him and straight away they added the stimulator of labor: pitocin. And I tell you, within minutes, the whole process started. The whole grapefruit stood up!

CM: What grapefruit?

CH: Well, I guess the bottom of the baby when it starts to get into position. It looked funny, that grapefruit shape. Bunker had his eyes wide open watching it.

CM: What did the medicine feel like?

CH: It didn't hurt. It was the first contraction. They listened to the heartbeat. They have this special machine that amplifies the sound. It was pounding through the whole room! Tsch...schut...tsch... schut! Within ten minutes it started hurting because the drug brings it on so fast. Instead of dragging on for hours, it's within minutes. Like very bad period pains down in the back and I said, "All right Doc, I don't want to be around anymore!" Bunker had to leave and the doctor said, "All right, this is going to take thirty seconds and you will be out. It's going to burn first." It burns in your veins. It's the Demerol to put you to sleep and Sparine. They never had to give me another shot or anything. It all goes through that needle. From different bottles, into the needle, out into the veins through various exits, peculiar! I thought, "Surely it can't take thirty seconds." And then this thing started burning and I said, "It really burns!" They told me to close my eyes and I did. I promise you that within fifteen seconds I was floating.

It's a great feeling and I wanted to tell them I could still hear them talk, my mind was still working. I could not actually make any sense out of what they were saying. I wanted to tell the doctor he had been fooling me because it didn't really take thirty seconds, but I couldn't form the words. It came out like a blur. I imagined or maybe heard the nurse saying, "Mrs. Hoover you are just drunk, you are an old drunkard." And then I was out. I remember waking up a little bit when they moved that table to the delivery room.

CM: How about the breaking of the waters?

CH: Oh, I have forgotten to tell you. The doctor broke my water before. I had asked him if he had to do it while I was still awake, usually they do it after you are out. But he had to examine me anyway to see if the medicine was really working, if I had dilated enough. He put a couple of fingers in, I guess, and said it was dilated a lot. He was examining me and it was hurting a lot. You know how it is to get touched at that point. He put in a small instrument and caught the membrane surrounding the waters and broke open the bag. Fluid came rushing out and I said, "Jesus Christ, that hurts!" And then it was finished, it took a second.

CM: Back in the delivery room . . .

CH: I was completely out. Apparently, they wait until the baby starts to come down the birth canal to wheel you into the delivery room and they give you gas and oxygen as the delivery happens.

CM: Now the contractions are going on and the baby is on its way out but, since you are not pushing, do they have to deliver the baby with forceps?

CH: No, they had to with my first baby because he was all twisted, but since the muscles are still working, they can expel the baby. It's your mind that is asleep.

CM: How long did it take?

CH: The doctor came at seven at night. A few minutes later he gave me the drug to stimulate labor. The baby was born at ten. Three hours. I woke up in the recovery room. I had been there an hour. The first thing I remembered was being wheeled out of that place into the corridor. It

was around eleven at night. They took me by the nursery and pointed through the glass separation saying, "Look, there is your baby." Bunker was there and some other people. I remember someone saying, in a cute tone, "Isn't this a happy moment?" I was completely groggy. Bunker was holding up my head and I kept saying to him, "I can't see without my glasses." He went to get them. I felt very much as if I was very drunk and all I could say was "Oh! It's a little boy, how nice! Bunker, are you disappointed?" I knew he wanted a girl. His answer came back but I forgot it the minute he said it and I would ask again. I was taken to my room and slept all night. I did not see my baby until the evening of the next day. You know, I had cramps after this second baby for two days afterwards. They had to give me a lot of codeine and it also hurt from the episiotomy. While I was out I was also given a shot to dry up the milk.

CM: So, for two days you were loaded with medicines?

CH: I loved it. I felt good. People would come with flowers and I'd welcome them happily. I didn't feel any pain. I really don't like pain.

CM: How do you know you are going to be in pain?

CH: Because it was painful enough before I got the shot. I didn't want to hang around, really. Bunker was very disappointed. He wanted to see the birth. I could watch you having a baby but I couldn't watch me having a baby!

CM: You thought about having natural childbirth?

CH: I thought about it for a very short time, like two seconds. You know the only trouble when you are put out is that you cannot connect the baby with yourself. It's like going to a place, you go to sleep and the next day are given a present of the baby. I could not put the womb and baby as part of each other because I did not see it happen, I suppose. That's the only thing I sort of regret. But I would much rather endure that than worrying about being around. I am a different kind of person than you.

It was very difficult for me. I kept on looking at that baby and saying, "I cannot believe it, I cannot believe he came from me." It was not a big thing but I thought about that for awhile after I had been put to sleep to have my first baby.

DATE (MO., DY., YR.) | LOCATION | SERVICE

Williamson

AGE | DOCTOR

IF NO PLATE, PRINT NAME, SEX, AND HISTORY NO.

Parents' Copy

TAPE NO. | SEX

DATE OF BIRTH | RACE

PRINTS TAKEN BY

DATE

BABY'S LEFT FOOTPRINT | MOTHER'S RIGHT INDEX FINGERPRINT | BABY'S RIGHT FOOTPRINT

THE NEW YORK HOSPITAL | NEWBORN IDENTIFICATION

Jill Williamson
Hospital delivery, prepared childbirth with complications, first child

Jill Williamson took breathing and exercise classes in England. She happened to be in America during her last months of pregnancy and decided to give birth in the hospital. In the middle of labor it became obvious that the baby was presenting the back of its head rather than its face. Jill breathed right through the cross-cut incisions that became necessary in order for the baby to be born without ripping her.

Caterine: Your baby took a long time before it decided to come out?

Jill: It was right on time. He was born three weeks before due date but the doctors thought that it would be more premature so it made the wait a little longer. In the true Williamson tradition he had to do it his own way. The whole development was so extraordinary. Friday night we were supposed to go out (the baby was born on Saturday). I felt very heavy and I did not feel like moving, so I stayed at my parents' apartment and my husband went to the theater and to dinner after the show. My mother was making me something to eat but I felt I had better not eat anything. I couldn't. And then my husband came in at about two in the morning and offered to prepare cereals for me, but I did not feel like eating at all.

In the morning, at about a quarter to eight, I got up and went to the loo. I felt a pain, a contraction I suppose. I looked at my watch but I didn't have a second hand on it and I thought, "Well, at the beginning of labor the pains are supposed to take place every fifteen minutes or half-an-hour apart or something." I went to the bedroom and then got another contraction almost straight away. Also, I started to bleed. I took my husband's watch, it was phosphorescent with a hand for seconds and I timed them. The contractions were three minutes apart. I remembered that the doctor said I should get to the hospital when they were five minutes apart! I woke up my husband and I said,

"Darling, I have started labor." He said, "Well, just relax, do your breathing and relax between contractions." I said, "I don't think that's possible, they are three minutes apart!" He jumped out of bed, went to get my mother and then went to take a shower. Meanwhile, I was sick, sick to my stomach, vomiting. I called the doctor and told him. He said, "Are you sure you don't have the flu?" "No," I said, "I am sick with every contraction and they are coming every two and a half minutes now!" He said, "Get your ass in here fast!" And Nicol is singing in the shower!

We arrived at the hospital and, for openers, you have to fill out all sorts of forms while you are doubling over with contractions. They ask you for a $600.00 deposit before you can get any further! It's insane! They could ask for any amount and you would say yes because you want so much to go and lie down somewhere! Luckily, my mother had a hospital credit card. Can you imagine that? It's like going to shop for a very expensive toy in a big department store.

I was put in a little room and the nurses started preparing me. When they saw how advanced I was they immediately called the doctor. Nicol was marvelous, he kept reminding me to take the contractions on, to relax and breathe and I kept on being sick all over him and everything else. The doctor arrived and examined me. The water hadn't broken yet but there was a lot of blood. The baby had turned the wrong way. He was facing upwards instead of down and the contractions were coming on so fast that they had to slow them down with medicine and monitor the heartbeat. Something was slipped inside of me to attach to the baby's head and register the rhythm. I was huffing and puffing but there is really no description for it all. It seemed to happen in another dimension. The first time I looked at the watch it was a quarter to eight and the baby was actually born at four minutes past four in the afternoon and that was the next time I looked at the clock! I thought, "Where did the time go?"

Finally, they could not turn the baby around. He was blocking off my bladder. They broke the water bag and took me up to the delivery room. Meanwhile, the baby turned sideways, presenting the broader side of himself. The doctor had to cut me lengthwise and sideways, all the way into the muscle of the leg. That is the only pain that I feel now, the stitches.

It was the most incredible feeling when the baby came out. I had to pant and hold it as they were making the incisions. It didn't hurt because somehow the pressure of the baby had numbed the area. I was given a paper bag to breathe into because of hyperventilation and they told me to push.

C: And Nicol was with you the whole time?

J: No, he had a matinee performance scheduled at the theater and the doctor told him that it would be a difficult birth. So, around one o'clock, they suggested that he go to the theater to perform and come back afterwards. The moment the curtain came down, at the end of the play, Luc was born.

I hadn't realized that anything was wrong. I was so much in my own little world. Nicol knew and he was so fantastic all the way through. It was so good having him there. At one point, he hugged me really strongly as the contraction was shaking me and that felt really good.

When the baby was actually being born, there were five people in attendance: the doctor, a young Chinese doctor, an English midwife, and two nurses. They were all helping me with the breathing. It was like a group of friends around me. But at one point, when the baby was actually being born, someone pressed and pushed hard on my abdomen and that really hurt. I would take a very deep breath, and then scream it out and, oh! the ecstasy when the baby came out!

C: At the time you were in pain, did they give you any pain-killers?

J: They tried to give me an epidural but it didn't work. It must have been too late in the labor. It was all right in a way because I wanted to feel the pushes my body demanded. I was so busy concentrating on what I was doing that eventually nothing mattered. I didn't want to do anything else but get the baby out. It was painful but when he came out, it was the most incredible feeling and the tummy popped right down again. When the cord was cut, they gave me the baby. It was fantastic! Nothing else like it! And I said, "Oh, what a beautiful boy, isn't he? What a pleasure and I would really love a cup of tea."

Zilina Luc
Giving birth in the fields, fifth child

Zilina Luc lives in a small village in the countryside of Haiti. She has five children and works as a housekeeper at the Episcopal Center.

I had Wilfred, Sheila, Leslie and Madeleine at home with the assistance of a midwife. Nene, my husband, was there too and a neighbor friend who held me under the arms when I felt weak. I always gave birth standing up except for Leslie. With Leslie I sat at the edge of a chair, one knee down, the other up, legs apart. It was all quite easy except for the first one. There I had pains. After the fourth one I was soon pregnant again. I went to the dispensary because I was feeling very ill and when I was examined they said I had to have an operation because this was an ectopic pregnancy. So, when I was pregnant with Zulimen I thought it would be better to have the baby in the hospital.

When I was ready to give birth I went to take the bus. As I was walking to the stop place, the baby decided to come out. After she was born, I sat down by the side of the road in a ditch. It was late afternoon but there were quite a few people walking to the village. Somebody went to get the midwife. She cut the cord; she always does it with a Gillette razor blade. Someone else took the baby to our house and I walked back holding my skirt between my legs. I was bleeding so much! But I was feeling all right. The midwife is paid ten gourdes ($2) for her services. Besides helping in the delivery, she prepares three herbal baths to be taken the following days. The palma Christi leaves mixed with various other leaves helps the contraction of the body's dilated parts and keeps the body warm.

Sandy Field
Certified nurse-midwife, home birth practice

Sandy Field has been a practicing nurse-midwife for over twelve years—after several years spent in the hospital system and half a year at a birth center she has opted for a practice of her own in home birth.

Caterine: You are a certified nurse-midwife who has practiced in hospitals, birth centers and in people's homes. How are the midwife's abilities actually affected by the setting?

Sandy: In my experience, the hospital was the most restrictive of all the places, in terms of midwives fully reaching their own potentials. You see, there is constant competition for power and superiority going on in the hospital system between resident doctors and nurse-midwives and also between midwives and nurses. The hospital units in a way limit a midwife's spontaneity and her ability to practice and interact with her client. The atmosphere of a hospital in general is one of so much caution, tension and anxiety, especially now when they are so concerned about lawsuits and malpractice insurance that it is projected onto the staff, who in turn transfer that anxiety onto the clientele.

C: And the clients don't understand why there is this rigidity and this uncomfortable feeling in hospitals.

S: In a sense. The hospitals operate under fear, they are constantly afraid of the result of their actions because of the liability factor. This is less so in the birth centers, primarily because there is not a power play going on among the practitioners. They know who they are, they've defined their roles, there is nobody there trying to tell them what midwifery is all about and limiting the scope of their practice. So the birth center has a much more relaxed atmosphere than the hospital. But still, birth centers are also institutions that operate with a degree of fear, primarily because there is always the fear that their license could be taken away from them and the institution closed. The criteria they use in accepting or rejecting potential clients is affected by the fact that they have to meet outside criteria in order to keep their doors open. So they will turn away people who they don't really feel are at risk, just because they have to maintain standards imposed from outside. That pressure is then filtered down to their staff, from the administration on down to their clients. What I found in working in the birth center here was that oftentimes clients would come in with a reluctance to be as candid as they possibly could. They were afraid of admitting to any symptom or past illness or family problem, or anything that might make the center reject them.

C: Do you view the role of the home environment as essential to the woman's ability to release and open up in order to give birth with more ease?

S: Well, I think that no place can compete with the home for that situation. When you go to somebody else's home, you still cannot open up and feel as relaxed and comfortable as you can in your own home.

C: How many years have you been practicing?

S: Twelve now.

C: And how many babies have you delivered, more or less?

S: Well I haven't delivered any, but I've assisted parents at well over five hundred births, which I don't consider a whole lot for twelve years. I'm not interested in quantity of experience, I'm interested in quality. There is no place like home, that's an old expression, but it is most poignant when it relates to birth.

That's why I say I've never delivered anybody. The home allows you familiarity, when you are in familiar surroundings you feel more in control, when you go to somebody else's place you still feel as though no matter how hard they work to make you feel relaxed, it's still their place. So when you have to ask whether you can go to the bathroom or whether you can eat or who can be there and who can't be there—it becomes inhibiting. Whereas in your own home you don't question these things, you assume them as your right. And this releases you from burdens in other areas. If you have invited the people that make you most comfortable to your birth, then you'll feel more inclined to open up and release your fears and anxieties among them because you trust them. But if you're in an institution you may be attended by a midwife who you've seen only once in your pregnancy, at the most two or three times. It's not somebody with whom you've established an ongoing relationship throughout the pregnancy. If each time you've envisioned what your birth would be like, you've always envisioned that one midwife, who you know, and you've envisioned your friends, and there were no other strange people there, then you have to some extent already prepared yourself to open up for these people. If you cannot open up emotionally in labor, you have a very difficult time opening up physically, and that's what labor is.

C: The relationship of the emotional let-go with the . . .

S: With the physical let-go, it's a let-go. And you cannot let go physically if you cannot let go emotionally. And that's where the problems are cropping up today and why you see so many cesarean sections. It's because women today are approaching birth from another place, as opposed to women twenty and thirty years ago. Today's woman has more freedom of choice, but this has also placed upon her more responsibility, so she's in constant conflict during her pregnancy about whether she's made the right decision, whereas thirty years ago a woman did not question that this was the right thing for her to be doing. Thirty years ago I'm not so sure women spent as much time wondering whether they were going to be good mothers or not, they sort of assumed it, all of their lives they were being prepared for this role—whether it was good, bad or indifferent, who thought about it. Today's woman thinks about it. When she goes into labor she goes in with a lot of anxiety, not so much about pain, even though that's what's expressed. She says, I'm afraid it's gonna hurt, but that's not what's really going on. She's afraid of opening up, she's afraid of letting go. After eight or ten years she's finally in control of her life, she's able to control aspects of her life that her mother was never in control of. So now she's being asked to let go of control. To give in and to surrender to a new experience, and that's frightening. And it's that type of fear that slows down the progress of labor.

C: Many women today are scared that home birth may not be a relatively safe choice. Are birthing centers and hospitals necessarily safer environments?

S: Well, neither is really. Hospitals have never had to prove their safety, it was just assumed. They've never had to document or justify any of the procedures or techniques or even recommendations that they've used. A lot of the procedures don't even stand up to common sense. Most of them come from another era of hospitalization and if you work in the institutions and ask why this is done they say, hospital policy, or this is the way it's always done. Home birth is the safest way to have a baby if you are dealing with a healthy mother. And I'm not just saying that because I'm prejudiced, but because home reduces the fear factor and that's a big cause of complications in pregnancy and delivery. It also limits the number of physical contacts that you have, and certainly the more people that are involved in your care the more likely you are to be a victim of negligence or malpractice or transference of germs or whatever. When you give birth at home you must share the control and the responsibility so that if the person attending you recommends something that does not feel right, you feel more comfortable questioning that decision and refusing it, whereas in a hospital you're intimidated. Even in a birth center there is a certain amount of intimidation just because you're not in your own place.

C: Is it the same for birthing rooms?

S: To me a birthing room is nothing but a hospital room with curtains on it. Of course, if you're talking about the lack of stirrups it's certainly nicer to look at flowered curtains and no implements than the traditional delivery room–operating room type of environment.

C: And also positionwise you're more at ease in a birthing room than you would be in an obstetrical room.

S: It's a step, but one of the things I'd like to say is that this step was made because of the availability of home birth. If there were no such option as home birth, none of these changes would have taken place, there would be no such thing as an out-of-hospital birth center, and if our out-of-hospital birth centers hadn't developed, then there would be no in-hospital birth centers for clientele. The birth center was developed to provide an alternative to do-it-yourself home birth, which came around again because people were so fed up with the hospital system. If you lead a healthy life, you don't need to give birth in a hospital, you don't need to be in a birth center either, and safetywise there is no difference between a birth center and a home. The birth centers tell you that you are so many minutes away from their backup hospital by ambulance. But they have to call the ambulance. Well if I had an emergency situation at home I would do the same thing, but my car is sitting right outside the house. I carry the same emergency equipment that's available at birth centers, all that stuff is portable. I have portable oxygen, portable newborn resuscitation equipment, a portable IV bag, the IV tubing, and the same medications that are used to prevent hemorrhage, all of those things can be brought to the home.

C: And you would call a hospital that you're affiliated with or the closest hospital?

S: If you're talking about an out and out emergency which to me means life or death either for mother or baby, we would go to the closest hospital. I've never had to transfer anybody in an emergency and I really don't think that's a fluke. I've never had to take anybody anywhere but my backup hospital because I don't wait for an emergency to take somebody in, and I also don't do anything to cause an emergency. That's one of the things that people don't understand at all about these so-called complications associated with labor—99 percent of the time they are caused by something else that was done to the woman while she was in labor. Even if it's no more than the position she was made to deliver in, that can be a cause of complications. The drugs that they give her have a potential risk. People don't question these things.

C: Because they don't understand what is being done to them...

S: Because they assume that hospitals are safe, and that anything other than the hospital has an increased risk factor. But that's the wrong assumption. It should be understood that birth is normal and that home is the place for birth, and that anything that deviates from that has a potential risk. That's the way it's seen around the world. We have a false image here in this country.

C: When you think more than half of the world delivers at home . . .

S: You mean 80 percent of the world still delivers at home, and they are attended by nonphysicians. In the countries whose childbirth safety statistics and outcomes are much better than ours, home birth is the norm.

C: So what varies is the experience and how safety is assured?

S: I think it will be many years before women in this country adopt a mentally healthy attitude toward childbirth. There has been too much brainwashing going on, scaring women into believing that they cannot handle birth themselves, they cannot do this, that this is dangerous. Women have been told so much nonsense, and often for reasons that have nothing to do with the issue of birth and birthing.

C: The awareness of sound nutrition and of the hazards of pollutants is a strong factor in the healthy development of the fetus. What are your recommendations to mothers in general, and to home birth candidates in particular?

S: The primary emphasis in my practice is on prevention. And my definition of prevention is nutrition. It is the most important aspect of prenatal care. Without adequate nutrition, I don't care what else you do for or with that mother, you are going to have high risk factors. Really all the complications of pregnancy, birth and the newborn are associated with poor nutriton—prematurity, intrauterine growth retardation, poor growth rates after birth, allergies, maternal hemorrhage, most complications associated with perinatology (the baby's development from about twenty-eight weeks in the pregnancy to the first month of life)—those complications are associated with prematurity and the cause of prematurity is poor nutrition. Hypertension and toxemia are associated with inadequate protein intake, it's all nutrition. You have to pay particular attention to the needs of the body during pregnancy, and if you do that then you have wiped out 99 percent of all the complications associated with childbirth. Now you're talking about 1 percent risk factor and there is no other avenue in life that offers you a 1 percent risk factor.

C: And you believe in the properties of herbs?

S: You mean natural remedies, yes, I use them in my practice. I recommend natural remedies for any of the discomforts associated with pregnancy and I use herbal remedies in labor. I also strongly recommend herbal teas during the last six weeks to prevent against perineal tearing so that women don't need episiotomies. Also so they do not have stretch marks on the abdomen, which are associated with poor tissue tone and reflects on poor nutrition. It's almost like a hyphenated word with me, pregnancy-nutrition, because the two of them are that closely related.

C: I understand that you're the only licensed midwife in Manhattan who can legally deliver babies at home?

S: Well I don't know if that's absolutely true. I was hearing recently about another midwifery practice downtown that just started doing home births. I can certainly say that there are very few nurse-midwives interested in doing home births! If you take all the certified nurse-midwives in this country, and then average out the percentage of those nurse-midwives that are interested in home birth, it is a very small percentage of the total. Midwives evolved from home birth to begin with. And for them to categorically deny that aspect of their heritage means that they don't know who they are or what they are doing or why. And that's sad.

C: How long is the study period before you can qualify as a nurse-midwife?

S: It depends on what type of educational program you go to. I went to a four-year nursing school, I practiced for two years as a nurse in a hospital maternity department, I went to Columbia University and studied midwifery for a year and have now been practicing for twelve years. That is four-and-a-half years in a hospital system, six months at the birth center and then seven-and-a-half years on my own in home birth.

C: How did the huge increase in malpractice insurance affect your own practice?

S: It doesn't affect me at all; in fact, I'm probably the only practitioner in this city that's not the least bit concerned about the issue one way or another. The rest of them are tearing their hair out.

C: Your insurance doesn't go up?

S: Mine was dropped just like the rest of them but I don't have to have insurance.

C: Why is that?

S: Because first of all, the law doesn't require that you carry malpractice insurance, the hospital requires it. I don't work at a hospital so I don't need it. The type of relationship that I have established with my client lets me sleep at night, I don't worry about them coming back and suing me afterward, I don't do anything to make them sue me. They make the ultimate decision as far as health is concerned. They are not following my instructions and then ending up with a problem, they are making their own decisions. They have no grounds to sue. I don't worry about it. I even suggested to one midwife who's practicing in a hospital, if you're so worried about losing your job, and being unemployed, why don't you do home birth? She gave me five thousand excuses and when I broke down all the excuses she says, Sandy, I don't have the patience you have, I can't be traveling all over the place and staying up all night long sitting with ladies. And I wanted to know, what are you doing in the hospital then? Why are you in midwifery, if you can't do this, why are you where you are?

C: So you really have to have a calling, you really have to have the patience . . .

S: To do it correctly you should, otherwise I question your motives.

C: Why did you become a midwife?

S: I'm a naturalist in general, I'm also not easily manipulated or easily deceived either. And though I had the same type of training that the other midwives did, and that the obstetricians basically did, I just didn't swallow it whole. If something doesn't make sense to me, then I'm not going to deal with it, and a lot of the stuff just didn't make sense. I was in constant conflict with myself, working in hospitals. I was constantly asking why, why do they lock out people's relatives, to me a husband has more right morally to be in the room with his wife delivering than I have, because this is his wife and his child.

C: Michel Odent suggests that maybe fathers shouldn't be there at all because he has noticed that often fathers tend to take over and start telling women what to do like the doctor would, because it's deep down such a patriarchal society.

S: I've never seen that happen. I saw Michel Odent's film and quite frankly I felt that Odent's own role was too dominant in his relationship with his clients, that he took on this fatherly image which in general is not allowing the woman to grow and develop herself.

C: You don't feel like the mother figure.

S: No. I think my role is background. Certainly if she's not getting whatever support she needs emotionally or physically from those people around her, then I come in, and actively participate in that area of support.

C: In other words you don't want them to be dependent on you?

S: Right, when you promote dependence you are restricting the growth and development that should take place during birth. Having a baby is a growth experience. You grow from one phase of life into another one, and you need to be allowed that space and that emotional energy to do that.

C: Which is what he says, too, he definitely feels that, as a man, he's interfering.

S: Notice in the film the midwives are up against the wall with their hands behind their backs. This is essentially where they should have been, out of the way, not interfering, and allowing the couple to grow and have their baby, but being there to allow them to know you're doing well, everything is fine, your baby is well, this is just the way it goes, I know it seems tough, but you can do it. That's the role of the midwife. Not to be in there directing people, telling them what to do, even hand-holding, unless there is nobody else to do it. That type of emotional exchange should take place between the woman and her husband, or the person that she's deemed the significant person in her life. It should not be the attachment between the woman and her midwife; I think it's an ego game, it's not healthy. It's part of the thing that I reacted to working at the birth center, they promote that type of maternal takeover and I think that's dangerous for anybody.

C: Too much responsibility on the midwife, and then the women don't tap their intuitions . . .

S: Also once they separate from the midwife they are lost again. They are not capable of making their own decisions and being responsible for their own health. That's what you should be doing as a health care practitioner, promoting the growth and development and responsibility and not taking it over.

C: You choose who you are going to deliver. How do you screen prospective mothers and parents?

S: Pretty much they're self-screened. I think if the day came where home birth got to be the norm then a more active type of screening may become necessary. But in today's society where there is such a negative attitude toward home birth, for somebody to want a home birth they have to have thought about it carefully, they've read up on it, they've considered their options, certainly if they have a disease or an illness or something like that they're not even going to look for a home birth. So with very few exceptions, women who want to have a home birth are good candidates for it, because these are women who are confident in their abilities. As a practitioner you use your knowledge and your skill to help them develop, you're not here to do it for them.

C: In other words you reinforce how they follow their intuitions?

S: They follow their intuitions, you help promote health but you don't do it for them. There are very few people I've ever had to turn away. Most people, even though they don't follow a textbook definition of absolute health, will come with a willingness to improve their health habits, to work with me to effect the maximum potential that they have. I had one lady come to me who was rejected by a birth center because her hematocrit (the percentage of red cells in her blood) was only twenty-six, she was very anemic, and they told her she couldn't possibly eat enough food or take enough iron pills to get up to their minimum of 34 percent by the time of delivery. They discounted this woman's abilities, according to their own criteria. The woman came to me with a hematocrit of twenty-six, when she delivered it was up to thirty-eight. She was a healthy woman, she was a confident woman, and she felt good about herself because she knew what to do to improve her own situation. This is what private practice and home birth can offer, that institutionalized care cannot. They cannot offer you the personal, one on one type of involvement, so that you know that you've got somebody you trust who is helping you to become better than what you are. The majority of the population can deliver at home. It's the minority that should deliver in the hospital.

C: Are there some homes that you would deem not appropriate for home delivery?

S: Absolutely not. It's just common sense. Why is it not right for you to have the baby there, but okay for you to bring the baby there a day after birth or two or three days after? If the conditions are so intolerable for giving birth or for a newborn they are also intolerable for a three-day-old. I think any home that's appropriate for the person to be living in is appropriate for their child to be born in.

Nancy Richardson
Home birth, third child

A mother of three children and a successful career woman, Nancy Richardson chose to have her babies born at home, in Manhattan, New York.

Caterine: You are a mature, working woman, living in the middle of a busy city. In spite of the choice of hospitals you chose to deliver your children at home. Why is that?

Nancy: I just had my third baby a few months ago at home. It is a habit by now! When I was living in California, through my Christian religious group, I met with some friendly medical personnel who could help me have a baby at home. I felt that it would be the safest, something not necessarily easy to set up or arrange, but I felt that it would be the most congenial setting.

C: What are the names of your children and how old are they?

N: Phillip is ten, Caroline is seven, and Isabelle will be six months next week.

C: What was your husband's reaction when you told him you wanted to give birth at home?

N: He had attended Harvard medical school and had worked on cadavers, he had worked in obstetrics and attended various births and he felt that women who had their babies in hospitals were not in control of a process that was natural and healthy. He agreed with my choice.

C: How did your mother react?

N: She gave birth to my brother and me under painful conditions with drugs. She told me about her mother having all of her children at home and that it was a good alternative.

C: How did you go about finding a midwife that would assist you at home?

N: I found that if you want to have babies at home you go to certain categories of people; women doctors are more accepting of the idea than male doctors and also older women who have seen much of it when it was not so common to go to a hospital. So I found an elderly German lady who came to my house and delivered my son. When I came to New York City seven years ago I asked around and found a midwife who was living a very beleaguered life in the Village. She has since gone on to become a professor of midwifery at Yale. And for the last birth I found her in the Yellow Pages, a truly wonderful and patient woman, really unique.

C: Since you were in your early forties when your last child was born, did you have any anxieties?

N: Many people say that after thirty-five there are risks, so I did have some anxieties in the middle of the night, but in moments of wakefulness and a settled frame of mind I knew that home was the safest place for me.

N: What would you have done in case of an emergency?

N: I would have walked a block to the nearby hospital's emergency room, or the midwife would have taken me in her car which would still be faster than calling an ambulance.

C: How did you prepare yourself? What extra nutritional care did you take?

N: I followed the midwife's nutritional advice but I also have experience now, I ate well, gained a lot of weight because I did not feel the baby should be thin and I needed the strength that food can bring.

C: How did you prepare your bedroom for the birth?

N: That is probably the most important thing to do once you have understood the importance of nutrition. I had the bathroom washed with antiseptic, I placed a dropcloth under the bed, I had dropcloths made of canvas for the top layer on the bed and a sheet on top; you have to be careful with plastic because you can slip when you are pushing hard, and underneath I had rubber pads.

C: Had you organized for someone to help you afterward?

N: I had a baby nurse I found at my church, a qualified certified postnatal nurse who was also present during the birth as a birth coach, along with my husband. You could spoil the joy of a home birth because you are so tired afterward. It is a bit like running a marathon, it's a very athletic thing to do and you need to rest.

C: As an apartment dweller did you find yourself holding back from screaming while giving birth for fear of disturbing your neighbors?

N: I was quite concerned that they should not be part of something that was so intimate, but I don't think anybody heard. Though the workmen came in the morning and asked my son if they could see me, the apartment was not quite finished at that time, and my son said no, I am sorry she is very busy having a baby and they all flew out.

C: Were there any problems at any time?

N: My second baby came very fast, and the third baby did not come as quickly so there was one moment of discouragement in a process that took several hours, but everyone was very supportive and with patience Isabelle arrived.

C: Did you breast-feed?

N: I breast-fed her for the first two months around the clock, then for five months I gave her a bottle at night. We both enjoyed it.

C: Among all your friends you must be one of the few who have given birth at home. What are their reactions to your choice?

N: I do not talk about it much, I feel it is not my business to proselytize. My decision to have babies at home was based on a practical practicing religion which would support me mentally, spiritually, in terms of my daily life through something like this.

Mary Salter
Hospital delivery, cesarean, first child

Mary Salter, thirty-four, is a film and television producer in Manhattan. Her husband is a sculptor. Max is their first child.

Caterine: Mary, today you're five days overdue. How does it feel?

Mary: Well, being overdue is really difficult. This is my first baby, so there's a lot that's unknown to me. If I had been through the whole thing before, I wouldn't be so anxious. I'm sure every time you have a baby, it's different, but I think the first time is potentially much more anxiety-provoking, just because you don't know. I'm also feeling sick.

C: What a week! You've had bronchitis.

M: I've had bronchitis—maybe I'm thinking that this baby is a lot smarter than everybody put together! The baby may be waiting till I am well to come out! I'm glad I'm not in labor feeling like this. I was taught all these breathing exercises in the Lamaze class, but I don't think they told me what to do when you *can't* breathe! My breathing is not under control in any way. If I can gasp out a few breaths, that's fine.

C: You're now thirty-four, therefore your decision to wait to have a child comes after much reflection. Why do you feel now is the right time?

M: I don't believe I was ready *before* now to have a child simply because up till now I didn't decide to do it. I've been living with my husband—although we weren't married—for twelve years. So it was a very long-term relationship. But our relationship wasn't ready for a child. I have a very active career—I work as a film and television producer, and I've been very busy, living, working. I've always wanted a baby, and I'm sure I could have been very happy having a baby when I was twenty-seven or twenty-eight, but it didn't work out then for a lot of reasons that I'm sure are the right reasons. It just became clear that there was a right time to do it. Quite frankly, I didn't want to wait any longer. A lot of my friends are having their first babies or have just had them in the last few weeks and they're thirty-eight, thirty-seven; I didn't want to wait quite that long... I'm a practical personality, I think the older you get, the more complicated things are for the first time.

C: So it was a conscious decision?

M: Yes, it was.

C: And did that require a lot of give and take on both of your parts?

M: It's not something that hasn't been discussed for many years, it just became an inevitability, I don't know how to explain it. You see, I had had an ovarian cyst that wrapped around one of my ovaries about four years ago. So I had surgery and only had one ovary left. And I was thinking, it's possible that there are going to be complications here—you hear so many stories about people that have blocked tubes. I told Mel I think we should just try now, so we stopped using contraceptives. And I became pregnant within two days. It was remarkable! And I am grateful for that. I see some of my friends that are struggling with that problem, and it takes a very serious toll on their relationship. I think that their love life isn't quite as spontaneous, number one; number two, I think there are all kinds of questions about responsibility, and I know... a lot of people take the responsibility upon themselves. They feel guilty when they shouldn't. So anyway—yes, it was a conscious decision.

C: Did you have an amniocentesis?

M: No.

C: So you don't know whether you're going to have a boy or a girl?

M: That was a really big struggle.

C: Why?

M: On the one hand, the odds are really against you having any problems like Down's syndrome until you're thirty-five. That's really the cutoff point when the curve goes way up. On the other hand, it would be really comforting to know that the baby was not a victim of that disease. And my husband and I went just nuts on it, because the need to be reassured was really important. I also felt if I gave in at that point, to this neurotic compulsion to know everything—to have everything figured out up front, it was not a great way to start. It was a really hard decision to make. And now, especially since I'm late, I go through these moments of neurotic terror. But then you calm down, you assume everything probably *is* okay; now at the end, I'm having these nightmares about the possibilities of a child that's not perfectly healthy, even though I don't have any real reason. But . . . I also think that there's a danger, in the test itself. My doctor told me quite concretely that the chances of complications for the test at my stage in the game were greater than the chances that they would find anything on the test. So, you weigh all of that and you make your decision. It was a really difficult decision. I'm glad that we made it.

C: What kind of a place have you chosen to give birth?

M: Well, I'm going to have the baby at New York Hospital . . . and I came about it in a relatively passive way. When I had had ovarian surgery before, it had been a really negative experience—the whole thing happened too quickly—there was some medical mismanagement of my case. That is my own responsibility in a way. It's just like hiring an accountant when you're seeking medical advice—you really are responsible to make sure that you've got the best person, and the whole thing happened in a way where I didn't make the best choices. So then I got another doctor, after my surgery, who is truly a remarkable person. He followed up because I was having ovarian cysts on the other ovary at that point. The whole thing got to be unpleasant and this doctor really helped me in many ways—both medically and psychologically. When he started having heart problems and stopped practicing obstetrics he referred me to another doctor. So by this time I was kind of locked into that scene. Right now I'm feeling very oppressed by the technology of the whole medical situation, even though the decision to have a doctor, not a midwife, to go to a hospital and not a birthing center, is mine. For this first child the traditional setup is right for me because deep in my heart there's a conservative element to me. So I will go to New York Hospital with this doctor who is a really fine physician and quite conservative, and yet noninterventionist at the same time. He's not a great communicator, though. And there have been little complications in this pregnancy. For example, I was tested for gestational diabetes, it's borderline whether I had it or not, so now I'm on a completely sugar-free diet. But I had to go into the hospital for tests— going to a hospital is not a good experience. I lost weight in the hospital; I don't flourish in there.

C: Do you feel the maternity aspect should be separated from the hospital aspect?

M: When there is no need for medical intervention, probably. I don't know if you're familiar with gestational diabetes. Since it's very borderline with me, and my blood sugar now is very low just by avoiding sweets, it probably isn't an issue, but there have been immediate complications. So in my case, yes—it is good that there's medical facilities to handle the crisis.

Technology saves the lives of many teeny babies—a technology that has seen serious situations in the making, and helped alleviate them or confront them at the appropriate times; it's become sort of like a master of the whole profession. I don't love that aspect of the hospitals and the machines. But on the other hand, it's foolish to say it's not good because there are times when you really need it. The most important thing is to be yourself though, the one that's making the decisions. You know, I think the medical profession is unwilling to give up a certain amount of power. I don't feel like I'm being victimized by a doctor who doesn't want to do his work; by a doctor who is mean or a money monger. I feel like my doctor is a very fine, gentle man, who has lived a very traditional life as a doctor, and he doesn't really know what I mean when I say I'm taking responsibility here. I don't think all women necessarily feel that way about their pregnancy and birth. And I don't even know how much I feel that way. But I do know that I've been around long enough to resist having decisions made for me. And when you get into a hospital, it's not even people that are making your decisions for you—it's the tests and the results from the machines and that's rather frightening.

C: How have you prepared for the birth?

M: I took the Lamaze class at the hospital. I thought I'd like to really see what the attitude of the hospital is—get a sense of the way this place operates, and I'm glad I did. I came out of the classes knowing what the hospital procedures are, and that's critical information. I have been able to talk to my doctor and say, well, I don't want to be on a fetal monitor until this point in time, how long can we wait—I found out that I *have* to have an IV at New York Hospital at a certain point in delivery; I think it's after 8cm, if there is any chance that they're going to do a cesarean.

C: Is there any chance, in your case?

M: At the moment, no.

C: Are you actually considered a risk factor?

M: Well, not really, only if they ascertain that there's some kind of cephalo-pelvic disproportion, if after eighteen hours of labor, this baby isn't coming out, then it has to be. I don't even mind the thought of that, I just don't want any decisions made without my approval, and I don't want them made too quickly.

C: Is your husband going to be with you during the birth?

M: Yes.

C: Can he stay there?

M: Yes, he can stay in—even if there is a cesarean, they can go into the operating room. I don't think they let men in if the woman is under general anesthesia. Other than that, if it's epidural or for any other major complication, the father is right there, and he's allowed there for the whole time. They can be in the room with the mother and child from morning till night, there are no visiting hours.

C: Can he sleep over?

M: They can't put a cot in the room. I asked about that. They're considering doing it, it's a matter of gearing up facilities.

C: Can the baby stay with you?

M: Yes, that's what rooming-in is. At New York Hospital, the baby will stay with you. If you have a cesarean, they take the baby away for six hours. There are places that are much more organized for the kind of conveniences that I think we'd all like to have. But a big New York City hospital is not one of them.

C: Do you intend to breast-feed?

M: Sure.

C: That means you are going to have to reconsider your work pattern for quite a while.

M: I'm taking the entire summer off, at least until September. My work is freelance so I have control over it. I can make my own decisions. I think you either feel this intense need to get back to work because you're going crazy or you just don't want to leave the baby. And I do think that's something you don't understand until it's upon you. I figure by September I'll have my feet on the ground. My husband is a relatively successful artist so we have enough money to make whatever decisions we want. It's lucky to be able to make those decisions. Some people don't have a choice.

C: What are your worst recurring fears?

M: My worst fears are that the baby won't be healthy or that there'll be some abnormality. It's a very basic sort of neurotic psychology that there is something about me that will cause this baby to be ill or not be born normally, which is just a reflection on my own genetic structure—those are my worst fears—I guess my only fears.

C: Do you think your mother recounting her birth experiences is affecting your own?

M: My mother had two children. She had me when she was thirty-one, she had my sister when she was forty-four. She's a physical therapist and always had a very active career. My sister was two weeks late and I was three weeks early. I was a very little baby. But when both of us were born, there was no observation of cervical dilatation, no really significant effacement or anything. Labor began, she went into the hospital, and bang! The babies were born. I went to the doctor yesterday, and apparently the head is really quite far down now, so I think something should happen soon.

C: How does the change in physical aspects affect you?

M: I think that pregnancy is a very interesting time, at least in my life, it's been a very self-informative experience. I see myself in a different light. I'm surprised to see that in some ways I'm more vulnerable than I thought I was, and in some ways I'm not vulnerable at all. I thought I was going to have a very difficult time with my body changes . . . I'm a vain person but it hasn't bothered me at all. I don't mind the change in my shape. I don't look the same anymore, that's for sure. And my husband has been a great source of encouragement, he's very sweet about it all. And he's enjoyed it, too. I guess after you've known someone twelve or thirteen years when they look different to you it is a surprise. I was actually pleased to see that I wasn't a silly, jerky airhead about the difference in my form. And I really haven't had any emotional problems with looking like a blimp.

C: Rather than a sort of boyish figure.

M: Well I'm pretty skinny.

C: And suddenly, you become a full-blown woman.

M: Yes, I have huge breasts and this big stomach—it's been fine.

C: Blooming into a woman, in a sort of way.

M: I suppose it's that. I see it very directly as what the body is doing to make a place—a space for the baby and to make food. I see it very practically. I like that efficiency of nature, it appeals to me. But I guess the most important thing that I really learned about myself through the pregnancy was that at a certain point in time, I think if you're in a relatively comfortable, secure situation, and I have been, you become very satisfied with your life. I've been looking forward to it for a long time, partially because my husband has just been wonderful; our relationship has grown. I think that there's some hormonal stuff going on inside me, too. I'm much calmer. I'm in a bit of an odd way right now today because of these antibiotics, but I'm not a very calm person by nature. I've really calmed down through pregnancy, and I guess my priorities have shifted. I really hope that after the baby is born, I'm going to remain that way. Because in my business—which is media—you're surrounded by frantic people. It's very easy to become insane yourself. If you have any sort of perfectionist tendencies, you can live a very frustrating life. What has been the nicest thing about being pregnant, is just being able to see that some things matter, and some things don't, and some things that matter, you don't have any control over anyway. I hope I'm going to be able to take that with me into the world again. That's the big lesson. I figure it's good to learn this at thirty-four, not fifty-four.

C: What have you prepared at home for when the baby comes home?

M: It's a funny thing, because you get very superstitious about these things. At first, we bought just a little bit, then we bought the crib, but won't have it delivered until the baby is born. Then my husband's little teeny crib that he slept in as a baby was given to us, and we slowly started preparing everything. Everything now is sitting there waiting.

C: Can you sense whether you're going to have a girl or a boy?

M: No, the crib was blue—I don't know what it's going to be! That's the other thing about not having amniocentesis. It's been fun—not knowing what it'll be.

Three months after this conversation, Mary Salter is sitting in her office at a production meeting, with Max feeding at her breast.

C: Mary, last time I saw you was just before the birth and now you have a baby boy. How did it go?

M: The birth in my mind was wonderful, truly great and without a doubt the most wonderful thing in my life. However, it was a very long labor and then I ended up having a cesarean, it was tough. I was very exhausted. I prepared hoping for a natural childbirth and after twenty hours they put me on pitocin, then internal monitors. Then I had an epidural at about twenty-eight hours because they thought that might loosen up the cervix. It didn't but fortunately I was prepared to go in for my cesarean operation fully conscious. At one point I counted five sets of tubes in and out of my body, but I must say every step of the way the decision was mine and my husband's and we weren't rushed. I endured thirty hours when maybe I needed to endure only twelve. I was convinced that I was going to go as long as I could and deliver this baby the natural way. It did not work out that way. I do feel, however, that I was in control of my own labor and delivery, what came out was the best possible result. He was nine pounds and born with a very large head because his father has a large head, and I am not a big person.

C: By the time you had the cesarean were you under total anesthesia?

M: Oh no! I had an epidural so I was fully conscious for the cesarean and that was terrific.

C: How can it be terrific?

M: It was terrific because I was there for the process. The only thing I remember was the anesthesiologist trying to distract me while the team was doing all the cutting and the pulling and the shoving. You do have a sense of movement and activity. I felt no pain at any point after they administered the epidural. But you do feel they are cutting away to get the baby out. They try to distract you so you will not be too involved with the surgery. Of course you cannot do that to a very curious new mother. My mind was zeroing in completely on every sort of frown—I mean my eyes were glued to the doctor's face and to me the most important moment was when the doctor turned to the nurse and said "Oh! a beauty," and I sighed in relief. That was the moment I had been waiting for. I am sure everybody has this terrific moment when they first hold their baby in their arms! I was so obsessed with the child's health that when the doctor made one comment under his breath I was stretching to hear anything that would indicate trouble. Then they handed me the baby, right before I was stitched up, that was the greatest moment ever! We tried to put him to the breast—he was too busy crying and peeing all over the place, but it was fun and my husband was really happy.

C: How did the hospital's reality compare with your expectations?

M: They were very supportive all around. I think they would have stayed with me in the labor room forever if necessary. They were very careful with the monitoring and when it looked like there was some problem with the heartbeat they took me off the pitocin for a while and waited until the heartbeat went up again. When you and I spoke before, I was real defensive about having it my way.

C: Do you think being hooked up to an IV from the onset of labor impeded your movements?

M: I was not hooked up from the onset of labor. Only when I went in the delivery room did I let them use the IV. For most of my labor I was moving around and sitting up. By the time they started administering the pitocin I could not stand up or move around.

C: Did your husband stay with you?

M: He stayed the whole time. In fact when I got out of the recovery room for a couple of hours, they rolled me in the bedroom and there was my husband on the bed with the baby. After he fell asleep in the chair, I fell asleep. Eventually he went home to sleep. He had been up for forty-eight hours.

C: I can see you are still breast-feeding, how does that interfere with your work?

M: Not very much. I hired someone to stay with Max in the mornings. I come to work around 11:00 A.M. and the sitter brings Max to the office around 3:30 and we leave around 6:30 or 7:00 o'clock. He only misses one breast-feeding and gets a bottle then. There's never any problem, he likes both.

C: What would you do differently next time concerning labor and delivery if you could?

M: I probably would not wait thirty hours if this problem of pelvic disproportion occurred again. There are certain genetic things that can not be changed. In my husband's family they all have big heads. So if there is not a great deal of progress after twelve hours of real labor I am

not going through a long labor again. Ultimately, you know, the line they drive into your head is that no matter how you go about it, all that counts is that you end up with a healthy baby. That's what is important. I decided not to feel defeated. If you think about how things were thirty years ago I might have died and the baby, too, and for that I am grateful to modern obstetrics.

C: Do you think too much emphasis is put on people to go through natural childbirth?

M: In a way I do. I have been thinking about that. Perhaps one of the causes for my tension was that I was really determined to do this the way nature intended. Well, in life nothing goes the way "it should." It just goes the way it goes, and I think that is the proper focus. You sort of roll with the punches.

Anna Pastoressa
Clinic delivery with midwife, first child

Anna Pastoressa, twenty-six, has taught Italian at language schools in Rio de Janeiro, New Orleans and New York. During Anna's pregnancy her baby's Brazilian father was denied entry into the United States. After the birth, Anna plans to travel to Brazil. The following conversation took place two weeks before delivery.

Barbara: Anna, when is your baby due?

Anna: They're saying to expect it any time. The midwife told me, you could have it now, you could have it in two weeks—which is really the due date. But now the head is down, already engaged. Maybe it's going to be a left-handed baby. They say that usually the baby's back is on the left side. My baby always has its back on the right side.

B: You feel that there are things you already know about your baby?

A: It's hard to say. I know that it will like music, because when there is music it moves a lot. And I dance sometimes, and I go to bars at night. I don't drink but there's music. I'm a night person, so the baby's active at night.

B: Where will you have your baby?

A: Bellevue Hospital in New York City, with midwives—and friends. The doctor is in the hospital, but he doesn't have to be there, because I'm giving birth, not the doctor. And I prefer to have midwives and friends there who can help me more and support me.

B: In what kind of room will you give birth?

A: They will put me in the labor room, and at the last moment they move you to the delivery room when the baby's coming out. The doctor is there to cut the cord. I think the midwife will be with me in both rooms.

B: Have you seen these rooms?

A: Yes. I don't like the delivery room. It's kind of cold, lots of lights. You know, it looks like a table where they cut you, a surgery room. I can do what I like there, I can have friends, music, I don't have to lie on the delivery table, but still, it's a hospital. The other room, the labor room, is much nicer. Nice lights, nice colors. I hear that sometimes they let you have the baby in the labor room. I hope they let me stay there as long as possible. And then I want to have the baby on me as soon as it comes out. I don't want the doctor to take it and clean it and show it to me clean. I don't care, I'll take it dirty.

B: Have you ever seen a delivery?

A: Only on film.

B: How have you been preparing?

A: I've been going to birth classes, doing respiration.

B: Exercises?

A: Only the breathing exercises.

B: Do they tell you what to expect of the birth itself?

A: Yes, yes, they told me everything. I know pretty much what is going to happen. The only thing is I don't know if I will really follow the breathing exercises through pain. I will try but . . .

B: You have a coach to help you?

A: Yes, I have a coach, a friend. They also tell me I can have other people besides the coach, other friends, so I will have two more in. My coach has been going to classes with me, so she will have full responsibility for me, she'll be my voice. The other two friends may not be there at the same time because there might be too many people.

B: What about medication?

A: No. It's natural, you know. A long time ago women didn't have medications to take, they just did it. So I will have a natural childbirth, and I will breast-feed, like my mother did with me. She told me not to take any medication. She was afraid that they would give me or inject me with medication without asking. I said no, no. My father was a gynecologist, and he wasn't for medication at all.

B: What are your own objections to medication?

A: I don't know exactly. It's better to keep the pain and work it in another way.

B: Are you aware of any differences between childbirth here and childbirth in Italy?

A: I think it's pretty much the same. Except in Italy, like in many other countries, they give you a sonogram every time you go to see the doctor. Every month and then every week. I think that's too much. Everyone in Italy is asking me if it will be a boy or a girl.

B: Because there they know from their sonograms?

A: Yes. When I tell them I haven't had a sonogram they ask why. My midwives say it's no problem, it's not necessary. As long as they tell me the baby's growing, it's fine. It's strange they do it so much there.

B: A new technology, perhaps.

A: Yes, it's new so they have to use it.

B: Whereas here, they're now wondering what influence regular sonograms might have on the baby.

A: That's what they told me at the clinic. Not that it would hurt the baby, but it might be irritating.

B: In your classes, do they tell you about problems that might arise?

A: First they told us about a regular birth, and then they told us about the possible complications.

B: To be informed, to practice the birth, the breathing, it seems almost like experiencing the birth before it happens—do you think so?

A: Yes, and also from talking to friends who have already had babies.

B: Do you think that helps, to know so much?

A: Yes, because I know that there's a lot of pain, I'm ready for it. I'm not scared. When I get heavy contractions—I already have light ones—I will look at my watch. I will try to be as calm as possible and go to the hospital late, when I'm ready to go. I don't want to be sent back home. So I will try to stay home, relax, try to do some breathing exercises.

B: You seem very confident about the delivery. You have no fears?

A: No. I don't feel I will have complications.

B: Do you find it hard, doing all this alone, without the father?

A: No, because I don't know how he would be through it. I haven't seen him for a long time. I've been by myself the whole pregnancy and I'm going to finish it by myself. The father will have the baby when I go to Brazil.

B: How do you think it will be to be a mother?

A: I think it'll be a lot of work, because everybody tells me so. I'm ready for it. I think it will be nice. It'll be a completely different life. I'll have to dedicate myself to the child, but I'm still going to carry on doing my things, and be independent, take care of myself. And I want to involve my child, not leave him with a nanny—if that was what I wanted I wouldn't be having a baby. I want to have the baby because I want to raise my child. Wherever I go that I can take the baby, I'll take it.

The following conversation took place three weeks after delivery.

B: Last time we spoke, you were expecting your baby at any time. Did you have to wait long?

A: He was born May 1, a little over two weeks later. In Europe May 1 is Labor Day—so I was in labor on Labor Day.

B: This was a few days after your due date. How were those last days?

A: I couldn't wait. But I had a feeling he was going to be born May 1 because the night before, I prepared all my things, even my Medicaid card and clinic card—I had a feeling that I was going to have the baby the next day. In fact at four in the morning I started labor. I started timing the contractions and I had them every fifteen minutes until five. Then they started to come every five minutes. But I still wanted to wait because I didn't want to go to the hospital and find it was a false alarm. But around 5:30 A.M. I started having contractions every three minutes. I thought they were going to be further apart for longer, not so quick. I had called my coach at 5:00, and she arrived around 5:30. Then I also called another friend with a car to get ready. I was still walking around. After my friend with the car arrived I still waited around a little to be sure it was really happening. But with contractions every three minutes I thought, I'd better go to the hospital. I arrived there about 6:00. I was only 2cm dilated and was told to go walking. I walked for an hour, but now with contractions every two minutes it was crazy, I was walking from one end of the corridor to the other, and stopping for every contraction. It was terrible. And there was a lot of blood. So I went back in and told the midwife, look, there's too much blood. They checked me again, I was 4cm dilated, and they realized that my water had broken. I didn't know it had happened, so I couldn't tell them when it did. And then I thought back, and remembered that when I went to the bathroom at about five, there was blood with a lot of white mucus, so maybe this had been the moment when it broke. So now, at about 7:30, they kept me in and I had to wait around until I dilated more.

B: Where did you wait?

A: In the labor room. They kept me there because the waters had broken.

B: And who was there with you?

A: My coach was there, and she wasn't much help though she'd been to classes with me. After a while my other friend, Beverly, came in, and she helped me a lot.

B: How did Beverly help you?

A: She was breathing in front of my face, really getting into it, not just telling me how. In those moments you just look at the person and you imitate, it's easier. She treated me like a little kid, just letting me follow her examples. And she was telling me that I was doing very well. The best thing my coach did was to put some ice in my mouth.

B: How did you feel while you were in the labor room?

A: I felt a lot of pain, but I felt good, I felt fine with the people around. The midwife came and went, she was very good; I liked her. I felt very comfortable with her and I'd never seen her before. She helped me with my breathing and then let Beverly take over. She also gave me a massage.

B: What were you thinking about while you were in labor?

A: I was thinking about me. I wasn't thinking about the baby. I was thinking that it was painful, it was just me and the pain. All those things I'd talked about—music, friends—I forgot it all. I thought about the baby when I started pushing. Then I was thinking, the baby is pushing, too, I have to help him. We were working as a team.

I had to push for about two hours. I was lying down and Beverly was helping me to sit up and push. Actually I was pushing more than they were telling me to because I wanted this baby to come out. So when the midwife said, go back down and rest, I kept pushing. It took a long time, he didn't come out easily. And then, probably when he was almost out, they took me to the delivery room. All the way I was feeling like pushing and the midwife was saying, don't push because we have to cut you. I said I didn't want to be cut but she said I was too small, I was going to tear, and I trusted her. So I said, hurry hurry, because I have to push. We got there and she cut me. I felt the cut but I didn't really feel any pain. There was so much pain already. After that he came out fast. While he was coming out Beverly was describing him to me: a lot of black hair . . . big eyes . . . it's a cute baby . . . and finally, it's a boy. They put him on me right away, and I was shocked. I saw this baby and I couldn't believe it that this came out of me, it was a strange feeling. But he didn't cry at all, he was just there, looking, and I was looking at him.

B: What felt good to you in labor—besides the end?

A: Beverly massaged my back—that was good. Also the midwife was pushing with her fingers on one side of me, like shiatsu, in one spot, and that felt good.

B: You didn't mention medication. You didn't have any?

A: Toward the end of the dilating the midwife gave me something to make me feel better. I told Beverly to tell her to drug me up, and Beverly was saying no, no, but I said they have to give me something, so the midwife said okay. She gave me an injection in the arm, glucose in one arm for energy, and then something else.

B: What was it?

A: I don't know what it was [Demerol]. But she said it would make me feel a little spacy, and it wouldn't hurt the baby at all. It didn't knock me out or anything. Maybe it helped, it made me a little dizzy, and then soon I had to push.

B: What made you change your mind about medication?

A: The pain. But you know, I had a long labor. It was eight hours.

B: Eight hours isn't very long with a first child.

A: I felt it was long. I felt it was too much pushing and it really made me tired.

B: What did the midwife do in the delivery room?

A: She did everything. There were no doctors, only two residents watching how she did things, and I didn't mind that. She cut me and sewed me up, cut the cord, sucked the mucus from the baby's nose and mouth with a little pump. After I had the baby for a while she cleaned him with the help of a nurse. I didn't like the delivery room, but after the baby came out I didn't care because I knew it was all over.

B: How long were you in the hospital after the birth?

A: Three days.

B: Some women welcome the rest, others are impatient to leave.

A: I couldn't wait to go home. It wasn't a rest. I was always tired. There were four women in the room, so they were waking us up every two hours, turning on the lights, bringing babies, food, juice, medications. I was glad to go home. The morning after I brought the baby home, I shampooed his hair, cleaned him, washed all his clothes. It was as if I wanted to wash the hospital from him.

B: How are you feeding him?

A: Breast-feeding. I think it's the best. I started in the hospital, about two hours after he was born, after they'd checked him. I was still in the recovery room. After that they called me at regular times to feed him, or sometimes before, if he was crying. I couldn't feed him in my room, there was too much going on, so I had to go to the nursery. Now, at home, it's completely different. I can have him with me when I want.

B: Was the birth as you had expected?

A: Now, thinking back, I expected worse. You forget about the pain. I had a sort of amnesia. I forgot a lot of things that happened just before the birth. I had prepared everything, paid some bills, done all the things I had to do, but when I came out of the hospital I had forgotten that I did some of those things. This was because of the experience of labor. And now, I forget also about the pain. So in a way I was expecting worse.

Lynn and Alan Fliegel
Clinic delivery by cesarean, second child

Lynn and Alan Fliegel live in New York City with Judson, Lynn's six-year-old son by a previous marriage. Lynn is an artist-businesswoman who paints baby clothes and sells them. Alan, a criminologist, teaches special education in East Harlem. The following conversation took place two weeks before delivery.

Alan: Our pregnancy is a little unusual. This child will have taken about two years to be born.

Lynn: I've had two miscarriages in the past two years. This is the third pregnancy, so I've been in a pregnant state for almost two years. Also, I have a child from my previous marriage, Jud, who is six; he was born by cesarean after a long induced labor. I was three weeks late. I went into the hospital and they induced labor with pitocin, and the contractions started to come pretty fast. It was like having one contraction, it didn't come in waves. You reach a peak and you open up real fast. They used a fetal monitor, and with the monitor I could see the stress levels of the baby. I think the breathing went down and the heart rate went up, and they worried.

So after a while they said they'd like to use either forceps or do a cesarean. I thought, let's just get the kid out before it gets really bad. It's amazing, they told me to stop pushing and we had to wait about an hour for the anesthesiologist to get back from dinner. But I have a good memory of it.

A: So the chances of this birth being a cesarean are greater, and it remains to be seen if I'll be with Lynn during childbirth. If it's a cesarean, I'll have to wait in the recovery room. A lot of hospitals let you go into the operating room, but not this one. We're waiting for Lynn to go into labor and have the baby before the due date—that's the nineteenth. Then there's a good chance it can be a vaginal birth. I'd like to be present but if I'm not, well, I'll be with Lynn right after.

L: And actually you'll be able to hold the baby, you'll be bonding with it before I will.

This time if I have a cesarean I think it'll be with an epidural. I'd rather be at least mentally there, so I can see it come out. Last time, I didn't like the general anesthesia, but I was glad to be alive and to have a healthy kid. I had no regrets about the cesarean.

A: I wanted Lynn to have a vaginal birth this time. It seemed pretty important. But as I go along more and more, it's just that you want to get the baby out, you want to help the baby. It's not that the doctors are pushing for a cesarean. They're saying, wait and see. They seem to be for us.

L: I don't have a private doctor. I go to the doctors at the clinic, so I have three or four doctors. I get different opinions, and I like that.

The more I know, the better I can handle it, have some control over it. The idea of an epidural is frightening, but then you research it, find out the risk, proportionately. I talked to a lot of different doctors, nurses, everybody, just to get information. If I know what they're doing, what they're giving me—how they actually do an epidural—it helps. Three months ago I was pretty scared, but giving it a lot of thought, asking questions, learning about it in Lamaze class, the fear's gone away. It's amazing what you can do to prep yourself.

A: We saw a sonogram. I saw the four-chambered heartbeat. It was just . . .

L: Fascinating.

A: It was pushing and pulsating. It was an astronaut in inner space. Amazing, this little creature, attached with a cord, floating around like this. I couldn't understand very much of it. They had to tell me, here's an arm.

L: It's a very shadowy image.

A: I've only seen a birth in the movies—in our childbirth class and in biology classes in college. The babies had smashed faces, some were black and blue, they had this stuff all over them.

L: Vernix.

A: I don't know, I'll rise to the occasion, but if there's blood I'm apprehensive. I'm a little bit squeamish.

L: I saw my friend Margaret give birth to Alice at home and I just cried. Everybody standing there with tears running down their faces.

A: Home birth, I think that's the best thing.

L: It would be nice to be able to give birth at home, and to be there with your family, instead of in a hospital atmosphere. But I like hospitals too, I think they're interesting. And I think Alan can stay over with me. He has to wear those robes and things but they'll set up a cot. And I can have the baby with me as much as I want or as little. Jud can visit. He's been practicing putting on diapers, he's taking a big interest.

This one is going to be a girl. I had amniocentesis after four months. I was a little concerned about genetic factors, and I'll be thirty-five when the baby is born. We just wanted to get as much information as we could about what was happening. The hospital recommended it, but we could choose not to. It was weird. Just seemed like the wrong thing to be doing, to put a needle in to get fluid out.

A: I didn't like it either.

L: But we'd looked at the percentages, there's a 1 percent chance that something could happen or go wrong. And it seemed worth it to find out if the child was developing normally.

I don't know what I would have done. It would have been a hard decision if we'd gotten information that something was genetically wrong.

A: We're still worried. Here's a baby, after two years of, let's get something out. Like Yogi Berra said, it's not over till it's over.

L: Another week and a half. I feel much more confident now than in the beginning, to feel it moving. . . . But if I don't go into labor by a day after the due date, we'll check in and have a cesarean—because of my high blood sugar, and they don't like to induce because of the scar tissue from the first cesarean. I wouldn't like to risk it. Having a cesarean wasn't that bad at all.

The following conversation took place one month after delivery.

L: The end of my pregnancy was really suspenseful. I just couldn't wait for it to be over. My blood sugar was going up, and I had high blood pressure, too.

A: My blood pressure went up, too.

L: I was worried with the high blood sugar, and how it was affecting the baby. I wanted to schedule a cesarean for the day after my due date, because I just knew that I wasn't going to go into labor—I didn't with Jud, and he was three weeks late. Then I started talking to my mother, and she never went into labor, my sisters never went into labor. So I just figured, there's something in the family, whatever is necessary for labor to start is missing.

I went down to the hospital and I said, I want to do it today. But they said, wait, see if you go into labor over the weekend. They weren't anxious to do a cesarean if they didn't have to. And I felt that was a good thing, because you hear so much about doctors wanting to do cesareans for their convenience.

I had to wait until five days after my due date. I scheduled it for the twenty-fourth, Tuesday. I went in on Monday night and they prepped me. I was operated on about one o'clock on Tuesday morning, that's when they gave me the epidural, which didn't hurt. One of my major worries was, if I had a cesarean, how would I react to the numbness, the lack of sensation below the waist. But it was fine. I could wiggle my toes and that somehow made it seem okay. Then they started operating.

A: I was prepared not to be in the delivery room, but I thought maybe at the last moment they'd say okay. I held her hand all the way up, and I followed them in, but they wouldn't let me past this line outside the operating room.

L: I remember being wheeled into the operating room and there was Alan, standing at the line.

A: I felt okay about it. I trusted these doctors pretty much. But all of a sudden I didn't know where I was in relation to upstairs, downstairs. I was too excited to even sit. I just stood at the line near the operating room, and the lady said, why don't you have a seat, so I went to another room, got a chair and brought it to the line. It was as close as I could get.

L: The operation was real fast. They started cutting at 1:10, and she was born at 1:23. Five minutes to cut through all those layers. It was fascinating. I talked to them nonstop. They said I was the most talkative person they'd ever had on the operating table. I wanted to know what they were doing, and they told me in advance what I would feel at certain times—constriction here, nauseated for a minute— because I think that preparation takes the fear out of it. I would have watched in the mirror if I'd seen the operation on someone else, and knew what to expect. It would have been amazing to see her actually come out of my flesh. But I didn't want to freak myself out.

So she came out, and they handed her to me. I was crying, saying, this is wonderful, Alan's going to be so happy. She was crying like crazy, so she had good lungs, I could tell she was healthy. It was great. It didn't hurt, it wasn't too weird—I was really prepared for it after all that waiting. I got to hold her for a minute, kiss her, then they brought her out to Alan. They had to finish stitching me up. I was lying there cut open, it's amazing, a big slit in my body, but I didn't even think of it at the time, I was so rigged up with those machines.

A: All of sudden I hear, hey, aren't you going to look at your baby? The nurse gave her to me. There was blood all over her ears and neck. I held the baby in my hands, she started crying and I started to move—I thought, you're supposed to move, it was all cerebral. I held the baby for an hour; I was afraid to move much, her head seemed so fragile, and her neck. It was like a potato chip, if I dropped her, she might break. Just looking at this little kid yelling and crying, and smelling her, I was amazed—miracles can happen.

L: They wheeled me out into the recovery room at about two o'clock. We had Jannah with us for a while, and then they took her for tests. The numbness started wearing off. It didn't really hurt, it was like cramps or something. They kept trying to give me Demerol but I said I wanted to wait and see if it hurt first, and it didn't until eight o'clock. Then what had been a nagging cramplike feeling became unbearable. It was the first time I'd ever experienced unbearable pain. So I took some Demerol and went to sleep, which was what I needed after all that. I took some more during the night, and the next day I was fine.

They had me up and walking the next day. You feel like it might be impossible, but if you keep walking it eases the gas pains you get after the operation.

The staff was really nice. Alan visited all he could. I'd sit in the chair and he'd lie on the bed, holding the baby. It was like a vacation, we had fun. Jud was allowed in at times when he shouldn't have been, and that was good. I had the baby with me all the time, except for maybe two or three hours at night when I'd send her to the nursery so I could sleep. I was out of the hospital in about five days. The timing was good. That's how long I would have stayed if I'd had the choice.

A: They made allowances and broke some rules. The only thing in the whole experience I didn't like was the intravenous drip. Lynn had it for two days, walking around with it, while taking care of the baby.

L: I think it got me stronger faster.

A: Also, in the beginning, before Lynn was wheeled into the operation, a nurse came up and said, here's a shot. Lynn asked what it was for and the nurse said, doctor's orders, and I said, we're not taking that.

Luckily the doctor was right there and he said no, it's okay.

L: You have to speak up and know about everything. Now we're home. Alan gives her bottles of water. Soon I'll get a breast pump so I can express my milk for Alan to give her.

A: The bottle isn't as good. I have the baby early in the morning. I like Lynn to sleep as late as she can because she has a hard day. Then I have the baby when I come home, I take her out to the post office, things like that, just to give Lynn a break.

L: A half hour here and there helps.

A: I find that at school I'm more testy, working with delinquents, I don't have the patience I did. It's both the lack of sleep and having more to think about at home.

L: I'd like to work more. I feel a constant desire to paint, and I can't as much as I did.

A: I took off a week from work, to help and make sure she was okay. After that my mom came from Ohio. About two weeks after the birth, while my mother was still here, we had a baby-naming party. Both our families and our close friends came. It was a kind of religious thing, derived from the Jewish tradition, a mixture of reform and Cabalic, and different spiritual things. A rabbi came—he's a friend and he had married us; he's used to mixed marriages and mixed groups. In this ceremony we sang a song called "Dear God, thank you for bringing us up to this moment," we did it many times and everybody sang.

L: It was a welcome Jannah ceremony.

A: And we said prayers and blessings. Lynn and I drank from the same cup of wine and we gave a drop to Jannah. It was a high point, our families and friends came together. It provided a formal introduction of Jannah to everybody.

L: Jannah sat on my lap the whole time and cooed.

A: The party brought a lot of things out. It all came to a head—I started to say something and then I found I couldn't. I became choked up and cried. We'd waited so long.

Joan Weiner
Home birth, stillborn, first child

Joan Weiner prepared for a natural childbirth at home. She was in labor for a day and a half and her baby was dead upon arrival. Years later she gave birth to a healthy daughter and, at the time she wrote this account, she was seven months pregnant again.

It wasn't something anybody ever talked about. Stillbirth was not mentioned in the motherhood books, the subject was avoided like a colony of lepers. Mainly, the books stated how this probably wasn't going to happen to you anyway, how if it did it generally meant a defective baby anyway which was better off gone and not to worry your pregnant little body with something so morbid. Nevertheless, thinking about my own death in childbirth or the death of my baby was an integral part of that first long pregnancy. When it came up, I would think of how this was negative programming. But, suppress and repress as I did, it came up and up and up. In daydreams, in fantasies, in nightmares, and no list of positive statistics, no pooh-poohing by the childbirth mavens could make it go away.

I was still unprepared for it when the event actually happened. My labor was lengthy, a day and a half, only not extraordinarily long for a first baby pushing and pleading its way through unexplored territory. I labored in mid-Manhattan in the townhouse of a doctor who had agreed to let me have it in his home rather than make me take the alternative of a New York hospital. Depersonalized, redtape, 1984 assembly line tactics, gestapo nurses, accidentally injected labor room sedation, milk-drying chemicals. My good friends were with me and the room was set with candles and things I liked: a picture of Swami, a bas-relief of Siva holding Ganesh, afternoon summerlight coming through the window, incense instead of alcohol in the air.

Near the end, the Sunday bells of church on Fifth Avenue were ringing and the tiny heartbeat was becoming fainter and fainter and the pushing was taking so much time (half an hour, one hour, two hours), with so little progress being made. At 1:30 P.M. my doctor pulled out a beautiful nine-and-a-half pound Gabrielle. She was so perfectly shaped, so delicate, but completely void of the essence that gives meaning to such beauty and joy to the beholder. She didn't cry, except for a gurgle that was fluid being sucked out of her lungs by the straining of the doctor. After that, total stillness. No life. No cry of shock or pain as adrenaline was shot directly into her heart, piercing the bluish doll's chest. There was nobody home. The driver had gone, leaving us to cry over the perfect, unblemished, never-to-be-used vehicle.

Anyway, it was easier to have this trip go down in a home, rather than in a hospital. I was surrounded by the people who loved me, who cried with me and who didn't make me feel ashamed over so much emotion. I wasn't shut away in a sterile little room with a perfect view of beaming new mothers, their arms and breasts filled with babies while I lay all empty, aching, titties abrim with surplus milk.

While I healed, physically, spiritually and emotionally, a number of people came to visit me. This was the most difficult time. They were curious and ashamed of their curiosity. They talked around the event rather than discussing it directly and though they never actually accused me of being an accessory to the death of this being, it was implied.

Could she have been saved if she was born in the hospital? One never knows. I feel certain she had repaid her karmic debt and didn't have to go any further, but there is no way to prove intuition or satisfy those who don't believe it exists.

For me there was too much time and space after the birth/death. All those hours I had projected to be filled with being a mother and taking care of the baby. I had worked up nine months of fantasy, always the child. The closer the birth came, the more I thought about my time with the baby. My whole life was cut out for me and now there was this great emptiness, the laughing void. Here and now with nothing to do. I brooded for a number of weeks. Hating all new mothers wheeling their babies down Riverside Drive, resenting each smooth swelling baby on the

street, cursing the luck of every newly fertilized acquaintance, while my uterus lay fallow and discharging.

Nor was there anyone to relate to, no books on stillbirth, no magazine stories on mothers with dead babies. Miscarriage was the closest that friends had come to the experience. But it wasn't quite the same as nine months of growing, expanding, kicking, labor and term delivery. Not the same as this.

What I learned was how very precious, tenuous and miraculous life is. Truly a gift of God. When my second child, Daisy, was born, I was completely overwhelmed at hearing her cry. "Richie," I asked, "What is it?" He said, "It's alive!" We laughed and laughed. She was alive. A soft, hungry, naked, demanding individual ready to play baby to mommy, ready to let me live through that desire.

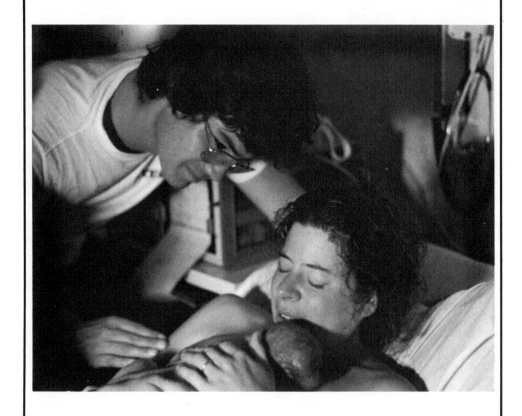

Daisy Hess
Hospital delivery, Bradley method preparation, first child

At age twenty-seven, I gave birth to my little girl, Clara. I was planning a natural childbirth, without drugs or pain-killers of any kind, and I looked forward to it with joy and confidence. Unfortunately, my labor progressed slowly and after twenty-four hours I was given a large dose of pitocin, a labor-stimulating drug. I found myself completely unprepared for the traumatizing effects of this drug on my natural rhythm.

I planned to give birth in the alternative birth room at the Brotman Hospital in Culver City, California. My doctor ran a birth center, but I chose the hospital, feeling safer in that environment. He promised that I would not be interfered with at all. My husband and I studied the Bradley method of natural childbirth, and I had also been practicing yoga and meditation for many years—so I considered myself supremely prepared for childbirth. Except for the possibility of an unforseen cesarean, I didn't see what could go wrong.

I went into labor at about 4:00 in the afternoon. By 10:00 that night the contractions were seven to ten minutes apart and remained that way through the night. I was sent home from the hospital twice—hardly dilated. I spent a lot of time in the tub, and in between was glad to be in my own bed, my husband snoring next to me, waking up to rub my back during the contractions.

At 2:00 the next day I finally returned to the hospital. I had been in labor for nearly twenty-four hours and was beginning to wear out, but continued nonetheless to be thrilled and exhilarated at the thought of the baby. I relaxed and breathed deeply with each contraction. My doctor finally arrived and announced that I was still less than 3cm dilated. He broke my water and the strength of the contractions increased (although they certainly seemed strong enough), but I still wasn't dilating.

At this point they hooked me up to an IV and began to administer pitocin. This was when everything went askew for me. I wasn't aware of an abrupt change in the nature of the contractions, I can only say that my physical experience was transformed from the difficult but exciting work of keeping myself together and allowing the pain to flow through me to a nightmarish ordeal of unendurable, practically unceasing pain. I was told later that pitocin-induced contractions are very different from natural ones. One friend described them as more like a charley horse than a contraction—or Arnold Schwarzenegger kicking you in the stomach. I quickly discovered that crying and screaming were going to be of no help—the loss of control made it much worse. The Bradley method of relaxation and deep breathing was no longer applicable to my experience. I knew I had to find some way to see myself through the contractions without flying into a panic.

I tried several methods. First, I had all the people there—my husband and a couple of friends—gather around me and count from one to fifty and then back down again, screaming the numbers into my face. I would yell orders at them: "faster!" "backward!" "louder!" This had the effect of both distracting me and giving me a stronger notion of time—a sense that the pain would indeed be ending. Later, my doctor had me hold my thighs up and push, even though I was not yet fully dilated and ready to really push out the baby. This saved me—giving me something to do other than simply "endure," and also putting me in touch with the whole purpose of these overwhelming contractions, the dilation of my cervix. With each contraction I closed my eyes and pushed gently, counting inside my head and visualizing my cervix widening to let through my baby. I found that counting to ten over and over was also a big help. I remember thinking to myself that I could count to ten only so many times before the contraction had to end—and each countdown was possibly the last.

All this counting and shouting of numbers was helpful to me insofar as it went—and indeed I may have continued counting to ten over and over to myself during the entire final stages of my labor—but these methods also had the effect of keeping me hooked into a minutes-and-seconds conception of time, a rigid sense of the beginnings and endings of things, especially these terrible contractions, which kept me in a state of near panic. I finally found myself losing my grip on sanity, feeling that if the pain continued any longer I would go mad.

At this point, somewhere during the "false pushing" stage, I sank into a state of utter withdrawal, a state in which time took on a different meaning; a meaning less in tune with the clock, and more in tune with the experience of childbirth. Through a combination of tremendous effort and utter surrender I found that I was able to live only in each succeeding moment of consciousness; to forget that there had ever been or ever would be any other moments. My experience became an endless string of separate existences, each a lifetime in itself, unconnected to anything else in the universe. And, mercifully, in each of these separate moments I was able to fully accept my pain, over and over again, without fear and without desperation. Between contractions (that is, for five or ten seconds) I fell instantly into dream-filled sleep.

I remained in this state, as far as I can tell, for at least an hour and a half, maybe even two hours or more. Then from one moment to the next, everything changed. My doctor asked Jon to turn me onto my left side and hold up my right leg. It was time to push the baby out. I felt like I had returned from a long, lonesome journey. I snapped out of my zen-hell and began to push. I was wide awake and each contraction came as a blessing—one step nearer to the end. I was beside myself with ecstacy, not just because I was giving birth to a baby, but because I could live again in the knowledge that this experience was actually going to come to an end. I remember feeling especially thrilled when Jon announced to me that they were getting the scale ready—*proof* that the baby was actually going to come out. I could hardly believe it.

Even now I can put myself into a good mood at any time by simply recalling this pushing stage. The contractions continued to be painful, but the pain now had meaning, as it had had in the beginning stages, and I didn't mind.

Finally, at 11:00 P.M., thirty-three hours after my first contraction, Clara emerged into the world. Somebody propped me up and she was handed over to me—a tiny, squiggling, slippery bundle of flesh and limbs, looking up at me in bewilderment and blinking her little eyes. She was like a little star come through me from heaven.

Frederick Le Boyer

Frederick Le Boyer is a French doctor, author and filmmaker who has developed some revolutionary techniques for welcoming a newborn into the world. From intense observation of newborn reaction at birth, F. Le Boyer (who prefers not to be labeled as a doctor) has devised various ways to make the passage from life in the uterus to life outside a smooth episode. His prime concerns, besides safety for mother and child, are breathing, light, sound, touch and the spine. Gentleness is his primary objective. He has made a half-hour film, "Blissful Birth," documenting the evolution of the newborn from a state of primal panic to one of calmness, written a book on the same subject and produced a record especially for future mothers to play for soothing the newborn. Here he discusses how he developed his theory, what he does during and after the delivery and the astonishing results of his work.

Caterine: What made you become so interested in the newborn?

Frederick: It's a long story, a long road. I realized that modern medicine had concentrated on the woman giving birth. The technical snags, that is, have been resolved for the most part and a lot of care and attention has been showered upon the mother. Methods and drugs have been developed to alleviate her suffering (if any) and most women feel much more secure now about giving birth. This is probably the reason why so many women today want to be active and conscious participants in the birth of their children. So-called "painless childbirth" in fact aims at birth without fear. Women learn about the process of birth and gain a better understanding of human reproduction. At the centers associated with birth, anxieties and fears are aired and eventually disappear.

Each of us carries within, throughout life, the imprint of birth. As I was delivering those thousands of children I kept on wondering why those babies cried so much once they were born.

One day I started to get very interested in the newborn baby. This baby is born, cries and often the more he cries the happier people are.

They say, "The lungs are developing," or "This is a sign of strength," or some such inconsiderate conclusion. So I started looking at the newborn with a different eye. I thought this child should be content, feeling good, since at last he can move freely again as he did before he was in a tight prison.

C: What do you mean by a "tight prison"?

F: Well, there are two different periods for the fetus in the womb. In the first period of pregnancy the baby feels at ease. The egg and fluid develop at a faster rate than the fetus and he has lots of room to move, he is weightless. During the second half, movement becomes more difficult. The baby is still growing but his environment does not expand anymore at such a rate. The little one's universe gets smaller and smaller. It is a constriction after the early freedom. He has to bend over, fold arms and legs. The pressure on him comes to a paroxysm when labor starts. He is pushed all around, his head is squeezed and at last he is born! At that point he should be able to feel relief and enjoy his new freedom. It seemed to me to be an extraordinary paradox, that life should begin with such a contradiction. It must be an error on our part somewhere!

How could we make this newborn feel well upon arrival?

How could we let him feel that his new condition is so far better than his previous one?

All right, we each interpret other people's actions and reactions according to our own social structure. Some people will see a newborn's cries as a manifestation of triumphant life, others as cries of torture. All I can tell you is that I have seen and listened to a lot of newborns. It became evident that what we have there is a kind of heavy sobbing. I wondered why the baby breathed so well but cried and cried. Why such screaming and lamenting? It was like an unlimited sadness. So I tried to understand what the suffering of being born was all about and how it could be helped right then and there. There is no doubt that the suffering stems from the huge contrasts between what the infant has been through before and what he experiences at birth. But also, I am convinced that the lack of understanding with which newborns are welcomed is one of the prime causes.

Most of the time babies are regarded as if they were living objects, something that does not see, hear or have a consciousness, and because of this there is no need to treat them with the respect due to a human being. I thought again and again, if this child in his mother's womb can hear, see and feel he must continue to do so when he emerges outside of his mother. It is as if, without preparation, we found ourselves on the moon. It is total anguish, first-degree panic. Out of the uterus, the body has a different weight and density. Its surroundings are vast and unfamiliar. The sounds it hears are tremendous and the air it breathes is different in substance. From then on it came to me that this child was frightened by all this. Fear is mostly brought on by the unknown, something that we do not recognize as being familiar, such as in the case of the newborn.

I sought to make the transition from internal to external life a gradual development by prolonging some of the sensations felt in the uterus, and by slowly introducing the baby to the new ones.

All new babies are, in fact, hypersensitive through the skin, the eyes and the ears. They are in a raw state.

From the moment one realizes that being born is a tidal wave of sensations, it becomes very easy to help the newborn. Let him have the new sensations as slowly and progressively as possible and not all at once.

Light and Sound. To begin with, I deliver babies in dim, indirect light to save the eyes. My whole film was shot in black and white in extremely low light. I ask for silence from all of the people around. In the womb the sounds are absorbed and softened by the amniotic fluid, but when the baby is born sounds and noises are explosive.

Breathing and the Spine. At the same time I let the newborn slowly enter the world of breathing. Air is brand new and it burns as it goes down. I wait awhile before cutting the umbilical cord to allow him two ways of breathing. He still receives oxygen through the blood pulsating in the cord while he is getting used to the air outside. Another very important area to the newborn, very often overlooked, is the spine. All the life energy goes through the spine. You become very conscious of this doing yoga, any of the martial arts or T'ai chi. The spine should be handled with the greatest of care. A newborn is held delicately and not jerked upside down as a welcome! The first gesture shouldn't be one of brutality. Whatever the treatment given to this little person at birth, the first contact outside the womb is bound to stay in a corner of his mind all of his life, and even though we cannot remember it in words, it becomes part of us.

We have quite a hard time understanding each other as adults. Children we understand even less and babies not at all. We cannot enter a baby's mental structure. I went through psychoanalysis and retraced many decisive moments in my life, all the way back to birth. Freud, W. Reich and Rank expressed it well in their work: distress stems from that first anxiety brought on by the separation from the mother. It is manifested in two aspects: one physical through oxygen deprivation when the cord is cut too soon and second by the emotional separation.

Touch. It is considered normal to put a baby into cloth wraps straight away. But, after having been in such a slippery environment, the contact with clothes for the infant is as if he were being scorched. I put the newborn on the mother's abdomen, naked, since only skin is alive and sensitive enough to be bearable. He first lies on his tummy, so he will open very slowly from the fetal position, following his own speed and rhythm. The mother puts her hands on his back and so does the father (or myself) and the newborn feels security, being held closely once again as it was in the uterus for such a long time. The baby, once outside the uterus, suddenly feels that nothing is holding him together and has a sensation of bursting at the seams. Figuratively speaking, we are holding all of the pieces together. When he begins to stretch, I turn him on his side and only once he is comfortable in that position do I turn him on his back. A little later the mother props up the baby in a sitting position. His internal attitude has changed in some way.

I am dealing here with the first few minutes of his life when all feelings are so overwhelming. His first problem is with breathing. He should be allowed to tackle it by himself within his own rhythm. Therefore, he can slowly come to terms with breathing. When the cord has stopped pulsating and is cut, I make sure that the first separation from the mother is associated with something wonderful. This is so important because it is this very separation that causes human beings the most problems. Ninety-five percent of all people are still children hung up with their mothers; it has been replaced by other things like offices and cars but they are all dependent!

I thought for a long time about what could be the first pleasant thing for a baby besides a kind hand. It became evident that the only acceptable element was water.

A bath is made ready, the water is a little above body temperature. The newborn is slowly immersed up to his neck. What happens then is wonderful: the child truly relaxes. You can see he feels at ease, often a real smile appears on his face. The child, having experienced this heavy new world, suddenly regains some of the liquid weightlessness he used to know. His eyes open and he starts looking all around. All I do at this stage is to hold him under his head at the nape of the neck, he does the rest.

C: Do you mean that the umbilical stub is immersed as well?

F: Yes, that's quite all right. The dangers of infection nowadays are minimal. As the child is taken out of the bath, a little antiseptic can be applied on the umbilical stump as a measure of safety. I have bathed over a thousand babies at birth and there has never been an infection. For the bath, hot water from the tap is fine. If it seems too hot simply pour cold water in it. Dip your elbow in the water to check the temperature. The baby in the warm water literally begins to play and to discover inner and outer space, moving arms and legs. You look at him and you really get the feeling of someone discovering the world. Often I turn my eyes away so as not to impose my gaze upon the child, their searching is so great that it almost brings tears. Some babies become calm straight away, stop crying and play at stretching their arms and kicking their legs; others take longer. The baby remains in the bath for three to six minutes. You can see the tension disappear, the

spine is loose, a smile appears. We then take him out, dry him and wrap him very loosely in cotton cloth. Then another important moment comes: we let him experience stillness. It is quite an unknown feeling for the baby since he has lived in a storm for nine months.

C: What did you say?

F: In a storm. In other words, aboard a ship constantly in movement. Even when the mother is sleeping the diaphragm is moving. So for nine months the little being has lived in a tumultuous environment. He has never known one moment of respite. His sea of amniotic fluid is always in movement whether it is calm or stormy. So we lay him flat and suddenly nothing is moving anymore. Since the baby has gone through all these experiences slowly and lovingly he accepts his new stage, even being immobile which is one of the reasons why whenever the baby cries in the following months he will have to be picked up and rocked each time this primal panic seizes him. Often this panic is provoked as the child wakes up and realizes the world is still. This and the breathing factor are the two main contradictions between life in the uterus and life outside. But in this gradual coming to life you can really see the difference in the infant's reactions: the eyes open wide, he touches himself and the things around him. No more screams and tears but a smile. When a child is born this way everything becomes voluptuous instead of painful. Not only do the babies not scream, but there is a whole special newborn language going on, babbling and funny little noises.

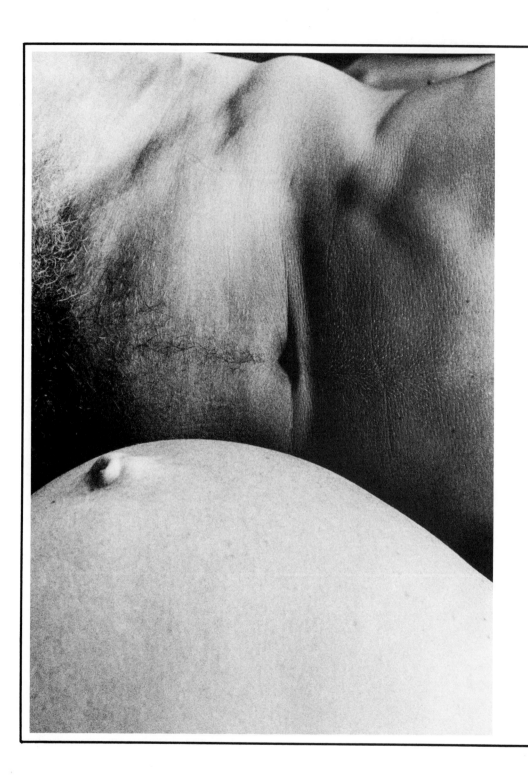

Fathers

In trying to give, you see
that you have nothing.
Seeing that you have nothing,
you try to give of yourself.
Trying to give of yourself,
you see that you are nothing.
Seeing that you are nothing,
you desire to become.
In desiring to become,
you begin to live.
—Rene Daumal

There was a time when men did not recognize that semen contained the nucleus of paternity. It was generally believed that the source of a baby was engrained within the female, much like a seed lies in the earth. A good time was had sexually, but it was not related to procreation.

Could it be that, unconsciously through the centuries, fathers have been perpetrating this belief by leaving the total care of the newborn to the mothers? Well, the usual answer to this question is that men were hunting for food, making war, cultivating the fields, going to the office, etc., so how could they have had the time to look after their offspring? Besides, the infant needed mother's milk for survival so mother and baby, it seemed, belonged together. Until recently it was almost as if babies didn't have fathers until they were old enough to walk and talk. Women were feeding, changing, cuddling and walking the little ones. It's only in the last decade or two that men have tried, in increasingly greater numbers, to understand pregnancy and to be a part of the birth and care of the newborn.

To find the predecessor of today's actively involved father, we have to look at our own social origins, to a time when nomadic men and women moved from place to place, hunting and gathering wild food for their small families, sharing in the birthing and bouncing of babies. In recent times we, too, have tended to move away from our families, creating our own small households wherever we choose, bearing and raising our children with little or no support from our mothers, sisters, aunts or cousins. And like our nomadic forebears, men and women now have begun to share the economic responsibilities of family life.

The role of fathers in caring for their babies is changing radically, not so much because of inborn paternal feelings but rather as a result of a general life-style transformation. Perhaps, as we adapt to our new kind of society, we are beginning to realize what our predecessors knew—that the small, mobile family can work better if the elements of family life are shared. As people become more informed and enlightened, it becomes easier for a man and a woman to define the rules between themselves and society. We have begun to understand that in the fragmentation and loneliness of modern society lies the possibility for a new, closer kind of relationship between man, woman and child. In this increasingly impersonal society, men may be feeling a greater need to relate more intimately with the source of life.

Traditional sex roles are fading, but even now it is more common to see a woman carrying a briefcase than to see a man pushing a stroller. Some men worry that too close an identification with babies might compromise their maleness, while mothers sometimes feel that by yielding their traditional nurturing responsibilities to men they won't be "good" mothers. But, of course, the way we act as mothers and fathers shapes our self-image as men and women. The man who cuddles his newborn baby may be surprised to discover the power of gentleness.

Men gained a new consciousness when they realized that being part creator, a father, did not only mean fertilization. It also meant participation in making the pregnancy smoother, in giving strength and balance at birth and in caring for the newborn. There is the case of a teacher, Gary Ackerman, who claimed his rights to a paternity leave when his second child was born. This time he wanted to get acquainted right away with the new member of his family and share with his wife in looking after the infant. He won a three-year legal battle, reversing the policy of the Board of Education, and granting child care leaves to fathers on the same terms as it does for mothers.

The option of paternity leave is emerging slowly in this country. In Sweden, both mothers and fathers are offered leave from work at nearly full pay after the birth of a child, and parents of preschoolers are allowed to work shortened weeks to enable a system of shared parenting. Not only does the father stay home with the baby part time, but he also takes the baby to work with him—to the library, to the store, to the studio.

Men have an inborn capacity to nurture. If it is exercised, this capacity develops. The father who wants a close relationship with his child should establish it from the start. Once the baby toddles and says Daddy, she will already be accustomed to the mother's way of caring for her, and will find it hard to adjust to a father she barely knows. Just as the mother and infant need the closeness of the first days after birth in order to become intimately attached to one another, so the father and

infant need this early closeness to "bond," and the mother and father's relationship can reach a new intensity if this bonding experience is shared.

This realization, combined with the stark loneliness encountered by many women in hospital labor with neither the partner, mother or friend in attendance, has led to immense pressure on hospitals to allow the father into labor and delivery rooms. Fathers have also won the right in many hospitals to unlimited visiting hours. The blossoming of birth centers has given the father the opportunity, as with home birth, to fulfill his potential as a strong and loving partner and father. In the past ten years, the role of the father in childbirth has developed from passive witness to crucially involved collaborator. As one midwife put it, "the father has more right to be there than I do—it's his wife and his child."

Pregnancy

Men have very mixed emotions about accepting the shape and state of pregnancy. To some it's comforting, reassuring, beautiful.

Andrew Warner, a furniture salesman in Santa Fé, New Mexico, says, "It's not every day that you see a woman carrying a child. I am superstitious, to me it's a lucky day if I pass a pregnant lady on the street. You see, I know she is in a special state of grace." Another man who was sitting in a playground told us he thinks that "Sometimes pregnant women look a little sad... so do women who are not... but somehow there is something very special, promising, in the way a pregnant woman looks which makes me feel warm toward her." To Fred Sweeda, a filmmaker in New York, "Pregnant women are extremely sexy. My wife Indiana and I have three children and every time she started to grow I thought it added to her sensuality; but some people are really inconsiderate. I remember walking with Indiana (eight months pregnant at the time) and as she was going through a door, a couple in a hurry just pushed her aside, not even excusing themselves. It hurt me, too." Most expectant mothers have experienced the embarrassed, shifting gaze of

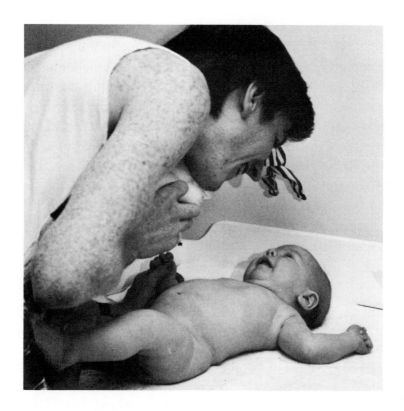

someone ill-at-ease with the sight of pregnancy. A few men interviewed at random said that "It makes me uncomfortable to be next to a pregnant woman; they just look so full, I would be scared if she lost her balance and fell on me." Or, "Oh! pregnant women are so unattractive, absurd looking!" Husbands are often also put off by their wives' bulging pregnancy in making love or feeling sensual toward them. Sometimes this has to do with the attitude that the woman has toward her own body.

Yet a man who is prepared to become a father and who wants to have a child with the woman he loves often finds the experience quite exciting. To Michael, "She really bloomed. I know it's not all easy for her, but seeing her grow made me feel more intimate, closer to the baby she was carrying."

Pregnancy and birth are an important life transition for both man and woman. But while the woman can rush off to prenatal exams, showers, baby stores, many men feel deprived of experiences and activities to mark their passage into fatherhood. For many men, the excitement of pregnancy is offset by apprehension, even loneliness. The father-to-be, besides worrying about his ability to provide for a family, may feel left out, even jealous. What is happening to his relationship with this woman who is devoting more and more attention to her developing baby, to her approaching motherhood? Some expectant fathers feel so excluded from the experience of pregnancy that they go through a kind of false pregnancy of their own, gaining weight, and suffering from mood swings and feelings of nausea.

There are many ways in which the father-to-be can involve himself in the pregnancy. Participating in childbirth classes, sharing in decisions about the birth itself, helping to prepare the home for the newborn, going out with his partner for special dinners to celebrate the baby's first audible heartbeat, the first kick, the eighth month, etc., are "rituals" that can bring him closer to his partner and to his unborn child.

One of the best ways for a man to share in pregnancy is by helping the mother-to-be to feel good about her own body. He can massage her, feel for the position of the baby in her uterus and for its movements, join with her and encourage her in her efforts to stay healthy and restful, help her to luxuriate in her physical blossoming and the growth of the baby. If he can share with his partner in all the pleasures of pregnancy, he will also be able to help her through the difficulties, especially if he can remember that the pregnant woman's highs and lows are often phases brought on by hormonal changes.

Assuming that this is the first baby, the new father has been learning, along with the mother, about the baby growing in her, following birth classes or reading the same books as she does. Often men feel the classes are comical and they feel a little foolish being in this elementary school situation with so many pregnant women. However, as the classes progress and there isn't much else to do but listen, they begin to realize that they are learning vital information. The new father begins to understand the process through which the baby is born. It's often a very abstract learning experience as he cannot feel any of the subtle

physical changes that the mother feels. He can see, in the last months, that her abdomen moves as the baby changes position; he can touch it through the belly, and he can hear the little fetal heart. New fathers are just like the new mothers, inexperienced but eager to find out how a new person develops and to discover how to make the procedure as easy as possible.

David, a musician, and Susan, a fashion coordinator, had decided together to have a child. When she became pregnant, they both went to see a doctor in her third month. David stayed in the room while the doctor gave Susan an examination as she had requested. The doctor explained to both of them how the pregnancy would progress. David was very moved watching her grow. He kept on repeating, "It's so hard for me to imagine that I was once in my mother's belly like our child is in yours now. When I try to think of myself emerging into this world from her, I find it almost impossible to believe!"

Birth

The phase of labor ending pregnancy is a weird period for many fathers. Tom and Lisa from New Mexico chose home delivery. He remembers, "We were there, both in silence, concentrating; I felt it wasn't necessary to talk. The look in her eyes and the way she breathed said it all. There were changes taking place for which there were no words. I chanted for awhile. When contractions came, her expression ranged from tension to relaxation, from bliss to grimacing. I massaged her back and felt very close to her physically."

Steven, another father who was with his wife during labor, felt more helpless than Tom. "There we were, Jane and I, in this blank labor room. She seemed to be in pain, but when I would ask how I could help she would say she was all right and she was glad I was there. We played some games of tic-tac-toe. We had prepared together, but nevertheless I felt a little lost just sitting there. At times I would breathe along with her and that would relieve my own head cramps. Keeping in rhythm with her kept me from wanting to do something else. Between contractions, when Jane's breathing quieted down, even a whisper sounded like a cry in this empty room. Jane would sometimes grab the metal railing on the side of the bed, her muscles tensing, and then reassure me that all was fine and I could help her relax. I caressed the nape of her neck until the next contraction."

Steven was very disturbed to hear women crying and screaming in other rooms. "I thought, is this the right place? Am I in a psychiatric ward or an animal hospital? It was the same kind of attitude you get in a

mental institution when somebody yells and nobody pays attention. It was a bit the same in that labor department."

The comfort a father brings during labor is invaluable. Ossie had visited the hospital facilities beforehand with Vicky. Realizing that the place lacked warmth and coziness, he brought along a recorder to play soft tunes. Many men sense that the better a woman feels during labor, the more efficiently she will be able to function; and they use their ingenuity (from poems to massages) in order to achieve that state.

Sometimes simple, loving eye contact helps a woman know that she is not alone in labor, and that everything is going along fine. If problems arise, it is often the man, the person closest to the laboring woman, who can best interpret her feelings into words and share with her in any decisions that have to be made about drugs or surgery. Probably the hardest part of labor for most men is the stage known as "transition," immediately preceding the pushing stage, when intense contractions come one on top of the other and the woman will tend to retreat into herself, not wanting to be touched, even becoming angry and abusive toward her partner. The man who wants to help his partner and baby through this brief storm and into the final stage of birth will calmly ride the insults. (She will forget she even said them.) He will find a way to stay close and distant at the same time, to touch without touching, speak without speaking.

Not every man chooses to be with the mother during labor. Joel O. declared, time and again, that he certainly was bored, felt out of place and not at all needed in this phase of life, which in his view belonged exclusively to women. Besides, the sight of a baby being born was not particularly attractive to his eyes. He would rather see the finished product in the calmness of a bedroom instead of standing in everybody's way not knowing quite what to do. Men can be quite scared at the idea of participating in this mysterious happening. One father said "It's not as if she were going to the clinic for surgery or something. She is going to have a baby and she doesn't even know which doctor is going to help her. She says she doesn't think I should stay too long because she doesn't want to

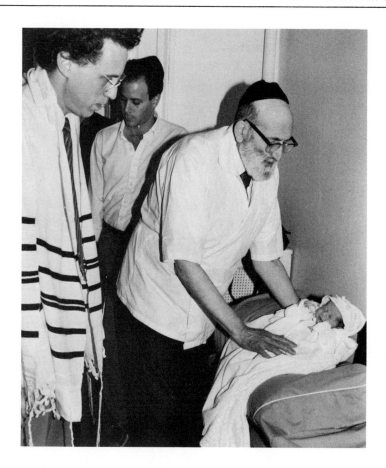

be seen in a funny state. She is darn right, I wouldn't know what to do if she started agitating or screaming!"

On the whole, however, for fathers-to-be who have prepared themselves, there is curiosity, excitement, high emotion. To fathers who realize that participating in and witnessing the birth of their own child brings them closer to understanding the meaning and the realization of a true union, becoming a father takes its full meaning. The enthusiasm, that shared intimacy of having a baby together, gives the new fathers the incentive to be with the mothers at the climax of the closest emotional and physical moment that can possibly be shared by a man and a woman: BIRTH.

There are a few fathers who have delivered their own babies at home, like Tom Law: "Catching this little being in my hands was the most extraordinary sensation I ever had." And, in hospitals such as the Nesbitt Memorial Hospital in Kingston, Pennsylvania, fathers have delivered their own babies. Both parents followed prepared childbirth courses. The delivery was expected to be normal. The mother was closely watched. A doctor was there in the delivery room in case he/she was needed, which of course does happen. The Supervisor of Obstetrics at the hospital reports that "None of the fathers crumple in the corner, many of the men experience deep spiritual feelings and the atmosphere creates a rapport between husband and wife."

In birth centers across the country, fathers are seen as a vital factor in the process of birth, since birth is seen as a family experience. Fathers help their partners through labor, and support their bodies in whatever birthing position they choose for pushing. The father may help to catch the baby, and he is usually offered the scissors to cut the cord if he chooses. In hospitals the father is allowed into the labor room (but generally not the prepping or exam rooms) and most hospitals admit fathers into their delivery rooms provided there are no complications, but the level of participation allowed varies.

Fred wanted to be there; Indiana wanted him in the delivery room, but she also knew the sight of blood made him feel uneasy. He said he would overcome it. At the hospital, every time the doctor examined Indiana, the nurse asked Fred to leave the room. Finally, the doctor called the head nurse to ask why the husband couldn't stay if his wife wished it. He was told it was because of hospital rules. Fred recalls that for the first child, "I went outside of the labor room to have coffee and a cigarette and five minutes later returned to get dressed in sterile hospital clothing, but a nurse stopped me and said 'Sorry they are already in the delivery room, you cannot come in.' It didn't make any sense and there was no way I could argue. I didn't know any better, and it was my first baby. I used to think of childbirth as an operation until I expected children, and hospitals were like churches that had a monumental crushing effect on me. I know nurses, on the whole, want to do their best; but they are harassed, sometimes without being aware of it, by an antiquated code of behavior dictated by the hospital system. Kira was born without me, and Indiana didn't see anything because they removed her glasses. For the birth of Elena, our second daughter, I couldn't be in the delivery room either because there were complications. It was a breech presentation and eventually the obstetrician had to perform a cesarean.

"For the third one, I got all dressed up again in that green surgical gear; it felt totally unnecessary. The windows in the delivery room were filthier than the soles of the shoes I had left behind. It felt dangerous because the baby was almost a month overdue. I was skeptical. Once I was in the delivery room, I felt there was nothing the doctor could do that would hasten or slow the process. Yes, I know there are all kinds of drugs, but in this case Indiana wanted to see if she could have a natural delivery before accepting anything. As the doctors thought there would be problems, there was a whole medical army on hand: the head of pediatrics, another pediatrician, a resident, two interns, an anesthetist and two nurses.

"There we were, Indiana with her legs up in stirrups, pushing away. All was going fine. The doctor was sitting on his swivel stool, and asked if I wanted to have a look at the top of the head coming through. I moved to the side of the doctor. I became very numb, feelingless, because of the lack of words for what I really wanted to say! I returned to stand near Indiana's head. I focused on her hand, thinking how beautiful it was. I wanted to help, but there was nothing I could do. I watched Phillip come out. The white sheets draping the vaginal area made the whole thing look very surrealistic, like a painting. The nurse said, 'Some fathers feel shaky at this stage. Would you like a chair?' Once the baby was born I felt a spiritual lightness, like a sigh of relief: a lifting that is only created by death or birth. Indiana wanted to know if the baby was all right. He looked strange from postmaturity, kind of grey-yellow, but otherwise in good shape. It was strange to see him disappear so quickly again. He was taken into the special nursery for observation. I was amazed to see the internal life support system. I asked the doctor if I could see the membrane. He lifted it and it was light and weird, but the placenta and all that didn't shock me. I went back to the maternity ward with Indiana and stayed with her that afternoon feeling really good. Everything was O.K. The doctor had been really great. On my way out I stopped by to see Phillip; his yellow, sunken looks didn't turn me off. I thought good welcoming thoughts to him: 'Get better. . . everything is all right. . . . Oh, gee you have a cute nose and I am happy you are here with us.' By that time I ran out of conversation and went home to feed the two girls, to tell them they had a baby brother and to collapse."

Fatherhood

To be a father with the same meaningful sense that is implied in the word "mother" is not all that easy. The expectancy of birth has been fulfilled, the congratulations are over and suddenly there is the realization that a baby is a totally helpless and dependent being . . . alive, gurgling, twisting, crying. It's quite a surprise; the prenatal classes do not exactly prepare anyone for the anguish that grips your stomach when a baby cries and you do not know how to calm him/her. As for feeding and keeping the infant in clean diapers, it is a task many fathers have had a hard time coming to terms with. Peter admits, "I found it quite disgusting the first time I changed my daughter's diapers. It was all over the place, I had to wipe her, wash her. Once I got the hang of it there were no more problems. After all, we all started that way! The feeding was easy. Bridgitt gave her the breast for six months, and I would give baby Monica one bottle a day because we wanted her to get used to it. When she started eating food I became pretty good at crushing bananas and feeding her with a little spoon."

Obviously, it is easier to be a full-time father if the profession does not require a nine-to-five attendance. John, a painter, says, "I always thought I would like to look after my own child. Since we both work from home it's easier. We make arrangements in turn with our appointments, and alternate getting up at dawn for the early morning feeding. We are each as capable, one as the other, to look after the baby. It suits me that way." Fred didn't feel like helping change, wash, or feed his first baby. "I would play with the baby, yes, but I had a job. I was gone ten to twelve hours a day. Indiana was left alone in the apartment. I wasn't even making much money. I was trying like a good husband to provide her materially so that she could be comfortable. With the second child the situation was reversed, I had lost my job, Indiana was working in an office and I was looking after the children all day. I fed, clothed, bathed and took the two girls to the park. It was really enjoyable but at times it was frustrating because I was trying to set up a business of my own and I couldn't make any serious phone calls to organize the new business because the children would scream or pull on the telephone. With the third one we both worked at home and both looked after the three of them."

Often, looking after an infant scares a father. He feels awkward with his first child. Stanley was so intimidated he wouldn't dare go near the child in the hospital. Back at home it was worse. He would only look from a distance at the crib. This went on for two months. His wife got so irritated with his attitude that she left him with the baby for a whole day. The baby was given so much to eat that he threw up a few times and Stanley had to call a friend who knew more about babies to help him out.

To some fathers who are deeply absorbed in their daily office business, the feeling of fatherhood is superficial or doesn't gain meaning for quite awhile. "Gregory only started to interest me when he started to crawl." Or, "It's not easy to look after children; they are sweet but I have little time to spend with them because I am away from home a lot." Or, "Mary Ann is so adorable, she looks like my wife. Having a child changes your daily life. It keeps you really busy, feeding and changing at all hours of the day and night. We are lucky to have a nanny." And, "The last of my four children is seven months old. He is fun, I give him the bottle once in a while; I even changed his diaper once or twice without wincing, but I don't get up in the middle of the night to find out why he cries. I am a heavy sleeper, my wife would hear it first anyway. I don't think it's difficult to be a father but unfortunately at the moment I don't have much time for the children."

Fathers are important to their child's development, adding texture and balance to the care given by the mother. A father provides his baby with a different view of the world and of his/her self. He handles the baby differently from the mother, plays and teaches in a different way. Even the father with little time at home can establish a relationship early on, initially through a pattern of shared nighttime feedings. In the first two months it is a good idea for the woman who wants to establish a good milk supply to feed the baby at night, but the father can then burp, change and settle the baby while the mother gets back to some much-needed sleep. After the milk flow is established, or if the baby is bottle-fed, the father can give at least one of the night feedings. Some fathers also give their babies bottles of water between daytime feedings (but never more than an hour before a feeding). In this way the baby gets used to the bottle, and to Daddy, and the father has the opportunity to feel the warmth and closeness of a sucking baby.

The father who shares parenting—who shares the decision at one in the morning whether or not to call the pediatrician for the baby's upset tummy, who takes his baby for a long walk on Saturday morning so the mother can relax in a warm tub—not only builds the love between himself and his child, but also strengthens his relationship with his partner. Because the less alone and exhausted she feels in her new role as mother, the easier it will be for her to feel good about herself as a woman and a lover.

Many couples find that even a half hour gives the mother a valuable break from the constant presence of the baby. Alan, who has the tough job of a full-time teacher in New York, says, "I take the baby in the morning before work. I like Lynn to sleep as late as she can because she has a hard day. A kid is really hard work to be with all day. And then I take the baby when I come home from work—Lynn needs a break from holding her. I try to hold her on my lap or in a snuggly and do something else at the same time. The bottle helps, but it's hard."

The new father acknowledges that unless he lets the baby know who he is, it's going to be quite awhile before the child calls him either Daddy or by his given name. This is no indication that fathers are ready to replace mothers in the total care of children (and who would want that anyway?). It means, more probably, a coming of age of men. An evolution in which fathers are not willing to repeat the painful oversight of their own fathers. As John says, "When you have a child, it's the beginning of a love story. But it is the only kind of love in which you have no right to leave the other."

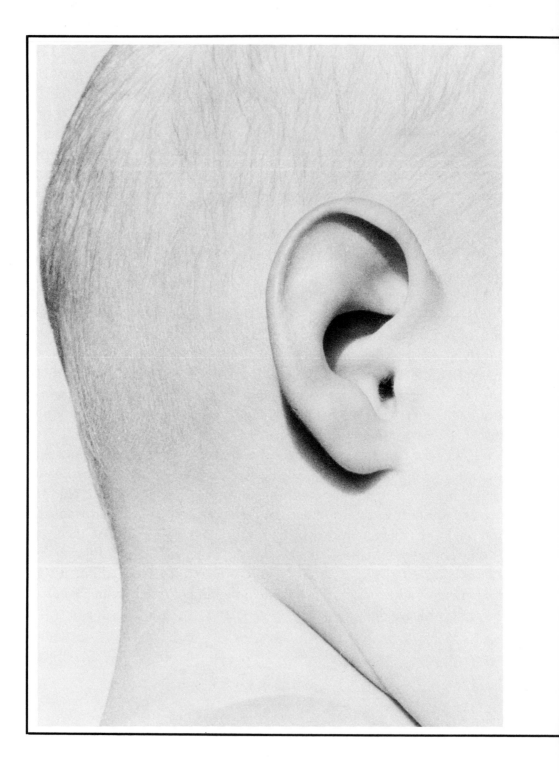

Caring for Your Baby

**What we have done
will not be lost
to all eternity.**

**Everything ripens
at its time
and becomes fruit
at its hour.
—Divyavadana**

New Mother

A week after our child was born,
you cornered me in the spare room
and we sank down on the bed.
You kissed me and kissed me, my milk undid its
burning slip-knot through my nipples,
soaking my shirt. All week I had smelled of milk,
fresh milk, sour. I began to throb:
my sex had been torn easily as cloth by the
crown of her head, I'd been cut with a knife and
sewn, the stitches pulling at my skin—
and the first time you're broken, you don't know
you'll be healed again, better than before.
I lay in fear and blood and milk
while you kissed and kissed me, your lips hot and swollen
as a teen-age boy's, your sex dry and big,
all of you so tender, you hung over me,
over the net of the stitches, over the
splitting and tearing, with the patience of someone who
finds a wounded animal in the woods
and stays with it, not leaving its side
until it is whole, until it can run again.

"The dead and the living"
Poems By Sharon Olds
Alfred A. Knopf publishers 84-Borzoi

After the Birth

There is a new person in your life, a baby. What a joy, what a shock! Even though you may have done a lot of thinking and preparing for your new friend, it's not quite the same as holding the child in your arms. In all probability, the baby does not act, respond or resemble, in any way, what you had imagined it would be. Most newborns come into the world looking somewhat strange. Some infants are round and full, others may be the average weight but still have wrinkled flesh on arms and legs, and many have grimacing faces. Observing a newborn during the first few days following birth is full of surprises. Nothing can quite prepare a woman for the first meeting with her first child (except, perhaps, witnessing another woman giving birth). Many men and women interviewed for this book said that seeing even the most explicit birth films had not prepared them for the tremendous personal impact they felt when first confronted with their babe.

It's not easy to know how to handle a newborn the first time around. Even with the second or third child, it is not that much simpler. But, approached with calmness and kindness, raising a child becomes a pleasure.

The sudden change from pregnancy into new motherhood throws many women off-balance. First, there is the internal readaptation of the hormones, tissues and organs. Second, there is the recovery period from the big effort of giving birth (also, perhaps, from minor or major surgery). Third, and at the same time, you must learn how to keep the nonspeaking new person comfortable and happy. It's a time when emotions run high and low like a scenic railway. However, unless there are complications, a more even temperament will soon return. The best healers are sleep, fluids and nutritious foods. The doctor or midwife will make a few recommendations according to the type of delivery that took place. In general, the immediate minor annoyances are usually caused by the uterus shrinking back to a smaller size, which causes cramps; various degrees of discomfort from the episiotomy; difficulties with bowel movements sometimes increased by painful hemorrhoids; and enlargement and hardening of the breasts as the milk forms. Of course, none of these may happen in your case but one thing that does happen after every delivery is the complete cleansing of the uterus. It expels the remaining bits of tissue and liquid in the same way as a menstrual period, and as the vagina and vulva are extremely sensitive at that stage it is recommended that you wear an external pad rather than a tampon. The lochia, as this discharge is called, can last anywhere from one to five weeks and shouldn't be a heavier flow than a regular period. After the flow tapers off there may still be irregular spotting for the next few weeks. If you have delivered at home or at a birth center or had a short-stay hospital program, ideally the father of the child is with you and perhaps a close friend or two will help you during the first few days while you rest. Your husband can hug the baby to his chest and change its diapers while you are still sleeping. He or a friend can prepare a meal and do some cleaning and shopping. The same situation applies for the mother's return from the hospital. Her companion could take a paternity leave from work and witness the baby's evolution from the very beginning of life as well as make it as comfortable for the mother as possible. In case the father is away and a friend is unavailable at the time, there are, if funds permit, specialized infant nurses who can help for a few hours a day or full time. If you have a good relationship with your mother or with the father's mother it is often her pleasure to help and she often has the best down-to-earth advice to offer you.

In fact, you will probably find in the first few weeks that every visitor has some word of advice to offer you. Even strangers you pass on the street as you walk your new baby in a snugli or stroller will give you some well-meaning but false tips on baby care, such as, babies don't like sunshine, it's crying because it's teething, etc. Much of the advice received by new parents is based on long-forgotten theories. Worse still, what your mother tells you will probably conflict with what your aunt, best friend or pediatrician says. In the end, you will have to decide for yourself. Go with your instincts, you know best.

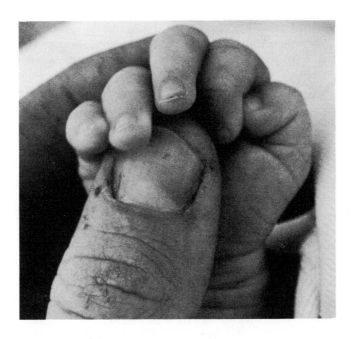

Every baby has its own rhythm and its own style. Your baby is not going to conform to any timetable of growth and development. There is no set chart on how to raise a baby, but from the moment of birth every new individual has universal basic needs. Some needs the baby can fulfill by itself; but, for the most part, your help is needed in order for the baby to survive.

Each father and mother has their own way of caring for a baby. Their knowledge may come from their own family's way of doing things, from instinct or from professional advice. There is no superior way, no definite rule. The only rule is what you think is best and what makes the baby and yourself happy. The parents' care and influence during the first years is what will determine the state of health, happiness and curiosity during childhood and adolescence.

In the following pages we will deal with general common sense guidelines and family tips on infant care practices during the first three months of the baby's life.

Prayer of the Newborn

*I am just born . . . listen to me!
Only a day or so ago I lay safely within the warm liquid
and quietness
of your inner domain. Steer me away from harsh lights,
noisy demonstrations and whiffs of cold air.

*I am just born . . . stay close to me!
A strong force has separated me from the body that
nourished my every cell. I am afraid you may forget me
in a glass cage, leaving me with strangers—hands full of
drugs—all for my own good they say, already changing
my natural equilibrium.

*I am just born . . . nourish me!
The food you took built every layer of what I am now.
Give me the best you can, as you give to yourself. Let me
feed from the strength of the sun and taste the fresh
water springs. Let the grass grow green and the sky
remain transparent.

*I am just born . . . be kind to me!
The new air filling my little lungs causes me to react, the
rush of oxygen agitates my whole frame. Understand me
if I cry, it is only a sign of being alive and expressing the
abundance of odd sensations I am feeling. It is hard to be
apart from you.

*I am just born . . . teach me!
Show me in playfulness what you expect of me. I will
learn from you and you can learn from my reactions
about your past. Relive your life through me. Tell me
where smiles stem from and caresses go and I will learn
mostly by imitating you.

*I am just born . . . give me strength!
The world you have brought me into is filled with beauty
and love but it is also made up of those out to kill and
destroy. Hold me well, guide me through each new
clearing, push me through the waves. There will come a
day when I will break away, but meanwhile show me the way.

THE FIRST FEW DAYS

Parents who are at home with their newborn infant within twenty-four hours of birth often feel a little helpless and unsure about the well-being of the tiny, unfamiliar being for whom they are suddenly responsible.

If you are giving birth at home or plan to return home early, select a pediatrician in advance, so that he/she will be prepared to deal with any questions you may have in the first few days. Many new parents panic at the slightest suspicion of a problem. A good pediatrician will accept your late night calls and offer understanding and reassurance. Within a week or so you will be more in tune with your baby, and will know almost intuitively when there is reason for concern. In the meantime the following may reassure you or alert you to problems.

Before Your Milk Comes In. Newborns don't require food for the first few days, but they do need water. The first substance to come from your breast is colostrum, which is mainly water with a little sugar, protein and valuable antibodies. So, beginning as soon as possible after birth, let your baby suck frequently for two to three minutes on each breast, increasing by a couple of minutes every day until your milk comes in (around the third to fifth day). This will both stimulate your milk production and enable the baby to get used to sucking while your breasts are still soft and relatively small. Once the milk comes in, the breasts fill and swell, and even the well-practiced baby may need help in dealing with them. You may have to soften them by squeezing out some milk just before a feeding, and by applying pressure just above the nipple with your free hand, you will make it easier for the baby to suck without having his/her breathing obstructed by the swelling breast.

New babies tend to be very sleepy, and sometimes take just a few sucks before dozing off. Don't try to wake him/her up, newborns wake themselves when they need more food—perhaps in ten or twenty minutes. The baby is still accustomed to life in the womb, where his/her food supply was continually available. This eat-sleep pattern may continue for a few days.

Some babies seem to know about sucking as soon as they are born, while others need to be educated in the pleasures of the breast or the bottle. If your baby doesn't take the breast because he/she doesn't know how or is too upset to remember, you can use the newborn's rooting reflex. Hold the baby close to the breast, stroke the cheek closest to it, and he/she will turn toward it, lips pursed, and immediately suck on the first thing to touch his/her mouth—the waiting nipple. Make sure that the baby takes not only the nipple, but the whole, darkened area surrounding it, called the areola.

Elimination.   The newborn should urinate within twenty-four hours of birth. Call the pediatrician if this doesn't happen. Until the milk comes, urination will be frequent. Once lactation begins, or if the baby is bottle-fed, at least five wet diapers a day will let you know that he/she is getting enough fluids and that there are no obstructions. The doctor should be told if the baby stays dry for more than six hours in the early days. Sometimes the first few wet diapers show a brick-red coloring—this is no cause for alarm.

The first bowel movements produce a sticky black substance called meconium. If your baby does not pass his/her first stool within twenty-four hours of birth, contact the pediatrician. If the baby is bottle-fed and produces hard, dry stools, he/she may be needing additional feedings of plain water.

Night-Day Reversal.   After the first few days of totally un-patterned existence, your baby may show signs of mistaking day for night and night for day, by sleeping more in the daytime and wanting company after dark. It is possible that babies adapt to the mothers' sleep patterns while still in the uterus. Unless night-day reversal suits you, you might be able to gradually change the pattern by very gently waking the baby from long daytime sleeps and feeding him/her. Feed the infant frequently in the evening so that he/she fills up for a longer nighttime sleep. While the baby makes the transition (it could take a few weeks), conserve your energy by sleeping when he/she sleeps—but not for more than two to three hours at a time so that you can wake the baby.

Newborn Jaundice.　It can take a few days for the baby's liver to function efficiently, and as a result many newborns develop a mild degree of jaundice beginning the second or third day after birth and lasting until the seventh to tenth day. Babies with severe cases of jaundice are placed under special lamps for treatment. In newborn jaundice the skin and eyes are tinged a very light yellow. If jaundice develops within twenty-four hours of birth or after the fifth day of life, or if the skin is more than very slightly yellow or worsens, call the pediatrician. The baby's coloring should be checked in full daylight near a window. It is best seen in the whites of the eyes, and by pressing on the nose, forehead or any other bony protuberance. If the yellow has spread to the lower parts of the body, especially the palms or soles of the feet, or if there are other signs of illness such as a disinterest in feeding, the doctor should be called.

Jaundice can often be prevented by offering the baby frequent bottles of water, and by taking the baby to a window and exposing his/her skin—as much as possible depending on the temperature—to indirect sunlight for about five minutes once or twice a day.

The Cord.　The stump left after the cutting of the cord will wither and fall off by one to three weeks after birth. The remaining scab will take a week or more to heal. The stump and subsequent scab should be kept clean and dry. If the baby is bathed, the navel area should be dried carefully with sterile cotton swabs and diapers should be folded down at the top so they don't touch the area. Some very slight and occasional oozing is common—treat it gently with rubbing alcohol on a cotton swab a couple of times a day. But if the area looks inflamed, or if the oozing is constant, or foul smelling, call the pediatrician immediately.

Cleanliness. There is no need to bathe the baby for the first week, especially if he/she is one of those newborns who cries when naked, or if you cannot make the room extremely warm for bathtime. Simply wash the face, neck and behind the ears daily, and the bottom and genital area during each diaper change. Many newborns have pimples (red with yellow centers) or peeling skin, but this is common so there is no need to be concerned.

Feeding

We are constantly getting lectures and advice about one way of feeding or the other. It almost makes you wish there was a third method. The way you choose to feed your infant—the breast or the bottle—depends entirely on your own feelings. There is always time to bottle-feed a baby, but if you decide to breast-feed you should make up your mind in the first days following the birth (in fact you should decide during pregnancy, so you can prepare your nipples if necessary). If you leave it till later, breast-feeding could be difficult to establish and you may even miss your chance.

Both ways—bottle or breast—are good, providing it is your own choice and you don't let yourself be influenced into doing something you dislike. If you feel strong and healthy, can ignore people's objections to seeing you nurse in public, if you are going to eat well and do not have to rush, then you'll probably want to breast-feed. On the other hand, if you feel fatigued from the birth event, if you are not ready to draw your breast out at any time or any place, and if you want to resume work soon, it is better to bottle-feed the baby. Of course, these are very simple guidelines to a complex dilemma. Many women find themselves confused over the advantages and disadvantages of each method.

Besides, neither one necessarily excludes the other. The mother who breast-feeds needn't think of herself as constantly tied to the baby. After the first few weeks of lactation the baby can be given the bottle instead of the breast at occasional feedings—by the father or sitter, for instance.

BREAST-FEEDING

Breast milk has the biological advantage of being the perfect nutritional composition for infant consumption. Along with its availability, warmth, and germ-free properties, the milk from the breast protects the baby in the first months against minor infections. Breast-feeding also helps the mother. It encourages her uterus to contract to its original size, and often helps her to lose weight faster. Breast-feeding becomes a sensual pleasure once the milk-flow is regulated. To ensure a good start, feed for short periods and often at the beginning. A good schedule is to start with a few minutes at each breast the first day, increase the feeding to five minutes the next day, ten minutes the fourth day and a quarter of an hour thereafter.

At the beginning the baby is happier if fed more often. This also prevents the ducts in the mother's breast from clogging up. If the liquid does not flow, the breasts may become swollen, hard and painful. Let the baby suck often the first days, but only a little at a time. Tender nipples which are not used to all this activity may become sore. If you haven't been able to avoid breast engorgement and they have become large, bumpy and heavy, try binding your breasts tightly between feedings with a large piece of cotton fabric fastened with big safety pins. This condition shouldn't last more than two days. The efforts you sometimes have to make in order to breast-feed are well worth it. Once the flow comes easily all you have to do is help the nipple into the baby's mouth, relax, and this weird, pleasurable, intimate sensation will take over. If you have trouble at first, don't panic. One of the main factors in successful breast-feeding is the relaxed state of the mother. Sit back, drink some juice or water and try again. As long as you are breast-feeding you should be sure to take plenty of fluids and to eat well.

The first substance to come out, as the baby suckles, is the colostrum, a thin yellow liquid, full of good proteins and antibodies. You can give the baby a little formula in a bottle if after a feeding it is crying and still appears hungry. It will get the baby used to taking a bottle at the start from the father or a babysitter if both parents want to go out. Be careful, however, not to give more bottle (one a day) than the breast or you may find the baby becoming disinterested in the breast, and your milk supply may be diminished since your body produces as much as the baby takes.

Sometime around the end of the second week, and again at five to six weeks, three months, etc., babies have a growth spurt. This means that for a day or two they want to feed more often than usual. By giving the baby as much as he/she wants, increasing her own fluid intake and resting, the mother will increase her milk supply in readiness for a suddenly heavier baby.

Remember that many of the substances you ingest will find their way into the milk and may affect the baby. Talk to your pediatrician about any medications you need to take.

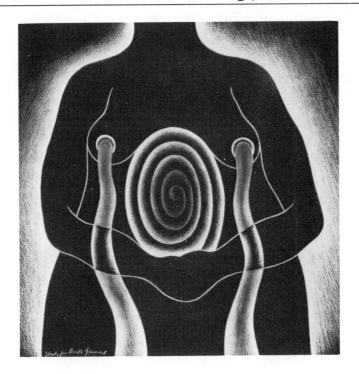

BOTTLE-FEEDING

You may have tried breast-feeding but disliked it, or you may not have the time, or may not be successful at breast-feeding. Whatever your reason, it is true that bottle-feeding can nourish your baby efficiently. It means a whole lot more objects and expenses, but it also allows someone else to participate in feeding the baby. If the baby is healthy, it does not make that much difference what kind of regular formula you prepare as long as you measure correctly and follow instructions on the can or packet. Ready-to-serve cans of formula are also readily available, as are soy formulas for babies who cannot tolerate cow's milk. "Emergency" formula can be made by mixing one part unsweetened evaporated milk with two parts boiled water, and adding a flat teaspoon of sugar to every four ounces of mixture. At the hospital, the doctor will recommend a particular formula for the baby when you return home.

If you think sterilizing teats and bottles is a must then do it. There are, however, many mothers who simply wash nipples, circles and glass bottles with a good soap and a bottle brush reserved for that use. It works if you are preparing one bottle at a time and are using previously boiled water to prepare the formula. When you are making a whole day's feeding at one time and storing all the bottles, however, there is time for the germs to multiply. It is advisable, when preparing more than one bottle, to sterilize, by boiling and keeping all the equipment in the water. If you happen to be in a place without a refrigerator do not prepare twenty-four hours' worth of feeding in advance, for the same bacterial reason. Instead, make each one fresh when needed. The glass bottles may be heavier and breakable, but for the first few months they are much easier to clean. And, since at that stage it is the parents who are holding the bottle, there is not much danger of the baby hitting itself with the bottle or of the bottle breaking. Several kinds of nipples are available. Pediatricians often recommend the strangely-shaped orthodontic nipples (Nuk makes the most widely available) that encourage a sucking action similar to that of breast-feeding and therefore help the baby's jaw to form properly.

Plastic disposable bottles have become very popular in the past few years. They are often made with plastic bags inside which are filled with formula, attached to a ring and nipple and then thrown away after use. The person feeding the baby should make sure that the bottle is held in such a position so that the rubber teat is always full of milk and the baby does not swallow air. It is very important for the baby to be held closely and cuddled while feeding rather than having bottles propped up and the baby left alone to feed.

Helpful Hints. As the baby drinks from the breast or bottle it will swallow a certain amount of air (not always, but most of the time), and this air should be brought up either in the midst of feeding or afterward. Hold the baby up against your shoulder and rub or pat its back until a little burp comes out.

The baby will take the amount of milk it needs at each feeding. You could begin with a four-ounce bottle and see how much is taken from it and how long the baby sleeps afterward. If the baby is still hungry an hour or two after a four-ounce feeding it means the child needs more nourishment. Give another two ounces and see how much it takes. If the baby only took three ounces or less and sleeps two to four hours it means that this was enough nourishment. During the first weeks feed your baby on demand, and as you get to know each other better, establish a rhythm that suits you by slowly increasing the amount of liquid given and stretching the time in between feedings.

Your baby may, at times, sleep for two-hour spans and want to drink again, or it may even (more seldom) sleep as much as five hours in a row. Do not wake up the baby. Rest, work, or play but leave the baby to dream.

By the second month many babies sleep longer hours during the night. The early morning feeding doesn't have to be dreaded. Five or six o'clock in the morning is a lovely quiet hour. It takes a little while to come around to it, but once you are awake, the first morning feeding can be the best moment of the day to think, babble quietly with the baby, exercise or read and then go back to sleep. If you can do without going to

work for the first three months, you should let your whole pattern of hours change without getting anxious about it. You could sleep in two shifts for a while; one at night, one in the afternoon when your babe is asleep (and the other children at school). You will be more relaxed that way than if you tried to sleep as you did before your child arrived.

When the baby seems no longer satisfied with breast-feeding, or thirty-two ounces of formula in a twenty-four-hour time span, you can start introducing solids, one at a time. It happens around four months in general, sometimes earlier, sometimes later. For four days try mashed bananas, another time applesauce, baby cereals, crushed peaches, almost any fruit purée is good. The idea of introducing them one at a time is for you to observe if your baby develops an allergic reaction to any of the new foods introduced.

There is a wonderfully handy little machine, "the happy-baby-food-grinder," which can turn any meal into a purée for the baby. It comes apart to be cleaned and is so small that it can travel anywhere. The food comes through easily, unlike when puréed in a blender where small quantities of food often get stuck at the bottom.

Do not get nervous if your babe does not take much liquid at one feeding. It happens to all of us that we do not feel hungry once in a while. But, if this is a repeated problem, it may be a sign of disorder and a consultation with your doctor may help clarify the matter.

Some people put their babies on whole pasteurized milk too early; it often results in intestinal disorders, as the infant has difficulty digesting it. Formula is designed for balanced nutrition and easy assimilation and should not be substituted until further discussion at the clinic or with your pediatrician.

Crying

The most difficult aspect of babyhood for most parents to accept is the crying spells. Somehow, when pregnant, a woman does not think that her own baby will cry half as much as some of the newborns she may

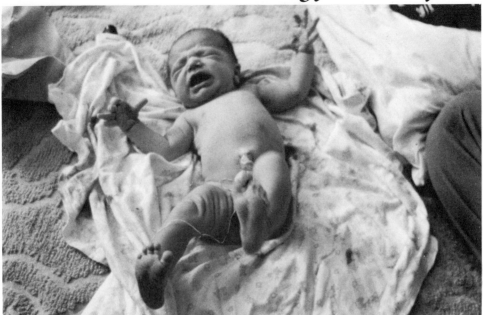

have encountered. But all babies do cry, even babes of the most calm and relaxed mothers, and there are no two ways about it.

When the mother returns home from the hospital with her baby, she begins to realize fully the demands the little one is going to put on her. At home, once the baby is born and crying a lot, you will find it very trying for your already shaken nerves. Try lying down with the babe resting on top of you, its head close to your heart. The heartbeat and the closeness of your body are two very familiar things for this little being and it often calms them all the way to sleep.

The first external day, the newborn is usually very active and certainly not likely to fall asleep very soon after the birth, as many women are led to believe. In the following few days the infant may be quieter but then may start fretting and crying again as it regains strength from food. It requires patience and understanding. As the child grows older this crying will dwindle and the tension and worry it often brings will diminish as you learn to discern the meaning and importance of each different cry. When you hear the baby cry, do not panic. Ask yourself these questions: Is the baby thirsty, hungry or wet? Too hot or too cold? Tired? Is it gas or does it need to be burped? Even after you have eliminated all these possibilities and think everything is taken care of, the baby will start again. You do not understand, there is no reason for this crying. Well, there is a lot of crying in the early months that we just cannot understand. It has to do with leaving that cozy internal life, with the body feeling strange and loose, with the new loneliness, with the food and the air, or maybe just releasing energy and a thousand and one reasons only the baby knows. All the parents can do is to take the babe in their arms and speak or sing softly, walk back and forth until the calmness returns. If the crying persists for long periods and you are getting tired and irritated it's better to put the child back in its sleeping area and rest yourself before trying again to figure out why. It's not easy to lie down and rest while a baby is crying, but it's far preferable to feeling angry and frustrated. Almost all babies go through fretful states. When the screaming periods follow a pattern, usually after feeding or at certain times of the day, it may be colic crying and should be checked by a doctor. A change in formula or in feeding schedule may do the trick. Sometimes what may seem like day-in and day-out crying with little naps in between tapers off by three months of age. It's important to remember that the most common causes for crying in early infancy are certainly not permanent and the best quality for parents to have during that short (but seemingly endless) period is patience! The main causes for crying are as follows:

Hunger. It's not easy in the first few months to establish the amount of nourishment that the baby needs and this accounts for some of the crying. You will come to realize what the feeding needs are if the baby wakes up after a small feeding or if it sleeps longer after a large feeding. Breast-fed babies often fall asleep on the breast before taking a large amount. If the child usually sleeps for a long time after a short feeding, but then wakes up early, you can be sure it is because of hunger. It's not advisable to give the breast or bottle at the first sign of crying an hour or two after a feeding. Check out some of the possibilities listed earlier, then if the baby is still fretting after a while try a feeding.

Sometimes a crying baby is not hungry but thirsty, especially in a very hot environment. If he/she was recently fed, or refuses the breast or bottle, try a bottle of boiled water instead.

Sickness. During the first three months of a baby's life there is a certain amount of immunity built up in the womb protecting the newborn against diseases. Acute infections are rare. However, colds are easily caught and manifest themselves through a runny nose, coughing, a change in bowel movements (generally runny). Breast-fed babies' bowel movements are generally loose and yellowish in color. Any change in consistency or color could alert you to your child's illness. Formula-fed babies' stools are usually darker and a little more solid, although no babies fed exclusively on liquid will have a really solid movement. If the long crying spells are accompanied by a change in general appearance and color of skin, take a temperature reading and consult with your doctor.

Wetness. Infants do not appear uncomfortable at first when the diapers are soiled or wet. It's only later, when the rejects start irritating the skin that they start crying. Check the baby often to avoid the problem of diaper rash and you will be one step closer to the process of eliminating the cause of baby tears. A period without diapers every couple of days will be an immense help in preventing a sore bottom.

Clothes and Accessories. Is the little blanket wrapping up the baby tight enough? Are the clothes too small? If pins are used, make sure that they are the safety ones created especially for that use. Check to be sure that you have closed them well if the baby is crying. Is there a toy in the way? Or a house pet wanting to get in the crib?

Indigestion. Try burping the baby again, even though you did it before successfully. If you suspect that it is gas, it should be relieved as soon as possible as it can be very painful. You can hold the baby against your chest, its head resting on your shoulder and rub or pat gently on the back. Another successful position is to prop the baby upon your lap with one hand over the baby's chest, holding it so that the face is in a down position, and rub the back strongly in an upward stroke.

Colic.   Colic, a common disturbance for infants up to three months old, is usually acute indigestion causing sharp pains in the intestines. The baby expresses this distress with shrill cries, tensing the muscles in the legs into a stiff position and agitating the arms. If gas swells the stomach it will perhaps be partially relieved through the natural way. Also, try holding your babe tight against you and walk about to pacify the child. If a regular pattern of lengthy crying develops, talk about it with your GP or pediatrician who can suggest effective remedies.

Certain herbal teas (already mentioned in the Body Care chapter) also apply for the baby, in a smaller dose, of course. Chamomile, the small yellow flower, is especially good for soothing the stomach and intestines, as are fennel and dill teas. Mint, or spearmint, also helps digestion. Catnip helps babies to sleep. It is a very distressing and helpless feeling for new parents to watch a child in discomfort and not know how to help. Herbal remedies were, at one time, the only aid our ancestors had and they are now looked upon as a lot of foolish nonsense. But, when a child is obviously uncomfortable, you want to try effective yet mild remedies to soothe it and well-known herbal teas cannot harm anyone. Some babies only have a few attacks of colic throughout the early months, while others have a great deal of trouble every day. Colic occurs whether the baby is fed breast-milk, cow's milk or any formula. The cause is not entirely known since several conditions may be present in the immature and nervous digestive system. Fatigue also plays an important part. The worst thing a parent can do is to fuss around a colicky baby. Stay calm, cuddle and rock the infant. If you can't stand the crying any more, try bundling the baby up and go for a walk together. The distraction may help you both.

Spoiling.   An infant does not premeditate its actions, they are spontaneous occurrences. The baby is reacting to the environment and to

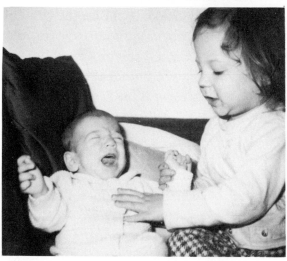

stimulation or lack of it. Basically the baby is relying on the five senses (taste, touch, smell, sight and hearing) rather than any intellectual or logical way of thinking. Therefore, an infant will not cry in order to be picked up. The first few months of life is a stage where no amount of cuddling and special attention can spoil a child.

Fatigue. Infants do get tired, just like children or adults, only their resistance is lower than ours and they sometimes express their fatigue by crying. When an infant has stayed awake for an unusually long period of time, being played with, passed from hand to hand, or just being in a room or public place full of noise and action for many hours, it may fall asleep right there or it may have a hard time going to sleep and cry in frustration or whatever. Instead of just putting the baby into bed straight away after an active period, shift into a lower gear of calmness and whispers. Sing softly and dim the lights; it will be contagious, the baby will probably quiet down. You can also let the baby cry itself to sleep if the wailing gets to be too much for your nerves. But, if after a period of time the baby is still crying, it needs more comforting and a check on any possible discomforts.

Whatever you do to relieve yourself from the frustration of not being able to stop an infant from crying, just do not take it out on the baby by shaking or hitting. The crying is absolutely not done to annoy you. All babies cry and all you would be doing is adding to their anxiety. Hit your fist against the wall instead, calm your nervous system under a hot shower, breath deeply, lie down . . . love your own babe.

Sleep

In the first month of their lives, babies usually do a lot of sleeping. However, the fourteen to eighteen hours of sleeping a day are spread over six to eight short sleeping periods within twenty-four hours. Some newborns rapidly adopt a pattern of daytime sleep and nighttime wakefulness, which can be quite frustrating for exhausted parents. It is up to you to encourage your baby to change his/her hours, if you wish.

A baby will wake up, cry a little to attract attention to its state of wakefulness, then cry a little louder if not picked up straight away. Once fed to stomach's content and burped, the child will either fall back to sleep or gurgle, stare, stretch, smile, yawn or cry or eventually nod off to slumberland again.

Once you have recuperated from birth, give yourself some time out. The baby can stay in the care of the father, a friend who knows about infants or a baby minder while you go out and air your brains for a few hours. Do it after a feeding, when the baby has gone to sleep. This way you can leave knowing that the baby is well taken care of. If you are breast-feeding, call an hour or two later to check that everything is all right. In case the baby is awake and you have an appointment that prevents your return, a bottle you have left beforehand can always be given. Also, it's best not to leave a babysitter you do not know in charge of your newborn longer than an hour or so or you may get anxious. Try the person out before you leave your baby with anyone for an evening. Until babies are much older, they don't really know that the person caring for them is not their mother or father. So as long as you are confident that the sitter can give the baby the comfort it needs, you needn't worry about infant anxieties.

Whether your baby is sleeping or not, never leave the child alone. If anything should happen while you went shopping around the corner or visiting a neighbor, you would be a lot more upset than if you took a sleeping or crying baby with you.

A baby can sleep just as well outdoors if the weather is fine. Fresh air is very important to the baby's health. If it is cold but sunny outside, bundle up the baby in woolies, blankets, bonnet, mittens and go for a walk together. If you leave your child to sleep outdoors during hot weather in a carriage, box or basket, make sure that the sides are not too high and that plenty of air is circulating to let the baby breathe correctly. Hot, direct sunlight is harmful to the eyes and to delicate baby skin after a few minutes on first exposures. In the summer, have a little tulle-netting over the baby's sleeping area outdoors to keep the bees, flies and other animals away.

Infants can sleep pretty well anywhere, but at home it is best if they sleep in a room of their own. Keep the temperature warm (a night and day average of 70°F. or 20°C.). Remember, babies come from a warm place. You could keep the baby sleeping in your room at night with you in the first weeks but you may find yourself listening to the baby instead of sleeping. It is cozy, if you are breast-feeding, to have your child by your side and just take the baby in your bed when it's feeding time. But, if you are bottle-feeding and one of you has to get up, the baby may just as well be in its own room so that at least one of the parents can rest. Sometimes newborns do not cry very loudly when they wake up and they may have been whimpering for quite a while before you hear it (not a desirable situation as it makes a hungry baby nervous and fretful not to be fed when ready). Therefore, it may be a good idea, in the first month, to leave the door of both your rooms open, or, if they are on different floors, to have an intercom system.

Once the baby is fed, changed and ready to sleep, lay the child on its side in case it should spit up some of the feeding. An infant sleeping on its back and throwing up its food may choke on its own rejects. The majority of babies, however, seem to feel more comfortable and secure sleeping on their stomach. Often the pressure on the tummy brings a relief to gas pains, if any. When a baby lies too often on its back, the hair at the back of the head may rub off, leaving a bald spot. It is nothing serious, the hair will grow back later, but it can be avoided by changing the baby's position often. Lying on its stomach, a child is more likely to develop its neck muscles, and therefore be able to hold up its head sooner.

A newborn does not need an elaborate sleeping arrangement. A large woven straw basket, a padded shallow box or a folded quilt will do quite well. If you put the baby to sleep on a bed, make sure it is on the mattress and not on the pillow, as a baby could suffocate while sleeping on the pillow. Babies should never sleep on pillows at all if you want the spine to develop correctly. Also, the mattress in their sleeping area should be quite firm. By two months of age babies are strong enough to turn over. Make sure that the place where you lay them is safe, even if it's only for a minute.

Young babies, once asleep, can stay asleep quite well through all sorts of noises. It is better to get a baby used to a certain amount of everyday noises such as telephones, music, conversations, cleaning-up cling-clang, instead of trying to avoid the noise and turning your child into a light sleeper. Quite a few people take babies to the movies. Until they are four months old, babies can sleep very well through the noisiest of films.

During their first six months, most babies seem to wake up at the early hour of five or six. Many mothers develop the bad habit of hardly ever falling into a deep sleep and then, at the slightest murmuring from their baby, the mother jumps up thinking that the baby is crying when in fact the child might have just gone back to sleep if it hadn't been paid any attention. During the first six weeks it is essential to be there all the time but from then on wait to see if the murmuring stops or gets louder before you go in to check. When a child is used to having company very early in the morning every day, it is going to demand such attention for a long time. Establish from the beginning of your daily rhythm that this is a feeding period after which everyone goes back to sleep, if that is what you want to have happen.

Infants' sleeping patterns change constantly. Just when you think you have established a regular feeding/sleeping pattern that has been constant for a few weeks, the baby will decide to forego the morning nap and your plans for doing a particular thing during that period are shot.

As mentioned before, unless you have to go back to outside work, give yourself at least a three-month period. Have a good time getting to know your own baby and get enough sleep yourself so that you can stay healthy and in a good mood to cope with all the intricacies of parenthood.

Cleanliness

A baby forced to live in a totally sterile environment would have little chance of survival on its first outing. That baby would not have been vaccinated naturally by the microbial flora and fauna of our usual environment. From complete sterilization to letting the infant wade in dirt, there is a vast range of possibilities. Babies should be kept clean without exaggeration.

During the early days, a newborn's skin should not be aggravated too often with soap. If plain lukewarm water can take care of the cleaning, leave the soap aside. Soap and other products used on the baby's skin should not contain detergents or harsh chemicals.

In the hospital the baby is cleaned and dressed for you. Later, a nurse will help you to change and care for the baby, if you wish. After birth at home, the newborn can be wiped clean of blood with a cloth dipped in lukewarm water. The person doing it shouldn't rub hard as the skin is very tender. Also, if possible, you want to retain and spread the vernix.

The stump that remains after the umbilical cord has been clamped will soon dry, shrivel and fall off. It may come off three days later or remain for as long as two weeks. It will come off in its own time, do not pull on it. The stump should be kept dry and clean with sterile cotton swabs and alcohol. It can be left to dry in the air. Make sure that the diaper does not rub over that surface, or cover it with gauze. Bandages, except in extreme cases, are not really necessary. Let the doctor or midwife know at once if any blood or pus is seeping from the stump.

Start bathing the infant with lukewarm water and a little soap. Too much soaping removes the fatty layer of the skin and leaves it open to

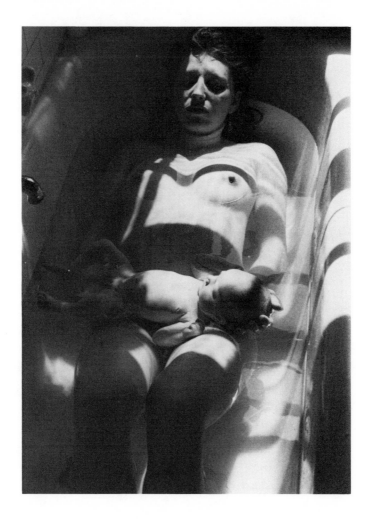

irritation and germ contamination. Fill the bath area with small amounts of water for the first baths. A few days later, when you are used to holding the slippery baby and supporting the back of the head as you are washing him/her, you can put in more water. The temperature in the room should be warm and you should dip your elbow into the bath water to make sure that it is not too hot, a tepid 95°F. (25°C.). Lay out a towel and a clean set of clothing nearby as it is impossible to leave the baby in the bath by itself for even a second, and walking around with a wet baby is not wise. After a good wash, going in and out of the neck, groin and underarm folds, over the face gently and around the head with a little shampoo, dry the baby well. Check the nails of hands and feet. They grow very fast and the baby will often scratch its face if they are too long.

Clean the nose and the ears and then dress the baby. Choose the time to give the bath according to what suits your activities best. Some parents like to give it in the morning after the second feeding, others prefer bathing the baby after the evening feeding, saying it sets the baby off to a good night's sleep.

Quite a few babies get cradle cap, light brown scaling of the scalp. It is harmless and can usually be rubbed off with a little oil (mineral or olive). Try it, gently, once or twice a day. If the cradle cap persists, your doctor may suggest other preparations.

Some of the toilet and bathing articles that you may need are: three bath towels and wash cloths, almond or other baby oil and lotion, sterile cotton swabs, a soft brush and a diaper pail.

Clothes

Clothes have other purposes besides following fashion or making babies delightful to view! Clothes are meant to make life more comfortable, a screen against capricious weather and perilous environment.

Clothes for babies should be practical first, happy to look at second. The best combine practicality with attractiveness. Practical baby clothes are comfortable to wear, with lots of room for bulky diapers, stretching and kicking. They should be easy to take on and off, should take into account that infants grow quickly, and should be easy to wash.

In temperate climates, you can start with a cotton undershirt that snaps closed in front or down the side. Infants find it quite disagreeable to have anything pulled over their heads at this stage. Undershirts are available with tabs which are meant to be fastened to the diaper so they won't ride up and will keep the stomach warm.

You really do not need all that much at first. If you're given bags of hand-me-downs, slightly yellowed shirts and gowns, you can make them new for your baby by dying or painting them (simple, washable fabric crayons and markers are widely available). Four to six short- or long-sleeved shirts will be enough. It's true that the more you have, the less frequently you have to wash, but a pile of soaked and milky shirts can smell quite unpleasant after a few days.

Disposable diapers have eliminated the most detested cleaning chore and a lot of diaper rash—although some infants' skin is very sensitive to the plastic and perfumes in disposables. Disposable diapers can be found in shapes contoured to a baby's bottom. Some come with elasticized legs to prevent drafts and leakage, and with refastenable tapes in case the baby wasn't wet after all. Supermarket brand diapers are cheaper but thinner so you'll end up using more of them. You are going to go through a lot of diapers anyway (about eighty to a hundred a week). Some discount toy stores and supermarkets sell disposables by the case, which works out to be more economical and saves you trips with bulky boxes. On the other hand, you may feel destructive submerging the planet with

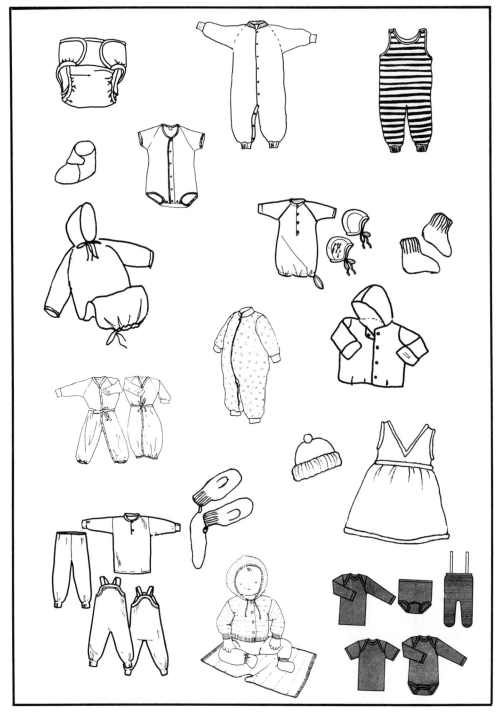

so many soiled disposable diapers which do not burn and take forever to rot! There is probably a good diaper service near you that has a pickup and delivery service if you can afford it. Some new parents request a year's diaper service as a gift. Cloth diapers are now available in contoured shapes, and with Velcro ties to save you using diaper pins. Instead of plastic pants over cloth diapers, you could try one of the many kinds of wool diaper covers now available. They let the baby's bottom breathe better and are wonderfully absorbent. Even if you choose to use disposables, it's always useful to have a dozen cloth diapers, a couple of baby pins and waterproof or woolen diaper covers on hand in case you run out. Cloth diapers come in very useful as infant feeding bibs, for wiping up after the baby, for burping after a feed or as soft pads on which to change the baby.

A stretch jumpsuit or stretchy, covering the baby from neck to toe, can go on next. The baby can wear it during the day and at night. It's an ideal all-round piece of clothing by the time the baby is one month old. Stretchies generally come with feet, so buy a size large enough for comfort. When the fit starts to get tight you can always cut off the feet, giving the suit an extra couple of months' use. One- or two-piece stretch diaper suits (without legs) are useful in summer months, but most have snap necks, so you may want to wait till your baby is used to over-the-head dressing. Just as practical as stretchies are the long john and shirt sets now available in 100 percent cotton and in a vast array of colors. The shirts come in many styles, short- or long-sleeved or sweatshirts. If you buy the set in a larger size, you can start out by rolling up the wrist and ankle cuffs. A word of advice: unlike many stretchies, long john sets are not intended as sleepwear, so they do not contain flame-resistant chemicals. In the first few weeks the baby might like to have the legs and hips wrapped tightly in a receiving blanket, giving a snug, womblike feeling of security. At night a sweater or blanket sleeper (styles without legs allow more room for growth) can be added if the temperature drops.

A nightgown with a drawstring is also very useful in the first months. It can be worn either when the baby is awake or sleeping. The drawstring makes it easy to change diapers, and sometimes these gowns have little mittens at the cuff which can be put over the hands if the baby has a tendency to scratch itself.

Sweaters for babies now come in the prettiest of colors. White, pale blue, pink and yellow are certainly babylike and adorable, but a little multicolored baby warms the heart just as much, if not more. Look for sweaters with buttons down the front or at the shoulders, for easy dressing. Knitted booties and ear-covering hats are most comfortable for their sensitive skin. Make sure that the yarn they are made from is very soft, and remember that some infants are sensitive to wool, while others are allergic to synthetic fibers. Avoid hats that tie under the chin. When selecting an outfit to be worn close to the skin, fine cotton and fine wool material should be favored. Dresses, as cute as they may look, are drafty in the winter and never quite as practical as shorts and tee shirts in the summer. If you think a child romping around in plain disposable diapers is not the most attractive sight (would you walk around parading your plastic underwear?), you could cover them with stretch terry cloth pants available at most stores. Or you could quickly sew a few printed pants large enough to fit over the diapers.

For outings in cool weather, you may find that the easiest thing is to throw a pram suit or bunting over your baby's indoor clothes. Buntings are legless, like zippered sleeping bags with arms. They allow for growth but can present problems in a carriage or car seat that straps between the legs. Pram suits usually have zippers extending down the legs for diaper changes. Both have hoods and are filled with an insulating fabric. The lighter and fluffier kind are more comfortable than the heavier styles.

Accessories

Modern nursery gadgets are numerous, but if you use your imagination you need to buy very little for your newborn. If you want to go all out and can afford to buy a matching set of baby furniture, it is available. But remember that after two or three years it becomes obsolete (unless you give it to new parents or save it for your next child).

Cribs. Chances are that someone around you has a crib with drop sides in which your baby can sleep once the first week's arrangements are outgrown. New cribs must meet federal safety standards. If you get a used crib, make sure that the slats are no more than 2⅜ inches apart, that there is less than a two-finger gap between the mattress and crib sides and at least 26 inches from the top of the rail to the mattress set at its lowest level. If you're choosing a new crib, bear in mind that cribs with adjustable mattress levels can be used not only for sleeping, but also as a playpen (at the lowest mattress level). Modern styles with straight, unmolded bars are much easier to clean after your baby has grabbed them with sticky hands.

In the first three or four months babies are often happier sleeping in a smaller, more confining space. If you already have a crib, try piling blankets around the sides to create a little nest. Otherwise, "moses" baskets are fine, or you might want to buy a carry bed—a light, portable, foldable bed with handles and ideally with zippered sides made of mesh so that the baby can breathe well and see the world. Baskets and carry beds can come in useful after the baby has graduated to a crib for visits or travel.

Bedding. Receiving blankets are fine for the warmest months. Otherwise you will need washable thermal blankets or comforters, preferably lightweight but warm. For babies who kick their bedding off, sleeping bags or blanket sleepers may be better. Crib sheets should be soft and warm. Babies tend to perspire and spit up in their sleep, so flannel sheets, which are both warm and absorbent, are ideal. Fitted sheets make life easier for the parents and are more comfortable for the baby. Unless the mattress has a waterproof surface, you will need to protect it with a rubberized cotton flannel sheet to be placed under the crib sheet. It is also a good idea to put a cloth diaper or waterproof pad between the crib sheet and the baby's bottom, to save you changing the bedding several times a day. Crib bumpers are padded cloth strips that fit around the inside of the crib to prevent the baby from knocking its head against the hard wooden bars, and to stop drafts.

Also available are lambskins made specially for babies to sleep on. They are sanitized, flame retardant and machine washable. Researchers have found that new babies sleep better on lambskins, gain weight faster and suffer less from colic, perhaps because the warmth of the lambskin closely resembles the warmth of a human body.

Other useful items you may need, depending on your life-style, include:

Baby Carrier. A baby carrier, strapped around you, leaves your hands free and the baby close to your warmth. Baby carriers now come in a variety of styles and fabrics to be worn in front or back (front is best in the first few months—in very cold weather you can button a big coat around both of you). Use your baby carrier outside or at home. The baby can ride around in it, sleep, wake, watch you and the world from a warm and secure position.

Baby Carriage or Stroller. Before the baby can sit up by itself it's not a good idea to use a stroller, except the kind that converts into a "bed." Carriages are ideal for leisurely walks with an infant, or even for older babies, and are ideal for piling up groceries, baby supplies, extra kids. But they are cumbersome on city streets and almost impossible to push up steps. After the first few months, your choice of stroller will depend on your life-style. If you have to climb steps to your apartment, ride buses or subways or plan to travel, choose an umbrella stroller that's light and folds easily with one hand. If your local streets and sidewalks are bumpy, the double-swivel-wheeled styles will wear best and be easier to push. Make sure that the handles are high enough to prevent back strain. There is also a stroller available whose handles can be tipped both ways so that the baby can face you as you push. Some strollers have built-in shopping trays underneath the seat.

Additional Accessories. A *high table* on which you can safely lay the baby to change clothes and diapers. There are many styles available, some with drawers. However, a bed with a waterproof pad is sufficient.

A set of drawers; a trunk or suitcase for baby's clothes; shelves or a box for oils, lotions and other toiletries.

A baby bathtub. Any kind of small plastic tub will do. For babies up to six months, the perfect bathtub is now available. It's inflatable, has a soft, bouncy base and sides to hold and cushion the baby's body, and a suction grip on the bottom to hold the tub firmly on any surface.

An infant seat. Molded plastic seats have adjustable heights, a safety belt and can be transported anywhere. Bouncing seats made of fabric stretched across a metal frame are also available. Most babies will stay longer in one of these since every time they move, they make it bounce.

Ultrasensitive sound-activated *transmitter and receiver* are convenient and safe between baby's room and yours.

A low-voltage lamp, or plug-in night-light, to check on the baby's sleep.

A diaper bag for carrying disposable diapers, bottles and change of clothes. They come with pockets so you can find everything quickly, and some styles are available with a detachable foldout changing pad, which makes traveling easier. Diaper bags should be machine washable since there are bound to be some leaks and spills.

Car seats are required for children in most states. Most car seats have minimum and maximum weight and height limits which you should check before choosing one.

Tiny babies are stimulated by the simplest things—the sound of your voice, your touch, the difference between light and darkness, the colors and patterns that you wear. To add sensory pleasure and distractions in the early months, you can buy, find or make: brightly colored mobiles; pictures or pieces of printed fabric (infants are fascinated by simple images of faces and by geometric patterns); soft things that jingle or rattle; a small plastic mirror to hang from the crib; a music box. For a much greater price you could go out and buy one of the special, developmental crib "gyms," or "rods," that attach across a crib and offer the baby a graduated series of exercises, first visual, then physical.

Infants enjoy rhythmic movement. They like to be carried, rocked, bounced, wheeled. There is also available a variety of swings for infants up to four or five months. They are manually or battery operated, and some give you a choice of speeds and sleeping or sitting positions. Swings can be calming, but cannot entirely replace the human element.

©K. Haring

Traveling

Traveling with your baby can be easy and require a minimum amount of fussing and care, or it can be the most chaotic, hectic and frustrating experience for everyone involved.

Whether it is a few hours in a car, a few days or a cross-country adventure, the ease of traveling has a lot to do with giving yourself ample time for preparation. An outing or a holiday should be just that and it should never be more work than if you stayed at home. If you have any doubts about your child's health concerning a trip, ask for advice from your baby's doctor.

Before leaving you should prepare a shoulder bag containing:

- Disposable diapers.
- Plastic bags for the soiled diapers, in case you don't have a place to throw them away.

- Tissues, cotton swabs, baby cream (or whatever else you use to clean the baby's bottom).
- A waterproof pad on which to change the baby. Many carryall nursery bags incorporate a flap on which to change a baby and have a separate plastic-lined compartment for soiled diapers.
- A snugli with padded shoulder straps, and baby head support for those early months.
- A yard of printed cotton fabric always comes in handy. Use it on top of the flannelette as a sheet, to cover a rough or dirty surface before you lay the baby down, to block off the sun from a car window, to wrap the baby against you, to give a happy touch to a blank environment, to throw over your shoulder for discreet breast-feeding.
- A bottle of formula ready to be given and as many disposable bottles (or cans and empty bottles with bottle brush and soap) as needed for the trip.
- A change of clothing and a little shawl or blanket for the night or temperature changes. A change of clothing for yourself in case the baby spits up or soaks you.

If you still have some room include one of those little music boxes. Some have very soft tunes which babies find soothing.

Other practical items to take along are a lightweight cloth or wicker carry cot with a removable foam mattress and quilt and a reclining folding stroller. This last item can always be checked with the luggage.

By Air. Call the airline in advance to find out their facilities on long distance flights. If you tell them you are traveling with an infant when you make your reservation they may be able to reserve a bassinet for you so that the baby can sleep in it rather than on you, leaving you more freedom of movement. The hostess or steward can warm the bottle if necessary. If it is not a busy period, one of the hostesses can hold your baby while you eat, take a stretch or go to the toilet. For takeoff and landing always have the baby in your arms, and the same applies when there is turbulence on the plane. If the baby is asleep during the flight you could lay it down on the little mattress, in between your feet on the floor if there is no bassinet. It's quite an experience to change a soiled baby in a narrow seat, sandwiched in between two strangers! If it is a large plane ask to do it in the space provided as a rest area for the hostess. It's certainly not possible to do it in the toilet-bathroom as they are far too small. If it is a flight over two hours long, the temperature in the plane can get very cool, and on transatlantic flights, after the cold it sometimes becomes hot and dry. Check the baby often for comfort. On most major airlines, infants and their parents can be preboarded on the plane before the main crowd rush. Also, ask for the seat with the most leg room (i.e., the first row). In flight, if your child is crying (due to pressure on the eardrum), do not feel you are stuck in one spot after the seat-belt sign is off. Walk up and down the aisle, rocking the baby to sleep. A pacifier also might help or a whole box full of earplugs for your sleeping neighbors. A snugli is a great help if you have to walk long distances in airports and wait at the customs office. It's better than a stroller because in the first few months the baby cannot sit in a stroller. Some airports now have unstaffed nurseries where you can clean the baby properly on high tables, lay the baby down in a crib and lay yourself down on a couch to rest while awaiting your flight connection. On national flights infants can fly for free and on international flights the price is 10 percent of your ticket.

By Train or Bus.   Have patience. Include in the infant bag moist towellettes as trains and buses are usually quite dirty (unless you can afford to travel first class). Don't forget food and liquid for yourself.

By Car.   If you are traveling by car in the United States or Europe you will probably be required to use an infant car seat. In other places, if a car seat is not available, put the little carry-cot or straw basket on the floor of the car to make sure it will not fall off the seat when you drive, or strap it to the seat with safety belts. It's better not to use the little mattress on the floor of a car because if you brake the baby might roll about. Besides, there is a lot of dust flying around down there. Do not plan to drive by yourself for long hours with an infant; the baby would probably not be able to take it. If you are being driven, watch out for drafts and put the baby in a safe position, either lying down or resting on your knees. You will probably be more comfortable in the back seat with your baby.

Infant Massage

Babies are such sensitive little beings that it is often difficult to pinpoint what stresses them. A good way to communicate and express a mother or a father's love is through massage. The nerve pathways are stimulated and appeased through touching movements and soothing sounds. After much research Ruth Diane Rice, Ph.D., has found that sensorimotor simulation by massage facilitates the development of premature infants, as well as decreasing the possibility of emotional disturbances.

Vimala Schneider, an expert on the subject, recommends five to ten minutes of massage a day for newborns to six-month-old babies, and fifteen to thirty minutes for older babies.

The room should be warm, and if you are outdoors choose a place shaded from the sun's bright rays. When you remove the diaper, place the baby on a towel or on an easily washable surface. The baby's stomach should not be full. If the baby is crying soothe the little one first.

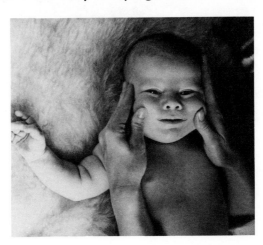

When choosing an oil to moisten your hands, select a natural vegetable oil; sunflower, coconut, almond, etc., since some oil may get in your baby's mouth. For this reason, mineral or baby oils are not recommended.

Alison Ozer, a baby massage instructor, suggests you breathe deeply and relax yourself first, so you may give your best and sense all the nuances of interaction that a massage can unfurl between you and your baby. She sits on a hard mattress, bed or on the ground with her legs extended and the baby placed between them.

Approach the baby gently. Put your face close to the baby's and establish eye contact. With a newborn start with gentle surface strokes; as the baby gets older the massage can get stronger. The baby's reactions should guide you. When time allows at the end of the massage, take your baby with you in a warm bathtub, it adds to the overall relaxation, particularly before bedtime. Put an infant seat covered with a towel, or a sleeping basket next to the bathtub, place your baby in it before you get out. It will make it easier for you to maneuver.

The Head.   Before putting oil on the hands the head is gently caressed in small circular motions.

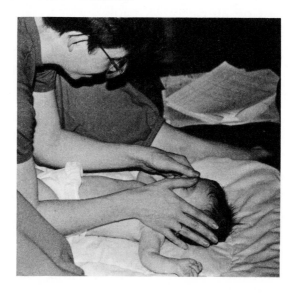

The Chest. Rub your hands with oil. Place your hands flat on the baby's chest. Move your hands from center to side in a smooth swoop following the lines of the ribs. Slide your hands back to the center of the baby's chest.

Be conscious of the rhythm of your breath and of the baby's breathing. Harmonize. It gives tempo to your movements.

As your baby gains weight over the months, use another form of chest massage. Starting from the sides of the chest, move one hand diagonally from the edge of the ribcage to the shoulder and back. With your left hand and right hand, one after the other, move across the chest in a crisscross motion at a slow and steady rhythm. Look your baby in the eyes and exchange gurgles and babbles.

The Arms. Lift up the baby's arm and, holding the wrist with your left hand, massage from the shoulder all the way to the little hand, give a "milking" and twisting motion with the edge of your closed right hand. Repeat the shoulder-to-wrist movement alternating your hands several times. Finish by massaging each little finger.

Loosen your own shoulders by moving them and massage the baby's shoulders with the palms of your hands with small circular motions, going in opposite directions.

The Abdomen. Wait until the umbilicus is well healed. If your hands are cool rub them together to warm them as the abdominal area is particularly sensitive.

Place your hands—palm to belly in horizontal but opposite directions—and in slow motion sweep the baby's tummy, one hand sliding after the other toward the legs.

Take both feet in the right hand and stretch the legs upward to relax the abdominal area. With your right hand flat on the tummy repeat the sweeping motion from the chest toward the lower belly.

The Legs. The movement is the same as for the arm. Hold the ankle with one hand and "milk" the leg, alternating your hands. Another

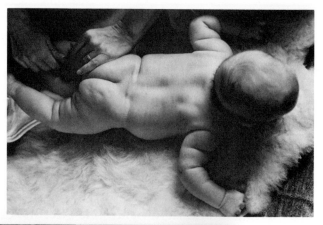

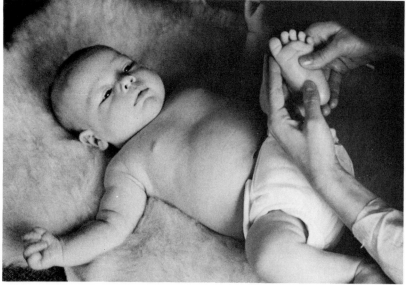

pleasurable movement for the baby is when you roll the legs in between your hands from knee to ankle.

The Feet. Recipients of a thousand nerve endings, the feet are key to many reflexes. Use your palms on the flat of the feet to uncurl the toes and then press your thumbs lightly all over the sole of the foot. Again with the ball of your thumbs press in and slide along each foot, from heel to toe, one thumb after the other. Then roll each little toe in between your fingers.

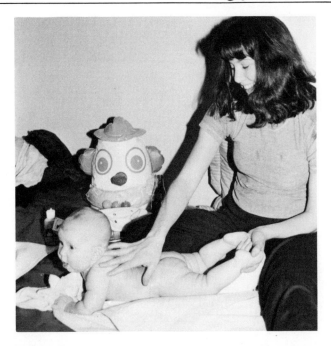

The Back.   With a little infant it is easier if you place the baby on your lap. In the first month place the baby's head toward your knees and as the baby grows straddle her across your outstretched leg. As the baby lies on the tummy, massage from the base of the neck to the buttocks with open hand strokes, one after the other.

In another movement hold the baby's buttock firmly with the right hand and with two fingers of the left hand slide down each side of the spine, from the neck to coccyx. Repeat also with the palm of the hand. With the baby still in the same position, hold the ankles firmly in your right hand and with your left hand rub down from the neck in a long sweep all the way to the ankles.

If your baby is still enjoying the massage you can end the session with an extended face massage. Place your thumbs in the middle of the forehead and move sideways along the eyebrows to the temple. Place your thumbs on each side of the nose and press slightly, sliding across the cheeks toward the ears. With your fingertips flutter along the cheeks, down the neck. Then holding the baby's head in your hands kiss her gently on the nose.

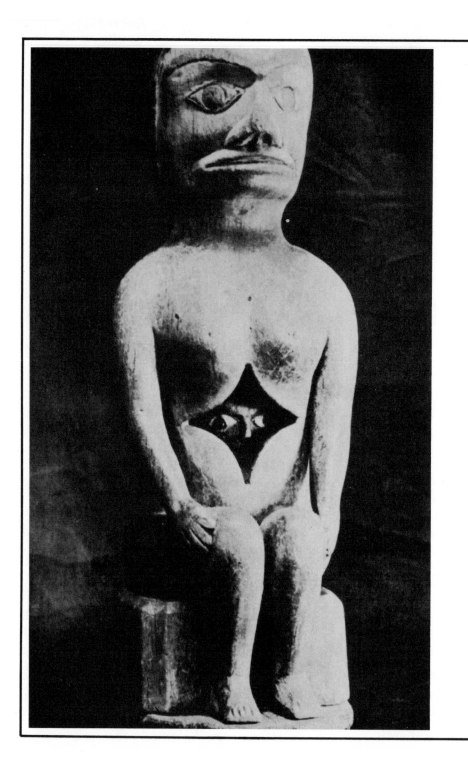

Birth Customs around the World

Human birth is the entrance of the ego with its qualities into a new body or vehicle of consciousness (while death is the exit of the ego from the body at any age). The first implies the outbreathing of the spirit and personality into material forms on the mental, astral and physical planes (while the latter implies the in-breathing of the same form out of the forms which then die and decay).
—G. A. Gaskell, *Dictionary of All Scriptures and Myths*

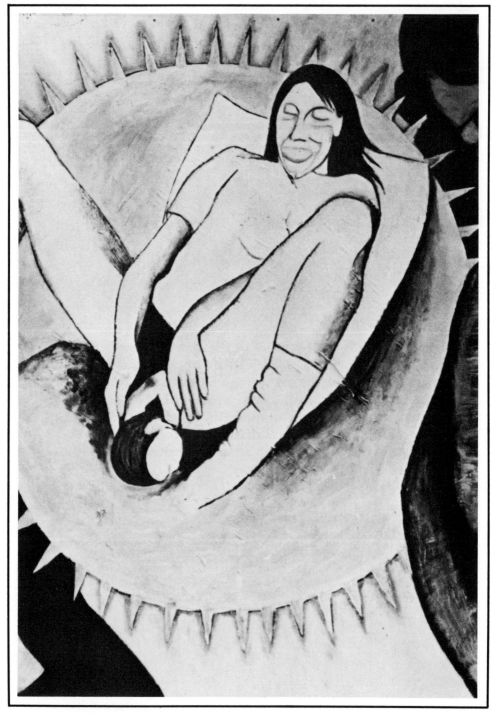

There is a vast variety of superstitions that revolve around birth. From prehistoric times to the present, people have concocted different ceremonies, rites and superstitions concerning birth. Each region or group of people has its own peculiarity, but their aims are usually common to all: luck, success and the warding off of evil spirits.

SOUL

Many women need help during childbirth to protect themselves and to ensure a healthy and safe delivery of their baby. But many people in many different countries also believe that the souls of both child and mother need special protection. The soul must not be forgotten or else it may escape.

In Sumatra, Indonesia, the midwife will sometimes tie a ribbon around the wrist of a woman about to give birth. This blocks the passage of her soul in case it should decide to leave her body. It would be nice to think that the plastic name bracelet you are forced to wear in a hospital serves the same purpose.

When a woman in the southern Celebes Islands is in difficult labor and needs help, the messenger who fetches the midwife always carries something made of iron. It is usually a knife or machete which will be delivered to the midwife. The midwife must keep the metal object in her house until the birth has taken place and then give it back upon payment of an established sum of money once the delivery is performed. The knife represents the woman's soul, which at this critical time is believed to be safer outside of her body. To make sure the baby's soul doesn't escape and get lost at birth, every possible opening in the house is blocked. The household pets and the outside animals' mouths are tied just in case they might swallow the soul. All the people present at the birth are asked to keep their mouths tightly closed.

Another tribe believes that before people are born, they are asked how long a soul they would like to have. According to their answer a soul is measured out. A person's life span is proportioned to the length of their soul. A child who dies young has asked for a short soul.

Identification of the soul's earth spirit perpetrates another ancient superstition among the peoples of Mexico, Central America and some of the Plains Indians of the United States. This superstition, known as nagualism, enforces the concept that each individual has a guardian spirit that watches over the person during his lifetime. One's spirit, or nagual (sometimes known as tonal), is joined in another being shortly after birth. Ashes are spread around the sleeping area of the newborn. The following morning, the father checks the ashes to identify any animal tracks which would indicate the animal spirit that has taken charge of the newborn soul. For some people that spiritual connection is so strong that they believe that the animal and the baby will share the same soul.

Other groups of people believe that they do not come from the earth in general, but from a very particular place such as a certain cave, the hollow of a tree, a bush, a rock formation or an ancestral site where souls of the unborn await incarnation and to which the dead return. The belief that women become pregnant when they come near these fertile shrines of souls is widespread. The souls are felt to be already waiting in the earth's womb and their human mother is considered a temporary vessel, acting on behalf of the great earth mother herself.

NAMING THE CHILD

In the language of the Kafirs of Afghanistan, the words "to name" mean literally "to pour into." It is the name that first gives the child identity, and this name is intimately linked with the child's soul. Since people in many cultures believe that a child is born with the reincarnated soul of an ancestor, naming ceremonies are often centered around discovering the child's true name, by finding out the identity of the ancestor. The newborn may be placed at the mother's breast while the names of its forebears are spoken; the name being spoken at the moment when the child begins to suck is deemed to be the child's ancestral name.

In parts of Africa, the placental cord is floated in water, and the name of the ancestor whose soul is reincarnated in the child is guessed by the cord's resting place. In New Zealand, the Maori blow snuff up the infant's nostrils, the list of ancestors is recited, and when the child sneezes the name being spoken is picked, since sneezing is held to be the way that spirits communicate.

Certain people of Hawaii purposely give their babies ugly names, such as "dung," in the hope that these will protect the child's soul by warding off evil spirits. There are several other cultures in which the infant is named after events or objects linked with the birth, partly as a way of chronicling time, but also perhaps because events and the nature of the soul are held to be linked by fate. In certain tribes, for instance, babies are named "thunder," "wind on water," "affliction" or "a tear" if the times were sad, or even "canoe" if the father finished making a canoe on the day of birth.

In northern Mexico, some people believed that the child's name could be found by walking the mother once around the room with her eyes closed, and calling the child by the name of the first object she saw on opening her eyes. A few cultures practice what is known as teknonomy, or the naming of the parents after the child. After the first baby is named, the mother's name changes to "mother of____" and the father's to "father of____." In Greece babies are named after the saint on whose day they are born, and in future years they share their birthdays, called "name days," with other people of the same name. And in some parts of the world all children are called by a common name, such as "thing," "child" or "little grub" until they receive their own name at puberty.

Naming ceremonies, which are accompanied everywhere by feasting and celebration, do not generally take place before the infant is a few weeks old, at which point the "discovery" of the name may be influenced by personality traits which the baby has already shown. Perhaps some parents in modern maternity wards would find it easier to find the right name for their baby if they had more time to get to know the child before filling out registration papers.

TREES

Trees serve an important function in the daily lives of the small villages all around the world. In certain communities the biggest and oldest trees are considered the place of residence for guardian spirits. In other places, the big tree is the meeting place, the central point in a plaza, a spot where ceremonies are held. In connection with the rites of childbearing, the tree represents growing life, the continuing cycle.

It's an old custom to plant a fruit tree for a new baby. In Switzerland, an apple tree is planted for a boy and a pear tree for a girl. In Haiti, a coconut or breadfruit tree is planted. In Sweden, a lime or elm tree was considered to be a guardian tree; anyone who damaged it would certainly be punished with bad luck, but a pregnant woman who clasped it ensured herself of an easy delivery. One can read in Greek mythology how Leto embraced a palm tree as she was about to give birth to Apollo and Artemis in order to facilitate her delivery.

In Africa, women from a Congolese tribe wrap themselves in cloth woven from the fibrous bark of special trees which protects them from dangers that can occur in childbearing. In Western Africa the people of the M'Benga tribe plant a new tree at childbirth time and then dance around it believing that the soul of the new child resides in that tree. In many cultures, the planting of a young tree at the birth of a child also helps the parents to keep count of the child's age as he/she grows up, since the age of the tree can be estimated by the number of rings in its trunk.

STONES

Stones have always played an important role in perpetrating good luck: gem stones, stone carvings, and spiritual dwellings such as Stonehenge in Britain. Some tribes also believe that a ceremony involving a stone at childbirth will ease a troublesome labor for the mother.

Among the Dayak in Borneo, the village magician is called to help a woman who is having a difficult time delivering her child. He arrives with an associate and a large moon-colored stone. The magician goes inside the hut to massage and soothe the woman. His colleague remains outside, attaching the stone to his stomach with a large piece of fabric (to simulate the birth) and, following the instructions shouted to him by the magician inside the hut, moves the stone in imitation of the baby's movements. Supposedly, he is absorbing the weight of the woman until the actual birth of the child.

There are also stones used to induce the flow of milk. In Greece and Crete the milk stone (probably a form of chalk-calcium) is dissolved with honey and consumed by the mother. This is supposed to produce an abundant supply of milk. In Albania the stone is worn on the body for the same purpose. In Haiti pregnant women ward off the evil eye of miscarriage by sewing a little polished stone from their magician into the hem of a seven-layered petticoat.

There are still some Arab women who perform an ancient superstitious tradition when they fear difficult delivery. Three days before their due date, they tie a fire stone wrapped in cloth around one of their thighs to ensure an easy delivery.

THE AFTERBIRTH

The afterbirth plays an integral part in birth ceremonies throughout the world. The afterbirth is made up of the placenta, the amniotic membrane and the umbilical cord. Many people believe that the afterbirth remains as an important part of the body, even though the physical connection has been severed.

From Baganda to the United States, many parents believe that the food that has nourished the baby is very special and should be disposed of with thought and care.

There are people in America today who eat the stewed placenta in a thanksgiving meal after the birth. In New Mexico the afterbirth is planted under a new Ponderosa Pine tree. An Indian tribe in Arizona makes a bracelet from the umbilical cord. After it has dried, bead stones are threaded on it and given to the child to bite on at teething time. The Incas of Peru preserve the cord and give it to the child to suck whenever it falls ill. In Europe the midwives used to keep the cord until it was dry and then give it to the father, instructing him to preserve it safely as the child would be healthy and prosperous as long as it was kept in the family. In the countryside of France, the navel cord was never thrown into water or fire for fear that the child would drown or burn.

One of the most poetic stories about the afterbirth comes from Queensland, Australia. The natives of Queensland strongly believe that a part of the child's spirit stays in the afterbirth. It is the grandmother's role to look after it; she takes it away and buries it in the sand. Then she marks the spot with a number of twigs which she sticks in the ground in the form of a circle, tying the top twigs together so that the structure resembles a cone. When Anjea (the being who causes conception by putting mud babies in the mother's womb) passes by and sees the place, she takes out the spirit of the baby and carries it away to one of her haunts, such as a tree, a hole, a rock, a shell or a lagoon where it may remain for years. At some later date, Anjea will put the spirit in another mud baby to be born again into the world.

On one of the Caroline Islands, in the Pacific, the umbilical cord is placed in a conch shell and treated in a manner that would be best suited for the child's future. For example, if the parents think that their son will need to be a good climber in order to survive, they will hang the conch on a tree.

In other places the umbilical cord, once dried, is reduced to powder and used as a remedy. In Iran, the powder was once used against trachoma (inflammation of the inner eyelid). It was a love philter among the Kalmucks, and in the Oceanic Islands some of the powdered cord was thrown in the sea to cast a good spell on their armaments at the onset of fighting.

It may seem a bit weird to eat the placenta raw, as some tribes from central Brazil do, but it is not any more odd than using any of the facial creams or rejuvenating injections that are made from placental extract.

KNOTS, LOCKS AND BONDS

The symbolic obstacle of a knot is sometimes associated with or believed to create a corresponding physical obstacle in the body, particularly during childbirth. For this reason, there are many ceremonies centering around knots, locks and bonds.

In Argyllshire, Scotland, for example, all the clothes of a woman in labor must be free of knots so that she will not be tied up inside. In the East Indies a woman must not tie any knots nor braid anything during the whole course of her pregnancy.

The Hos of West Africa call for their magician when a woman wants relief from a long labor. In certain cases he will declare that she cannot deliver because the child is bound within the womb. He promises to loosen the bond so that she may bring forth the baby. He orders someone to get a long creeper from the forest and with it he binds the hands and feet of the woman. He then takes a knife and calls out her name. When she answers, he cuts through the creeper saying, "Today is the day for the bonds between this woman and her child to be cut." He then chops up the creeper, puts the little bits in a basin of water and bathes the woman with the liquid.

In Chittagong, Pakistan, a woman in the same predicament calls a midwife. The midwife orders all the windows and doors opened, all the bottles uncorked, the horse is freed from the stall, the dog from the chain, the sheep and the fowl from the stable. This universal liberty accorded to animals and inanimate objects is supposed to be an infallible means of allowing the babe to be born.

When a woman is in labor on the Island of Sakhalin, in the North Pacific, her husband loosens up everything that can be undone: he undoes the braids from his hair and the laces of his shoes and unties everything around the house and outside. In the yard the ax is taken out of the log, the cartridge withdrawn from the gun.

WATER

Almost every religion has some ritual involving the use of water. As a purifying agent, as a blessing or to render fertility, the pouring of water and special ablutions are closely associated with the ceremonies performed after birth.

Ceremonial bathing in the ancient Greek civilization can be found in the Homeric story of the birth of Achilles. In the poem, the mother of Achilles took him for his first dip in the river Styx. She plunged him into the water until he was completely covered except for his heels by which she held on to him. His body was thereby rendered indestructible except for the famous Achilles tendon.

In the early part of this century, in the Chinese provinces of Kiangsu and Chekiang, a bathing custom following the birth of a baby was recorded. A member of the family would prepare the baby's bath. Two tubs were filled, the bigger one for the body, the smaller one for the head. Into the water of both tubs were put dragon's eyes and peanuts, ensuring success and long life for the baby.

The inhabitants of the Trobriand Islands of New Guinea involve the sea with each pregnancy. The mother, sister, father and other members of the paternal family of the pregnant woman go to the beach and two by two enter the water. Facing each other and holding hands, they form a human bridge for the woman to walk on without touching the water. She keeps her equilibrium by leaning her hands on their heads. Each couple whose hands she has already walked on runs from the tail to the head of the bridge until, at one point, she jumps into the water and everyone splashes, rubs and cleans her. Once this ceremonial bath is over, they carry her back to the beach where she is laid on a fresh mat of coconut tree leaves. A purification ritual ensues with magic incantations to prepare her for the event of birth.

The womb is often compared to the earth-soil as the place where seeds grow. Exposure to sun and water is therefore essential for the seed to grow. In Australia and South Africa, women who wish to become pregnant will lie in a shower of rain, thinking that the seeds of growth lie within them.

In the seventeenth century, baths from fountain waters, forest springs or river water were recommended after the birth. Into the bath were thrown leaves of ivy, sage, fennel, chamomile, rosemary, catnip and, for those prepared for an additional expense, two glasses of white wine were added!

During pre-Columbian days, pregnant women used to dye their hair purple and then, during the fourth and seventh month of pregnancy, they took special ritual steambaths, abdominal massages and light knuckling of the back to ensure a favorable position for the fetus.

In parts of present-day Mexico, women still receive regular abdominal, back and breast massage during pregnancy and in labor, and the postnatal seclusion cannot end before the woman has taken a series of about twelve herbal sweat baths, under the midwife's supervision.

COUVADE

Couvade is a very old custom that has almost disappeared. The name couvade is derived from the French word "couver," which means "to hatch," "to sit on." It is a custom whereby the father substitutes himself for the mother when labor begins. The ritual helps the father identify with and participate in bringing forth a new life and at the same time it is a protective measure to absorb or, at least, divide the interests of malign powers.

When the woman stops her daily activities to give birth, she will go either to a special birth house of the village or off into the countryside to give birth by herself and return a few hours later with babe in hand. The father, meanwhile, goes to his sleeping area and pretends to be greatly shaken and in need of attention, moaning and groaning. Sometimes the father will perform these ceremonial gestures for days before and after the actual birth.

In southern India the procedure used to be for the husband to dress as a woman when he was notified of the onset of labor. He would remain on a couch, twisting and turning until the baby was born.

Among the Bakairi in central Brazil the father has to lie in a hammock with the newborn baby while the mother goes back to her daily occupation right after giving birth. He is supposed to observe a very strict fast consisting only of cassava (a flat bread which is made of manioc flour) dipped in water. No meat is eaten until the baby's navel is totally healed. During this period the father is not allowed to touch his arms. According to the tradition, it would be fatal to the child if these conditions were not fulfilled. In parts of Brazil, the link between father and child is stressed by the word for child, which means "little father."

The requirements vary with different tribes in different countries. The Land Dayak of Sarawak, Malaysia, insist that the father stay out of sunlight during the four days following the birth. Also, he is allowed to eat only rice and salt for the next week. While the couvade is happening, the women of the compound who are not out working in the fields look after and care for the father in the same way that most people would care for the new mother.

GENERAL SUPERSTITIONS

There is an old Jewish superstition about not saying out loud that something good is going to happen to a person. If it is spoken, it is believed not likely to happen. If something good is happening it is paramount to keep it to yourself until it is well established. If a person says it out loud they are putting a *kanahara* on it. Many Jewish mamas, when wheeling their babies around, have a red bow attached to the carriage just in case someone comments favorably about the baby. The kanahara is then dispelled by the mother kissing the tip of her fingers and touching something red.

In China, a locket made of gold, silver and jade inscribed with the words "long life and riches" was put on the baby's wrist or neck after birth. Fearing that the child would be difficult to raise, this locket was used to encase the little life so that the evil spirit could not penetrate or harm the child. This locket was supposed to remain until the child was twenty or thirty years old.

Another way of preserving the child's life in ancient China was to have the baby wear a dress made up of small pieces of different colored cloth donated by the neighbors. Those donations were supposed to keep the evil spirits at bay.

In Uganda, newborns must be put to the breast within two hours of birth. If the child is slow to suck, the father's spear is laid alongside if it is a boy, the mother's cooking knife if the baby is a girl. In cultures where lactation is all important for the baby's survival, there are many such rituals connected with breast-feeding. The practice of these rituals usually does help the milk to flow and the child to suck, simply by putting the mother's anxieties to rest.

Among the Aztecs of Mexico it was (and still is) believed to be an ominous sign for a pregnant woman to gaze at an eclipse. This is thought to be a sure sign that the child will be born with a harelip. To counteract this malevolent influence, a small obsidian knife was sewn into the clothing, against the abdomen. Today, an iron knife is used in its place.

And, from Morocco, a real slapstick situation is reported. In the early part of this century, a Moroccan Jewish bridegroom would break a raw egg and fling it at his bride so that her future labors would be made easier! Perhaps this reflects the age-old use of raw eggs as a labor stimulant. In parts of Mexico, women in the beginning stages of labor still have two raw eggs broken directly into their mouths. The same is repeated if the placenta is slow to deliver. The eggs cause nausea and vomiting, which in turn stimulate stronger contractions.

CEREMONIES

The celebration of birth with ceremonial rituals is a common practice throughout the world. In many Christian families, for example, rejoicing is manifested in baptism. In Africa, certain tribes require purification ceremonies at birthtime. Many of these ceremonies are characterized by propitiation rites on behalf of the newborn child, and also on behalf of the whole community.

Among the Tswana tribe, animals are sacrificed at a birth ceremony and the skin of the beasts is used as a blanket for wrapping the newborn child.

Many traditional cultures kill an animal at the ceremony which marks the infant's introduction into the community. During the ceremony the mother is generally given the animal skin, which she will wear on her back daily as an infant carrier. Recently, while the animal may still be killed and feasted on, the mother may be given, instead of the skin, a piece of skin-shaped cloth similar to the infant carriers seen in Chinese communities throughout the United States. Anthropologists have found that in areas where the infant carrier is used, babies are more calm, visually alert, and walk earlier because they spend more time in an upright position.

The Sambas, on the west coast of Borneo, perform a ceremony for the firstborn child using two small figurines representing the parents. During the first part of the rite these figures are hidden beneath a veil. At a later point the veil is removed and the parents are invited to have intercourse in front of the statuettes. If the firstborn is a male, the old woman directing the ceremony rubs a little of the father's semen across

the child's forehead, saying, "Receive from your father the gift of engendering children." If the child is a girl, she takes a little of the vaginal mucus from the mother and, signing the baby's forehead, says, "Receive from your mother the gift of conceiving children."

The Thonga of Mozambique also practice ritual coitus with emission outside the vagina so that the semen moistens a cotton cord which is afterward tied around the infant's stomach in order to confer the gift of fecundity.

PRENATAL TABOOS

Most cultures have some form of prenatal taboo, some of them already described—foods that must not be eaten, things that must not be seen, activities to be avoided for fear of supernatural forces harming the unborn child. Some taboos are purely superstitious. Others are based on some form of logic. In parts of East Africa, for instance, the pregnant

mother must have no hot food or hot water for fear of scalding the child in her uterus. But in some cultures prenatal taboos are founded on a belief in the effects of the emotional environment, and particularly the mother's emotional state, on the growing fetus. The Mixtecans of Juxtlahuaca in Mexico, for instance, believe that bad gossip and aggressive talk are carried to the fetus. The African Akamba carefully regulate the mother's experiences in pregnancy, making sure that she remains calm and content. Among the Dayaks of Malaya, it's the father who must not involve himself in any violent acts—he cannot fire a gun, strike an animal or handle any sharp instrument except as needed for farm work. In the United States, we are only now beginning to discover the extent to which the mother's hormones, influenced as they are by her emotional state, affect the growing fetus.

CONFINEMENT

Many customs and taboos surrounding childbirth are actually very practical within their own cultures. People in traditional cultures all over the world believe that for a certain period of time after the birth a woman must remain alone with her baby in a place of confinement—sometimes

her own hut, or a structure specially set aside for the purpose. The period of confinement varies from about seven days to about six weeks, depending on the region, and during this time cooked food is brought to the woman and her hut is cleaned for her—sometimes by her husband. The midwife may sleep in the hut, instructing the woman on how to care for her baby and herself. If mother or baby should leave the place, or if the mother touches a needle, holds a broom, lifts anything, etc., bad luck will follow, usually in the form of the evil eye. In some cultures it is the infant who presents a danger to the community, since he is still too close to the world of spirits from which he came.

Whatever the reasoning, confinement is probably essential to the well-being of mother and baby. During these lazy days, the mother sleeps with her infant in her arms and the two develop an intense attachment that sees them through many separations to come. The woman cuddles, feeds, dreams, and produces enough milk so that when confinement ends, she and the baby will have the strength to deal with the relentless rhythms of daily life. And the infant, in its seclusion, is protected from disease—an important consideration where malaria, dysentery and many other dangers threaten the vulnerable newborn.

The end of confinement, usually marked by the falling off of the cord, the hardening of the fontanelle or some other noticeable change, is also the beginning of the child's life in the community. There is often a definite system to determine who first sees the child. Among the Ngoni of Malawi, it's the husband who first comes to the hut door where the mother awaits him. He announces "A new stranger has arrived," and gives one cry for a boy, two for a girl, before carrying the baby off to be seen by the male elders of the compound. In some cultures the baby's youngest brother or sister has the privilege of seeing the infant first—a good antidote to the universal trauma of "the new baby."

EARTH MOTHERS AND BIRTH GODDESSES

These are only a few of the female figures invoked at birth in ancient and modern times throughout the world.

Aphrodite Genetyllis. She was concerned with, and in fact embodied in, the reproductive powers and was worshiped to procure easy labor in ancient Greece.

Artemis and **Diana.** These two goddesses, one Greek and one Roman, are often mistaken for one another. Diana was an ancient Italian goddess; helper of women in childbirth. She was affiliated with Egeria and Virbius, divinities of childbirth. Later she was identified as the goddess of the crescent moon, identical with Artemis. This Greek goddess was originally a mother deity and goddess of lakes, woods and wildlife. She later developed into a goddess of fertility, marriage and childbirth, with the power of facilitating labor and delivery. The statue of Artemis at her temple at Ephesus, one of the seven wonders of the world, is sometimes identified as that of Diana. The upper part of the figure is covered with fruitlike breasts, identifying the goddess as a mother-deity and goddess of plenty.

Astarte. The Phoenician Great Mother—goddess of fertility— was pictured holding a child in her arms. Her head was usually that of a bull or cow, with crescent-shaped horns which identify her as a moon goddess.

Atargatis. Hittite mother goddess and fertility deity. She is pictured as a mother nursing a child with a cornucopia. Like some other birth deities, she was also worshiped as a moon goddess. Syria.

Cybele. The Great Mother goddess of Phrygia, she was worshiped as mother earth and goddess of all reproduction in nature.

Demeter. One of the twelve great Olympian deities, she was the protector of fertility and marriage; a mother-goddess; the deity of the harvest; the ruler of Virgo (in the Greek zodiac). She was usually portrayed as a tall woman with beautiful golden hair.

Diana
of
Epheseus

Êuret-Êpet (Tauret, Apet, Opet). An ancient Egyptian goddess who was the protector of all animals, and was preeminently helpful in childbirth. She was the giver of fecundity, guardian of women in childbirth, patron of the art of medicine and sender of fertilizing showers. She was represented as a hippopotamus with pendant breasts and paws like a lion, carrying a crocodile on her back. In other art she was pictured as a pregnant woman with lion's paws.

Ishtar. The Assyro-Babylonians believed the universe was created by a woman, and Ishtar was worshiped as the source of all life. Her name means "daughter of light," and was written with the character which stood for a house with the sign for a fish inside it; thus, a house filled with fertility. She was also called Ban Gula, Mama, Mami and Zerpanitum. Her image was represented in phallic symbols, such as a stylized tree or pillar, as well as in the human form of a queen wearing a crown.

Isis. The Great Mother goddess of the Egyptian pantheon. In art she appears as a mother suckling her son; wearing a crown with a disk and cow's horns on top; standing on a crescent moon surrounded by twelve stars.

Ixchel. Mayan rainbow goddess and Yucatan goddess of fecundity, invoked at childbirth. Mexico.

Kuan Yin (the Giver of Children). The Chinese goddess of fertility and motherly love whose special attention is given to women who beseech her to bless them with children. Her figure is often draped in long, flowing white robes while she sits on a throne of lotus blossoms or stands on a tall rock with a child in her arms. Some artwork shows her riding a dragon while she holds the twig of a willow in one hand and a bowl filled with the dew of immortality in the other; and she is sometimes represented as the thousand-armed goddess, showering mercy and consolation upon mankind.

The Goddess Tlazolteotl

Postverta (also called **Carmenta).** A Roman goddess who was a guardian of women in childbirth, and was invoked for aid during confinement.

Teteoinnam. Mother of all the gods; the midwives' patroness. Mexico.

Tlazolteotl. She is represented in the same clothes as Teteoinnam, and is therefore regarded as a manifestation of the mother of all the gods with special powers in the realm of fertility. Mexico.

Venus Genetrix (or **Venus the Birth Giver).** She was the special divinity of the childbirth bed for the Roman matron.

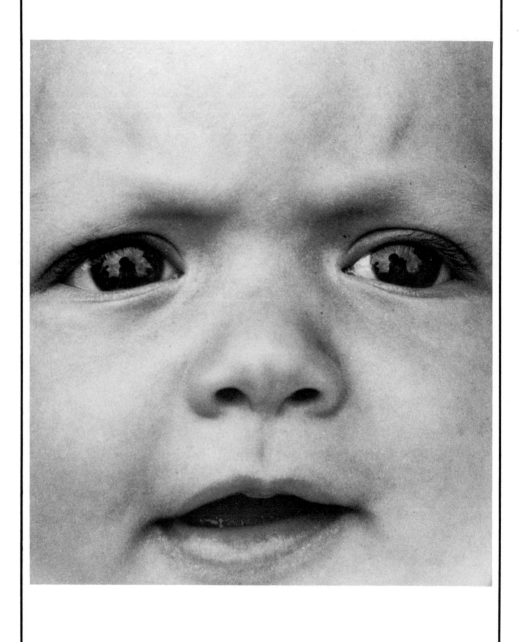

Resources

NATIONAL ORGANIZATIONS

Many of these organizations have referral services, information about childbirth education, methods of childbirth preparation, counseling. Call or write to find out the location of your chapter.

American College of Home
   Obstetrics
664 North Michigan Ave., Suite 600
Chicago, IL 60601

American College of Obstetricians
   and Gynecologists
1 East Wacker Dr.
Chicago, IL 60601

American Society for
   Psychoprophylaxis in Obstetrics
   (ASPO)
1523 L St., N.W.
Washington, DC 20005
(202) 783-7050
*Call or write for referral to Lamaze
   method classes.*

Association for Childbirth at Home
   (ACHI)
Box 1219
Cerritos, CA 90701

Cesarean Birth Association
125 North 12th St.
New Hyde Park, NY 10040

C-Sec International
15 Meynard Rd.
Redham, MA 02026

Cesarean Prevention Movement
   (C.P.M.)
P.O. Box 152
Syracuse, NY 13210

Compassionate Friends
P.O. Box 1347
Oakbrook, IL 60521
(312) 323-5010
Support groups for bereaved parents.

Home Opportunity for the Pregnancy
   Experience (HOPE)
P.O. Box 78
Wauconda, IL 60084

Home Oriented Maternity
    Experience (HOME)
511 New York Ave.
Tacoma Park
Washington, D.C. 20012
(202) 726-4664

International Childbirth Education
    Association (ICEA)
Box 20048
Milwaukee, WI 55420
(414) 445-7470
(612) 854-8660

ICEA Education Committee
Box 22
Hillside, NJ 07205

International Association of Infant
    Massage Instructors (IAIMI)
N.T. Enloe Memorial Hospital
West Fifth Ave. and the Esplanade
Chico, CA 95926
(916) 891-7300 ext. 7626
*Will indicate local chapters for
    instructors and further information
    for parents on the healing and
    bonding art of infant massage.*

La Leche League International
9616 Minneapolis Ave.
Franklin Park, IL 60131
(312) 455-7730

March of Dimes
P.O. Box 2000
White Plains, NY 10602
*Will provide a national listing of
    genetic counselors.*

National Association of Childbirth
    Education, Inc. (NACE)
3940 11th St.
Riverside, CA 92501
(714) 686-0422

National Association of Parents and
    Professionals for Safe Alternatives
    in Childbirth (NAPSAC)
P.O. Box 267
Marble Hill, MO 63764

National Midwife Association
P.O. Box 163
Princeton, NJ 08540
Will provide a list of lay midwives.

National Association of Childbearing
    Centers (NACC)
R.D. #1, Box 1
Perkiomenville, PA 18074
(215) 234-8068
*Send stamped self-addressed envelope
    for referral.*

National Organization of Mothers of
    Twins Clubs, Inc.
5402 Amberwood La.
Rockville, MD 20853
(301) 460-9108

Newborn Rights Society
Box 48
Saint Peter's, PA 19470-0048
(215) 323-6061
*Information on unnecessary medical
procedures.*

Parents of Premature High-risk
  Infants
33 W. 42nd St.
New York, NY 10036

Parents Without Partners, Inc.
7910 Woodmont Ave.
Washington, DC 20014

Pregnancy Aftermath Hotline
4742 North Sheffield Ave.
Milwaukee, WI 53211
(414) 445-2131
*For women who have experienced
  miscarriage, abortion, or who have
  had their baby adopted.*

REGIONAL ORGANIZATIONS

Every state and county has its own medical and health care societies listed
in the phone book. They can be contacted for referrals to ob/gyn doctors,
midwives and maternity centers in your locality.

Alaska
Better Alaskan Birth Experiences
  (BABE)
Box 4-381
Anchorage, AK 99509

California
Bradley Method
P.O. Box 5224
Sherman Oaks, CA 91413
(213) 788-6662

Coalition for the Medical Rights of
  Women
1638b Haight St.
San Francisco, CA 94117
(415) 621-8030

Nutrition Action Group (NAG)
2023 Oak St.
San Francisco, CA 94117
(415) 752-7934

Preparing Expectant Parents (PEP)
Box 838
Romona, CA 91769

Problem Pregnancy Information
  Center
Box 9090
Stanford, CA 95305
(415) 226-7846

3HO Foundation
1620 Preuss Rd.
Los Angeles, CA 90035

Florida
Council for Cesarean Awareness
5520 S.W. 92nd Ave.
Miami, FL 33165
(205) 596-2699
*Provides support for couples seeking
vaginal birth after cesarean.*

National Association for the
Advancement of Le Boyer's Birth
Without Violence, Inc.
P.O. Box 248455
University of Miami Branch
Coral Gables, FL 33124
(305) 665-9506

Maine
Maine Access to Alternatives in
Childbirth Care
RFD 1, Box 74
Dixmont, ME 04932

Massachusetts
Birth Day
P.O. Box 388
Cambridge, MA 02138
(617) 354-2385

C.O.P.E.
37 Clarendon Street
Boston, MA 02116
(617) 357-5588
*Coping with the overall pregnancy/
parenting experience.*

Maternal and Child Health Center
2464 Massachusetts Ave.
Cambridge, MA 02140
(617) 864-9343

The People Place
1465 Massachusetts Ave.
Arlington, MA 02174
(617) 643-8630
*Counseling for pregnancy, birth and
postpartum.*

New York
Center for Medical Consumers
237 Thompson St.
New York, NY 10012
(212) 674-7105

Father Focus
204 West 20th St.
New York, NY 10011
(212) 316-1414

The Fatherhood Project
Bank Street College
610 W. 112th St.
New York, NY 10025

Maternity Center Association
48 East 92nd St.
New York, NY 10028
(212) 369-7300

Single Mothers By Choice
200 East 84th St.
New York, NY 10028
(212) 988-0993

Women's Counseling Project
3001 Broadway, Reid Hall
New York, NY 10027
(212) 280-3063

North Carolina
Pregnancy Support Services
121 South Estes Dr. #204a
Chapel Hill, NC 27514
(919) 942-7318

Oregon
Portland's Woman's Clinic
3537 Hawthorne Blvd.
Portland, OR 97214
(503) 234-9774

Pennsylvania
Booth Maternity Center
6051 Overbrook Ave.
Philadelphia, PA 19131
(215) 878-7800

Rhode Island
Rhode Islanders for Safe Alternatives
   in Childbirth (RIFSAC)
P.O. Box 2593
Providence, RI 02906
(401) 438-2427

Texas
Houston Organization for Parent
   Education (HOPE)
3311 Richmond Ave., Suite 330
Houston, TX 77077
(713) 493-6792

Vermont
Vermont Women's Health Center
P.O. Box 29
Burlington, VT 05402

Washington, D.C.
The American College of Nurse-
   Midwives
Suite 500
1000 Vermont, N.W.
Washington, D.C. 20005
(202) 628-4642

Washington
Arcadia Clinic
1827 Twelve St.
Seattle, WA 98122
(206) 323-9388

Parents of Prematures
13613 NE 26th Pl.
Bellevue, WA 98005
(206) 883-6040

Canada
Prepared Childbirth Association of
   Nova Scotia
P.O. Box 5052
Armdale, Halifax, Nova Scotia
B3L 4M6, Canada
Also publishes "The Resource Kit"
   for pregnant teenagers.

England
National Childbirth Trust
9 Queensborough Terrace
Bayswater
London W2 3TB, England

HERBALISTS Write for catalogs.

Wishgarden Herbs
P.O. Box 1304
Boulder, CO 80306

Pan's Forest Herb Company
Route 1, Box 211
East Jordan, MI 49727
(616) 536-7445

Herbs, Etc., of Santa Fe
228 Griffin
Santa Fe, NM 87507
(505) 982-1265

The Herb Store
106 Gerard Blvd., S.E.
Albuquerque, NM
(505) 255-8878

Aphrodisia Prods., Inc.
282 Bleecker St.
New York, NY 10012

Kiehl's Pharmacy
109 Third Ave.
New York, NY 10003

Equinox Botanicals
Rt. 1, Box 71
Rutland, OH 45775

Meadowbrook Herb Garden
Wyoming, RI 02898

MAGAZINES AND NEWSLETTERS

Baby Talk
185 Madison Ave.
New York, NY 10016
(212) 679-4400

Mothering
P.O. Box 8410
Santa Fe, NM 87504
(505) 984-8116

Parenting
501 Second St.
San Francisco, CA 94107

Parents
685 Third Ave.
New York, NY 10017
(212) 878-8700

Parent Guide
Two Park Ave.
New York, NY 10016
(212) 213-8840

Working Mother
230 Park Ave.
New York, NY 10017
(212) 551-9412

Bibliography

BOOKS

Arms, Suzanne. *Immaculate Deception: A New Look at Women and Childbirth.* New York: Bantam, 1984.

Ashford, Janet Isaacs. *The Whole Birth Catalogue: A Sourcebook for Choices in Childbirth.* Trumansburg: The Crossing Press, 1983.

Bing, Elisabeth and Libby Coleman. *Having a Baby after 30.* New York: Bantam, 1980.

Bittman, Sam, and Sue Rosenberg Zalk. *Expectant Fathers.* New York: Dutton, 1979.

The Boston Women's Health Book Collective. *The New Our Bodies Ourselves.* Boston: Simon and Schuster, 1985.

Bradley, Robert A. *Husband Coached Childbirth* (3rd ed.). Boston: Houghton Mifflin, 1982.

Brewer, Gail S. (ed.). *The Pregnancy after 30 Workbook.* Pennsylvania: Rodale Press, 1978.

Brewer, Gail S. and Thomas H. *What Every Pregnant Woman Should Know: The Truth about Diet and Drugs in Pregnancy.* New York: Penguin, 1985.

Briffault, Robert. *The Mothers: A Study of the Origins of Sentiments and Institutions.* New York: Grosset, 1927. Reprinted by Johnson Reprints.

Caplan, Frank (ed). *The First Twelve Months of Life.* New York: Bantam, 1978.

Cohen, Nancy, and Lois J. Estner. *Silent Knife: Vaginal Birth after Cesarean (VBAC) and Cesarean Prevention.* Massachusetts: Bergin and Garvey, 1983.

DeLyser, Femmy. *The Jane Fonda Workout Book for Pregnancy, Birth and Recovery.* New York: Simon and Schuster, 1982.

Dick-Read, Grantly. *Childbirth without Fear* (5th ed.). New York: Harper and Row, 1985.

Dickinson, Robert Latou. *Atlas of Human Sex Anatomy* (2nd ed.). Baltimore: Williams and Wilkins, 1949. Reprinted by Krieger, 1970.

Duffy, Cynthia, and Linda Meyer. *Responsible Childbirth and Cesarean Prevention.* Saratoga, California: R and E Publishing, 1984.

Feldman, Sylvia. *Choices in Childbirth*. New York: Grosset and Dunlap, 1978.

Gardner, Joy. *Healing the Family: Pregnancy, Birth and Children's Ailments*. New York: Bantam, 1982.

Gaskin, Ina May. *Spiritual Midwifery* (rev. ed.). Pennsylvania: Summertown, 1978.

Heinowitz, Jack. *Pregnant Fathers*. New Jersey: Prentice-Hall, 1982.

Haire, Doris B. *The Cultural Warping of Childbirth: A Special Report on U.S. Obstetrics*. Minneapolis: ICEA, 1972.

Inkeles, Gordon. *A Daily Book for New Mothers and Fathers*. New York: Putnam, 1984.

Jones, Paul. *Sharing Birth, A Father's Guide*. New York: Morrow, 1985.

Kitzinger, Sheila. *The Complete Book of Pregnancy and Childbirth*. New York: Knopf, 1980.

———. *Birth at Home*. New York: Oxford University Press, 1979. Penguin, 1979.

———. *Birth Over 30*. New York: Penguin, 1985.

———. *The Experience of Breastfeeding*. New York: Penguin, 1980.

Lamaze, Fernand. *Painless Childbirth*. New York: Pocket Books, 1983.

La Leche League International. *The Womanly Art of Breastfeeding*. Franklin Park, Illinois: La Leche League, 1963. New York: New American Library, 1983.

Lappé, Frances Moore. *Diet for a Small Planet*. New York: Ballantine, 1971.

Leach, Penelope. *Babyhood*. (2nd rev. ed.). New York: Knopf, 1978.

Le Boyer, Frederick. *Birth Without Violence*. New York: Knopf, 1975.

———. *Loving Hands: The Traditional Indian Art of Baby Massaging*. New York: Knopf, 1976.

Levy, Janine. *The Baby Exercise Book: For the First Fifteen Months*. New York: Pantheon, 1975.

Lust, John. *The Herb Book*. New York: Bantam, 1974.

Maternity Center Association. *A Baby Is Born*. New York: Grosset & Dunlap, 1968.

Montague, Ashley. *Life Before Birth*. New York: Signet, 1977.

Nance, Sherri. *Premature Babies: A Handbook for Parents*. New York: Arbor House, 1982.

NAPSAC. *Directory & Consumer Guide to Alternative Birth*. Missouri: NAPSAC International.

Nilsson, Lennart; Ingelman-Sundberg, Axel; and Wirsén, Claes. *A Child Is Born: The Drama of Life Before Birth.* Translated by Britt and Claes Wirsén and Annabelle McMillan. New York: Dell Publishing Co., 1966. Rev. ed. New York: Delacorte, 1977.

Noble, Elizabeth. *Childbirth with Insight.* Boston: Houghton Mifflin, 1983.

———. *Essential Exercises for Childbearing Years* (rev. ed.). Boston: Houghton Mifflin, 1982.

Norwood, Christopher. *How to Avoid a Cesarean Section.* New York: Simon and Schuster, 1984.

———. *At Highest Risk: Environmental Hazards to Young and Unborn Children.* New York: Penguin, 1980.

Neuman, Eric. *The Great Mother: An Analysis of the Archetype.* Translated by Ralph Manheim. New Jersey: Princeton University Press, Princeton Bolligen, 1963.

Odent, Michel. *Birth Reborn.* New York: Pantheon, 1984.

Ohasi, Waturu, and Mary Hoover. *The Eastern Way of Natural Childbirth: Do-it-Yourself Shiatsu for a Healthy Pregnancy and Delivery.* New York: Ballantine, 1983.

Olds, Sally, and Eiger, M. S. *The Complete Book of Breastfeeding* (rev. ed.). New York: Workman, 1986.

Olkin, Sylvia Klein. *Positive Pregnancy through Yoga.* New Jersey: Prentice-Hall, 1981.

Panuthos, Claudia. *Transformation through Birth: A Woman's Guide.* Massachusetts: Bergin and Garvey, 1984.

Schneider, Vimala. *Infant Massage.* New York: Bantam Books, 1982.

Simkin, Diana. *The Complete Baby Exercise Program.* New York: Plume / The New American Library, 1985.

Spock, Benjamin, and Rothenberg, Michael. *Dr. Spock's Baby and Child Care* (rev. ed.). New York: Pocket Books, 1985.

Stewart, David. *The Five Standards for Safe Childbearing.* Missouri: NAPSAC International, 1981.

Stewart, David, and Lee Stewart. *21st Century Obstetrics Now.* Vols. 1, 2, 3. Missouri: NAPSAC International, 1977.

White, Gregory. *Emergency Childbirth.* Franklin Park, Illinois: The Police Training Foundation, 1958.

Williams, Phyllis S. *Nourishing Your Unborn Child.* New York: Avon, 1982.

CASSETTES, VIDEO TAPES AND FILMS

BABY BODY WORKS
P.O. Box 3668
Gaithersburg, MD 20878
Fun exercises to perform with baby on home video.

BIRTH IN THE NEW AGE
Star Enterprises
P.O. Box 10205
Austin, TX 78757
30-minute video of two underwater births.

BIRTH WITHOUT VIOLENCE
1975, a film by Frederick Le Boyer
21 minutes of peaceful delivery.
LOVING HANDS
1976, directed by Frederick Le Boyer
23 minutes of the traditional art of baby massage.
Both 16-mm films available for sale or to rent from New Yorker Films
16 West 61st St.
New York, NY 10023
(212) 247-6110

EXERCISES FOR PREGNANT WOMEN AND NEW MOTHERS
BABES (Bay Area Birth Education Supplies)
c/o Deanna Sollid
59 Berens Drive
Kentfield, CA 94904
Tape cassette and wall chart exercise program.

JANE FONDA'S PREGNANCY, BIRTH AND RECOVERY WORKOUT
1983, with Jane Fonda and Femmy deLyser
Karl Home Video
90 minutes of good advice and practical exercises.

MARIE OSMOND'S EXERCISES FOR MOTHERS-TO-BE
1983, MGM/UA Home Video
Designed by Elizabeth Noble, 60 minutes

NAN'S CLASS and FATHER'S
American Society for Psychoprophylaxis in Obstetrics (ASPO)
1523 L St., N.W.
Washington, DC 20005
Two films available for rental. One is of a Lamaze class, following the parents through to delivery. The other features interviews with fathers.

POLYMORPH Films
118 South St.
Boston, MA 02111
(617) 542-2004
This company has the largest selection of films and video tapes for rent or purchase on birth experiences.

PREGNANCY EXERCISE
CHILDBIRTH PREPARATION PROGRAM
POSTNATAL EXERCISE PROGRAM
American College of Obstetricians and Gynecologists (ACOG)
Feeling Fine Productions
3575 Cahuenga Boulevard West, Suite 425
Los Angeles, CA 90068
(800) 531-1212 ext. 165 in California
(800) 443-4040 ext. 165 in Continental U.S.
Series of exercises performed in an unreal setting and overly cosmetic. The childbirth program video tape gives a good idea of different hospital births in its real setting. The exercises are also available on LP records or audio cassettes.

RELAXATION TAPES FOR CHILDBIRTH... AND AFTER
Alliance for Perinatal Research and Services
P.O. Box 6358
Alexandria, VA 22306
Relaxation strategies set to classical music.

VIDEOS ABOUT LIFE
Academy Communications
Box 5224-M
Sherman Oaks, CA 91413
(800) 423-2397
*Assorted titles about home birth, breast-feeding, sibling presence,
nutrition, etc.*

WATER BABY
Point of View Productions
2477 Folsom St.
San Francisco, CA 94110
(415) 821-0435
The experience of water birth, 58 minutes, color video.

Catalogs available on request of various audio-visual titles:

Artemis Associates
P.O. Box 3147
Stamford, CT 06905

Cinema Medica
2335 W. Foster Ave.
Chicago, IL 60625

Educational Graphic Aids, Inc.
1315 Norwood Ave.
Boulder, CO 80302

Index

Credits

The author and publisher are grateful to the following for permission to reproduce photographs:

v. Barbara Nessim
vi. Keith Haring
viii. L. Pinsard
xiii. Lisa Law
xiv. Mati Klarwein
2. Ed Lettau
5, 6, 8, 9, 10 (illustration, top). author
10 (photos, bottom). Roberts Rugh, from Roberts Rugh and Landrum B. Shettles, M.D., *From Conception to Birth: The Drama of Life's Beginnings* (New York: Harper & Row, 1971)
12, 13. Roberts Rugh
13 (bottom right). Maternity Center Association
18. author
20. Toni Kent
24–29, 30–36. author
38. Ralph Sanders
41. Jodi Cobb
42, 44. author
46. Gilles Milinaire
47. Jodi Cobb
51. Steven Moore
70–75. author
76, 79. Pauline Pugliese
84. Judy Chicago
86. Alan Carey
91, 92, 93, 100. author (Beth Israel Hospital)
96. Maternity Center Association
103. New York Hospital
109. author
112. Jamie Smith-Jackson
119, 121, 123, 126. author
130 (photo). Barbara Johns
130 (drawings). Eastman and Hellman, Williams Obstetrics
134 (drawing). Eastman and Hellman, Williams Obstetrics
146. Beverly Skinner
148, 151. Vicky McLaughlin
152. Irving Penn, copyright © 1971 by Condé Nast Publications, Inc.
155. Mati Klarwein
160. author
166, 168. Reprinted with permission from *Birth Reborn* by Dr. Michel Odent, translated by Jane Pincus and Juliette Levin, copyright © 1984. Published by Pantheon Books, a division of Random House, Inc.
174. author
181, 183. Yona Nadelmann
184. Tony Curatolo
190. Barbara Cossy
196. Joe Lambi
202. author
206, 217. Connie Zalk
218. Francesco Scavullo
222, 228, 230. author
246, 255, 257. author
258, 266, 267. Steven Moore
274, 277. Weiner Family
278. Daisy Hess
288. Christine Amarger
290. Ralph Gibson
292, 295, 297, 299, 301, 303. author
307. Adger W. Cowans
310. Ralph Gibson
312. "New Mother" from *The Dead and the Living* by Sharon Olds, copyright © 1984, Alfred A. Knopf, a division of Random House, Inc.
315, 321. author
323. Judy Chicago
325. Adger W. Cowans
327. Alan Carey
331. Lisa Law
331 (bottom right). Fred Sweeda

333. author
337. Ira Cohen
338. Lisa Law
340. author
346. Keith Haring
349, 350, 352 (bottom), 353. author
354. The American Museum of Natural History
356. Monica Sjöö
359. author
361. Bernardino Luini, c.1500

365. L.A. Huffman, copyright © 1969, Jack Coffrin, Coffrin's Old West Gallery, 1600 Main St., Miles City, Montana
367. Lisa Law
371. Gravure Bernard
372. Adger W. Cowans
373. Peter Beard
378. Dumbarton Oaks, Washington, D.C., The Robert Woods Bliss Collection of Pre-Columbian Art
380. Aria Moore

About the Author

Caterine Milinaire is a French photojournalist who has traveled through Europe, Africa, Southeast Asia, Japan, Russia, Mexico and Venezuela. Her photographs and articles have appeared in *Vogue, Holiday, New York, Interview* and *Oui.*

Ms. Milinaire was born in Paris and educated at a convent school until the age of sixteen when she began modeling for a couturier and acting in films. She worked as a fashion editor of *Queen's* magazine in London and at *Vogue* in New York. While at *Vogue* she became involved in photography and film-making and subsequently left the magazine for an extended world tour in which she and another photographer traveled together and documented their experiences.

Birth is Ms. Milinaire's first full-length book, which she wrote after giving birth to her daughter, Serafine. "When I gave birth," she says, "it was the most exhilarating feeling I had ever had. I decided to find out even more about it and put it in simple words with lots of visuals for other people looking for such a book."

Ms. Milinaire has written two other books, *Celebrations* and *Cheap Chic.* She lives in New York City and produces and directs video documentaries.

The Beginning